W9-ADT-229

Hartness Library
Vermont Technical College
One Main St.
Randolph Center, VT 05061

From Front Porch to Back Seat

From *FRONT PORCH* to *BACK SEAT*

Courtship in Twentieth-Century America

Beth L. Bailey

The Johns Hopkins University Press

Baltimore and London

© 1988 The Johns Hopkins University Press
All rights reserved
Printed in the United States of America

The Johns Hopkins University Press
701 West 40th Street
Baltimore, Maryland 21211
The Johns Hopkins Press Ltd., London

∞

The paper used in this publication meets
the minimum requirements of American
National Standard for Information Sciences —
Permanence of Paper for Printed Library
Materials, ANSI Z39.48-1984.

Library of Congress Cataloging-in-Publication Data

Bailey, Beth L., 1957–
　From front porch to back seat.

　Bibliography: p.
　Includes index.
　1. Courtship — United States — History — 20th century. I. Title.
GT2650.B35　1988　　　392'.4'0973　　　87-46312
ISBN 0-8018-3609-3 (alk. paper)

In memory of my parents,
who loved each other very much

Contents

Acknowledgments

I enjoyed writing this book as much as anything I have ever done. Much of my joy in researching and writing came in solitude: paging through dusty decades of *Mademoiselle*, a cup of coffee and a clean page, the hard thinking and the moments when it all came together. Still, a large part of my pleasure in the process must be credited to others. I am grateful to the people and institutions that made the hard tasks easier, to the people who actively participated in creating this book, and to the sometimes overlapping set of people who have, over the years, given me their support and friendship.

I would like to thank the staffs of the Radcliffe College Archives, the Harvard University Archives, the University of Massachusetts-Amherst Archives, the Bentley Historical Library at the University of Michigan, the University of Michigan Housing Office, the Northwestern University Archives and Library Special Collections, and the University of Chicago Library Special Collections. The family of historian and biographer Harry Barnard supported this work through a fellowship established in his honor. Mary Sheila McMahon and Edwin Wheeler extended most gracious material and intellectual hospitality. And the Library of Congress offered me all a young scholar could desire: a room of (almost) my own and a stacks pass.

This work benefited greatly from the comments and questions of Neil Harris, Barry Karl, Beth Helsinger, Pamela Divinsky, Emily Harris, Sherry Bailey, Henry Binford, Robert McGlone, and Elaine Tyler May. Special thanks go to Mary Sheila McMahon, my "ideal reader"; to Ken Cmiel, for Medici coffee and conversations, and for reminding me that the man's role was no picnic either; and to David Farber, who asked the hard questions and helped me answer them.

I also want to acknowledge some of the people — and places — that have had an important, if indirect, impact on my work. This book was filtered through the landscape of West Division Street, Chicago, and through memories of Smyrna, Georgia. It bears the imprint of teachers who have, over many years and in different ways, inspired me: June Austin, Rima Vesilind, Henry Binford, Carl S. Smith, Bari Watkins, Robert Wiebe — and especially Neil Harris and Barry Karl, who taught me about history and historians. I offer my heartfelt thanks to both my families, the Baileys and the Farbers, and to my good friends, who will, I hope, recognize how much their friendship and love have meant to me. David Farber knows that this book is as much his as mine. He is a true partner — in my work and in my life.

This book is dedicated to the memory of my parents. They were fine people who taught me to treasure the world of ideas, and who set me an example of responsibility, love, and courage. I can never tell them how proud I am to be their daughter, but I can pass on their gifts to the next generation. Thus, this book is also for Max Warsaw Bailey / Farber, who is not afraid of the ocean.

From Front Porch to Back Seat

Introduction

When I was a senior in college I was on the Phil Donahue show. It was 1978, and I (along with a carefully selected assortment of other college students) was defending coed dorms to Middle America.

Isolated in youth culture, I hadn't realized that coed dorms might still need defending. On my by-no-means-radical campus, coed living was about as controversial as going to the library. Even my mother was perfectly satisfied with my living arrangements. She had been, to use her word, "charmed" on her one and only visit two years before. The first person we encountered in the dorm was stumbling down the hall to the bathroom clad in a towel about the size of a large washcloth. I performed a proper introduction, and he nearly lost his towel trying to shake my mother's hand. From that moment on she was — rightly or wrongly — convinced of the essential innocence of it all.

Anyone who has seen Phil Donahue in action can imagine how he maneuvered the audience through that hour: a current controversy, a little titillation, a little information, a few accusations, the exposure of generational conflict, some heavy nostalgia, one confession of envy, and finally a general reconciliation and an affirmation of progress. One of the few men in the audience provided closure. He hadn't liked the idea of coed dorms, he said, but the sight of us, so bright and healthy, had changed his mind. Afterward, with the ungenerousness of privileged youth, we asked each other, "What did he expect, tertiary syphilis?" Back on campus, I encountered the even less generous speculation that I had squandered my Warhol-allotted fifteen minutes of fame on a discussion of bathroom arrangements in coed dorms.

In retrospect it is clear to me that the controversy on Donahue that

1

day was less about coed dorms than about the transformation of American courtship. The audience was mourning the dissolution of the dating system and the death of romance. Person after person rose to tell of her college days — the waiting and the telephone calls, nervous boys clutching corsages, the exciting moments of risky privacy, the rush to sign in on time. In memory, the dating system became pure mystery and romance.

It's all too easy today, they said. You have so much freedom, so few rules, but it doesn't sound like much fun. Besides, one asked — to much applause — how can you fall in love with someone you see in the morning before he's even brushed his teeth?

And we countered: we see each other as people, not as dates. Our relationships grow from friendship and mutual understanding. Dating sounds so artificial — how could you get to know someone that way? We insisted: love is more than mystery, and romance can survive intimacy.

Of course, the brave new world of youth triumphed, and by the end of the hour representatives of our parents' generation had accepted the new and the strange. The new conventions of courtship, the rules and rituals and systems of meaning that structured the courtship of youth, had been rendered safe — knowable, and thus unthreatening.

But the essential conflict had not been resolved. Despite recognizable continuities, the two systems of courtship were fundamentally different. The differences lay not only on the surface, in the changing acts of courtship, but in underlying understandings of value and values, in presumptions about how the world works, and in ideas about the proper relations between men and women.

The new system of courtship had already won out, in life as well as on Donahue. And it, of course, was far from perfect. Critics of every stripe have found much to criticize in it. In our search for freedom, honesty, love, and equality, many of them claim, we have found only meaningless sex, loneliness, and lack of commitment. We have epidemics of teen pregnancy and sexually transmitted diseases. Some critics even say we have left youth without the rules that are essential for stability, much less for romance.

In the midst of such dissatisfactions and real problems, we find a valorization of the past. Self-described conservatives call for a return to traditional values, which often seem to be the values and sexual conventions proclaimed in the 1950s. From the highest office in the land comes the admonition "Just Say No," to sex, as well as to drugs. Even liberals and one-time leftists, drawing back from what they helped to create, call for more "traditional" arrangements between the sexes.[1]

American popular culture is rife with nostalgia for the old ways. Magazines document and promote it; they are full of analyses of our "return to traditional values and practices" and of invidious comparisons of today's dilemmas in courtship with the way "it used to be."[2] The conventions that have held sway for almost a quarter of a century are being questioned, and many calls for change are justified by visions of the past. In the midst of a heated debate about the future of American courtship, it is time to look more closely at its past. To what are we being asked to return?

This book is about America's "traditional" system of courtship — the dating system that flourished between about 1920 and 1965. It examines the origins of dating — how the system came to be and what it replaced. It details the rituals and conventions that shaped the courtship of several generations of American youth. It analyzes the understandings and beliefs on which dating was based, and shows the connections of private acts of courtship to larger changes in American society. And finally, this work offers a judgment. While some of the fruits of America's sexual revolution have not been sweet, we cannot simply look to traditional courtship for remedies. Just because the present is not satisfactory does not mean the past was better. Certainly we should seek our usable past, but to find answers to the current problems of American courtship we need to go not backward but forward.

In twentieth-century America, courtship became more and more a private act conducted in the public world. This intimate business, as it evolved into "dating," increasingly took place in public places removed, by distance and by anonymity, from the sheltering and controlling contexts of home and local community. Keeping company in the family parlor was replaced by dining and dancing, Coke dates, movies, "parking." In the twentieth century, youth increasingly moved their courtship from the private to the public sphere.

At the same time, a proliferation of public sources provided a new framework for understanding private acts and decisions. The growth of magazines and books offering advice about courtship was as phenomenal as the growth of the market for them.

This advice literature, which played such a crucial role in shifting courtship into the public world, was filled with the writing of a new group of experts — psychologists, sociologists, statisticians — who

studied courtship and interpreted "private" acts with reference to national norms. From about the late 1930s on, many young people knew
to the percentage point what their peers throughout the country
thought and did. They knew what was "normal." The publication of
such statistics helped strengthen and create a consciousness of national
convention, but it also altered the meaning and experience of private
acts and decisions. People compared their experience to public norms,
took their vocabulary and definitions from them. Increasingly, private
decisions were made with reference to a kind of public context that
had not existed in the previous century.

While the advice literature itself worked to place courtship in the
public realm, its content (and, indeed, the entire public discourse on
courtship) contained contradictory messages about the proper relationship between the public and the private. Experts and other arbiters
of convention drew on nineteenth-century understandings of those
terms, defining the relations between men and women, like "home"
and "family," as a sphere to be protected from the market values of the
public world. Many experts insisted that the "private" sphere of courtship should provide a safe zone — a respite from the too-rapid social
and cultural changes taking place between men and women in the
"public" world of work.

American courtship, nevertheless, was affected by the changes in
relations between men and women in the larger society, as women
took on new roles in the public world, and ideas about what was appropriate behavior for men and for women shifted gradually or were
jolted into new configurations. The rules and rituals governing dating
(and, for that matter, marriage) had been based on the concept of
man-as-provider. He paid; she didn't. (Assumption: he worked; she
didn't.) But as more and more young women entered the job market,
earning their own money and achieving the limited autonomy that
comes with economic independence, conventions based on the man-
as-provider model clashed more and more with the realities of men's
and women's lives. This dissonance produced tensions, which were
often manifest in struggles to gain or retain control within the courtship system. Many specific conventions of courtship behavior were
concerned with controlling these power struggles, with denying
change. There is perhaps no force so strong in the public conventions
of twentieth-century American courtship as nostalgia, the lure of an
imagined past.

Even as these arbiters of convention struggled to make courtship
safe by calling it private, they turned to the public language of the
marketplace. Gradually, a new cultural construct metaphorically sub-

stituted the marketplace for the home as the controlling context for courtship rituals. As it emerged in the twentieth century, courtship largely was construed and understood in models and metaphors of modern industrial capitalism.

The new system of courtship privileged competition (and worried about how to control it); it valued consumption; it presented an economic model of scarcity and abundance as a guide to personal affairs. The rules of the market were consciously applied; the vocabulary of economic exchange defined the acts of courtship.

This is not to say that in twentieth-century America, for the first time, courtship was understood through its relation to the marketplace. Through much of Western history, courtship was firmly based in the reality of the economy, and the definition of courtship as a system of exchange is common to many cultures. Even in the era of romantic love, writers such as Jane Austen vividly described the marketplace of courtship. However, in nineteenth-century America, public discussions of courtship commonly drew on metaphors of home and family.

Neither am I describing an economically determined model. Instead, these understandings of courtship reflect its passage from the home and the local community into the public world, which contemporaries defined as the world of the economy, the market. Perhaps the gradual adoption of these models shows a desire for unity in life, a willingness to generalize experience.

In any case, the new language of courtship had great symbolic importance. By shifting the analogies and metaphors through which individuals understood and described courtship, this new system changed the way courtship was understood in the culture, and actually influenced the *meaning* of individual acts and decisions.

In this work, I am not posing a unitary explanation for the forms courtship took in twentieth-century America. Instead, I am exploring some of the themes that emerged as important, in constellation around, if not in direct causal relation to, the emergence of modern American society. I explore the themes as historical and cultural constructs that framed the experience of individuals and groups in society. I try to play out the internal logic of the systems of courtship I define and to suggest the ways in which these constructs lent meaning to individual experience.

The understandings I lay out here were not newly created. They have roots that reach different depths of the past and that stretch to the soil of cultures other than our own. Likewise, some of these understandings, and even the specific conventions in which they were manifest, still flourish. Despite the strangeness of vocabulary or the occasional bald ugliness of a statement few would make today, the legacy of the system I describe remains strong. It is part of our culture's attempt to answer the basic question of what it means to be a man, to be a woman, to be a man and a woman together.

My arguments in this work rest on a cluster of concepts that require definition. First of all, I am writing about courtship. *Courtship* is an old-fashioned word. It summons visions of men wooing women with small tokens of affection and proposing on bended knee. Studies of courtship usually look at the process of mate selection; the proposal is what makes the preceding acts qualify as courting. In this work, I focus on the wooing, whether or not it culminates in a marriage proposal. I define courtship broadly; I mean the term to encompass a wide variety of conditions, intentions, and actions, for men and women woo each other in many ways, not all of which lead to marriage.

In twentieth-century America, the new system of dating added new stages to courtship and multiplied the number of partners (from serious to casual) an individual was likely to have before marriage. All this premarital experience necessarily had an impact on the final stages of mate selection. Thus, by my broad definition, the unattached flirt, the engaged college seniors, the eighth-grade "steadies," and the mismatched couple on a blind date are all engaging in courtship.

Second, I am looking at convention rather than experience.[3] In other words, instead of describing what people "actually" did I am laying out a public system of rules and understandings that provided a context for concrete acts and individual experience. I define *convention* here as public codes of behavior and systems of meaning that are both culturally constructed and historically specific. While convention may not *determine* actions, or exist in a one-to-one relationship with individual experience, it does *structure* experience. Convention supplies a frame of reference; it is a public system that lends meaning to private acts.

Thus, if a middle-class girl in mid-America in the mid-1950s picked up a telephone and called a boy to ask him for a date, her act existed on at least two levels. It was an individual, private act, but it gained meaning through a system of public definitions. She and the boy both knew she had broken a rule, had flouted convention. And both her action and his reaction necessarily were conceived and understood in relation to specific culturally assigned meanings. Whether they — or we — choose to follow rules or to break them, we still exist in relation to those rules. Even if we achieve total indifference to conventions that operate in our culture, others still will judge our acts in relation to those conventions.

This point raises another problem of definition. Convention, being culturally constructed and historically specific, is not universal. This, then, is a study of *national* systems of convention that governed American courtship from about 1900 through the mid-1960s.

The beginning and end points of this project are somewhat arbitrary, for I am not trying to pinpoint a moment of historical change and provide causal explanations for it but to examine an existing system, playing out its logic and analyzing its historical meanings and implications. However, the dates that set the boundaries for this study are both times in which long-term change solidified. By the turn of the century, "going somewhere" was beginning to rival "calling" in the American dating system. By the late 1960s, a new incarnation of youth culture and the beginnings of a new feminism challenged some of the values embedded in the dating system and undercut some of the public controls effected by convention.

It is difficult to impose beginning and end dates on changes in courtship, and the dates I have chosen to use here do not clearly mar ∿ the beginning and ending of an era. Change is marked by the persistence of older patterns — whether the new pattern incorporates the older values and customs or declares itself in opposition to them. And much of the story of the conventions of American courtship is of nostalgic calls on an imagined past and of lingering values directly contradicting the individual's experience in other spheres.

The emergence of dating does, however, parallel major changes in American culture and society. For my purposes, the most important of these is the gradual development of a national system of culture, made possible by the emergence of national systems of communication, transportation, and economy; the extension of education; and the forces of urbanization and industrialization. This national culture never was all-inclusive, but it was extended to an increasing percentage of Americans in the twentieth century through the democratization of education (7 percent of all 14 to 17-year-olds attended high school in 1900, 90 percent in 1960) and through increased leisure and expendable income for most Americans.[4]

Perhaps most important was the development of cultural media — mass circulation magazines (80.8 percent of all American households read popular magazines in 1959), radio, movies, television — that provided a common experience for most Americans.[5] The national media reached a much higher percentage of the American public in 1950 than it did in 1900, but even then a relatively coherent body of convention was being disseminated to and reinforced for a national "middle-class" audience through popular high-circulation magazines. Other cultures existed then, and others exist today, but this is the culture that gained the strongest public voice. The group to which this body of prescriptive literature was addressed — the American middle class — would grow and become much more inclusive through the period of this study. Through the twentieth century, even those unable or unwilling to participate in this culture increasingly felt its weight.

What weight the conventions of courtship had came through repetition. The rules were constantly reiterated and reinforced. The sameness of the message was overwhelming. Popular magazines, advice and etiquette books, texts used in high school and college marriage courses, the professional journals of the educators who taught the courses, all formed a remarkably coherent universe.[6] This universe of convention, moreover, meshed neatly with the systems of convention that operated on college campuses throughout the United States.[7]

On the surface, the customs of Radcliffe students would seem to have little connection with teen advice columns in *Good Housekeeping*, and the scholarly *Journal of Marriage and Family Living* would seem to have little relation to how-to-get-a-husband manuals. However, not only do all these sources present a fairly uniform set of conventions, they are interconnected to an amazing extent.

The new set of certified experts who appropriated the role of courtship adviser in the twentieth century attempted to make courtship a fairly uniform science. These scholars and social scientists wrote marriage textbooks, taught college courses, and authored many of the advice columns and articles that were staples of national magazines. Thus, a Mississippi teenager reading women's magazines in the 1940s and 1950s would receive much the same information and basic understandings as a college student at the University of California at the same time.

In addition, various groupings of magazines were more or less uniform in content; an issue successfully raised by one generally was picked up by the others. Some issues, such as the convention of going steady in the post–World War II years, were featured by virtually every major popular magazine in America. Advice books capitalized on these same issues and problems, and sometimes were even affiliated with a magazine (Esquire *Etiquette, The* Seventeen *Book of Young Living*, etc.). Other advice books were written by the experts who wrote the texts and scholarly articles, and by the 1940s one could count on most authors to quote from expert studies to validate their points.

Throughout these sources there were, of course, differences of tone and voice, of sophistication. Time lags existed, though not always predictably. Still, for most of the twentieth century, especially the period between 1920 and 1965, these sources were strikingly uniform. The conventions praised in *Good Housekeeping* were remarkably similar to the ones endorsed in the Radcliffe *News*. When differences and disagreements did appear, they generally centered around a uniform body of issues and questions. Challenges to prevalent conventions were accepted into a discourse that increasingly defined convention not as hard-and-fast rule but as custom. And when a magazine ran a disapproving article on the practice of petting or of going steady, it validated the conventionality of the custom by according it serious attention.

No matter how much this uniformity lends credence to the existence of national conventions, *national* is a tricky word. Here, it translates into white, middle-class, heterosexual, and young. This leads me to two more definitions — those for "youth" and "middle class" — and an explanation.

The new systems of courtship were inextricably tied to new understandings of youth and to the development of a youth culture. In the early twentieth century, a changing economic structure, a reform impulse, and new scientific and social-scientific definitions of youth led to "the massive reclassification of young people as adolescents and the creation of institutions to segregate them from casual contact with adults." [8]

Through the eighteenth and much of the nineteenth centuries, "youth" had been a loose classification, encompassing a wide and differing range of ages and an extreme variety of life experiences. Age groups were not frequently segregated, and the lines between childhood, youth, and adulthood often had more to do with physical size and social role than with age. As America became a mature industrial society in the late nineteenth century, the demand for specialists and technicians, as well as the widening gap between "careers" and "dead-end jobs," led to a prolongation of formal education for those who could afford it. This development, combined with socio-sexual fears — the legacy of a romantic view of childhood threatened by the onset of sexual maturity — led America's middle classes to redefine youth as a period demanding special institutions and protections.

Between 1900 and 1920, youth workers, educators, and theorists struggled to extend those protections beyond class barriers, to make youth a "universal experience." Through the first half of the twentieth century we see a gradual extension of the concept and experience of youth as a discrete and protected category. This "revolution" in the treatment and definition of young people was largely complete by 1950.

Within the institutions of youth, young people developed their own cultures, which, even before the 1920s, were chronicled for the nation by the national media. Youth cultures, however, were not usually discrete and parochial; they shared in a larger youth culture defined by common mores, experiences, and consumer goods. The music, the clothes, the dances, the courtship practices — all helped to define youth culture for its participants.

As youth culture grew in strength and size, it came to support its own cultural institutions and media. *Mademoiselle*, founded in the 1930s, focused on college-age women. During World War II, while paper stock was rationed, the head of Triangle Publications bought out *Click*, the third largest picture magazine in the United States (with projected ad revenue of $1 million for that year) and "buried" it in order to divert the paper stock to a new magazine, *Seventeen*, intended to tap the "hitherto unexploited market" of teenage girls. The response was "electric," and a host of imitators followed.[9] By 1960, one source estimated, America's eighteen million teenagers were spending $10 billion a year on their own culture, including magazines to "instruct them in custom, ritual, propriety, sex mores, and proper think."[10]

These years of segregation and protection of youth helped to transform courtship. Because young people were released, to a great extent, from adult responsibilities and decisions, the act of choosing a lifelong mate did not seem so immediately important. Within youth culture, the emphasis in courtship shifted to the social and recreational process of dating, but without giving up the romantic and sexual explorations that had characterized the final stage of courtship in the previous century.

Youth is an easier word to define than *middle class*, just as age designation is more specific than class designation. To a large extent, I am using a cultural definition of "middle class" — a definition that seems appropriate to mid-century America.[11] A culture that generally denied the importance of class defined participation in the general (middle-class) culture as a key factor determining class — thus offering middle-class status to the vast majority of Americans.

In 1952, the Purdue poll asked a large and representative sample of

American high school students to choose among four labels for their families' social class: upper-class, middle-class, working-class, and lower-class. When cross-tabulated with responses to other questions, this query yielded some interesting statistics. Forty-seven percent of all students whose fathers were unskilled laborers defined themselves as middle-class, as did 59 percent of those whose fathers held "mid-level jobs working with tools." (The job classifications were gained by collapsing twelve categories that listed specific examples from which students could choose.) Furthermore, 48 percent of all students in families with "low" incomes saw themselves as middle-class, and 52 percent of students whose mothers had no education beyond grade school believed their families to be middle-class.[12]

These responses seem to show that young people had a sense that class lines were flexible and not primarily determined by income or by occupation. I believe (and this is, to a large extent, speculation) that these otherwise puzzling class definitions in large part stem from a cultural definition of class. As students saw it, they and their families participated in the general culture – a culture *defined* as middle-class.

I am not arguing that allegiance to a middle-class culture or membership in the middle class (however defined) grew steadily and progressively from the late nineteenth century on. The 1930s, for example, saw a resurgence of working-class consciousness. But the middle-class culture maintained a strong public voice throughout the period, and by the post–World War II years, American culture claimed a middle-class consensus.

In any case, because I am looking at *conventions* publicly presented to and for a general, middle-class audience, and not at the *experience* of discrete and carefully defined class groupings, I am, in a sense, reading class backward. Since the cultural sources I use were, in general, explicitly aimed at the middle class, broadly defined, I accept that their audiences were, culturally, middle-class. Many studies and surveys presented within the sources themselves bear out that assumption. Still, what is most important is not that every individual who encountered these conventions was middle-class, but that the conventions were presented to the public as national conventions, that they appeared as uniform conventions of a dominant culture, and that they reached, directly or indirectly, a great majority of Americans.

I am very aware that, by choosing to examine the "national" conventions governing courtship, I am slighting both the experience and the conventions of many Americans: the very poor and the very rich; members of ethnic, racial, or religious groups that were excluded from the larger culture or that rejected its dictates; lesbians and homosexual

men; older people; divorced people conducting second or third court-
ships; and a wide range of individuals who, voluntarily or involun-
tarily, set themselves apart from this culture. Their conventions and
experience remain to be defined.

A study of national conventions of courtship, however, not only
reveals the conventions that structured courtship for the majority, it
also gives insight into the lives of other Americans. The culture I
describe was a dominant, even hegemonic, one. It informed public
policy; it was written into law and public school curricula. It was a
culture that judged both those it excluded and those who rejected it according to its own dictates. Almost everyone felt its weight. Those
who rejected these dominant conventions almost necessarily defined
themselves in opposition to them, and struggled to maintain or create
their own customs within this larger culture. This study, by providing
a context, a landscape of the dominant culture, helps to illustrate the
true difficulty and meaning of their struggles.

One final note: the word *love* scarcely appears in the following
pages. This is not because I have a cynical view of the subject but
because love was not so much the province of convention. Convention looked to a multiplicity of desires, not to love itself. It structured
and controlled the manifestation of sexual desire and the desires for
security, for status, for a clear role in society — even the desire for
love. Love and desire are intertwined, but I will leave love to lovers in
private and examine the public conventions of desire.

Calling Cards and Money

*O*ne day, the 1920s story goes, a young man asked a city girl if he might call on her. We know nothing else about the man or the girl — only that, when he arrived, she had her hat on. Not much of a story to us, but any American born before 1910 would have gotten the punch line. "She had her hat on": those five words were rich in meaning to early twentieth century Americans. The hat signaled that she expected to leave the house. He came on a "call," expecting to be received in her family's parlor, to talk, to meet her mother, perhaps to have some refreshments or to listen to her play the piano. She expected a "date," to be taken "out" somewhere and entertained. He ended up spending four weeks' savings fulfilling her expectations.[1]

In the early twentieth century this new style of courtship, dating, had begun to supplant the old. Born primarily of the limits and opportunities of urban life, dating had almost completely replaced the old system of calling by the mid-1920s — and, in so doing, had transformed American courtship. Dating moved courtship into the public world, relocating it from family parlors and community events to restaurants, theaters, and dance halls. At the same time, it removed couples from the implied supervision of the private sphere — from the watchful eyes of family and local community — to the anonymity of the public sphere. Courtship among strangers offered couples new freedom. But access to the public world of the city required money. One had to buy entertainment, or even access to a place to sit and talk. Money — men's money — became the basis of the dating system and, thus, of courtship. This new dating system, as it shifted courtship from the private to the public sphere and increasingly centered around money, fundamentally altered the balance of power between men and women in courtship.

The transition from calling to dating was as complete as it was fundamental. By the 1950s and 1960s, social scientists who studied American courtship found it necessary to remind the American public that dating was a "recent American innovation and not a traditional or universal custom."[2] Some of the many commentators who wrote about courtship believed dating was the best thing that had ever happened to relations between the sexes; others blamed the dating system for all the problems of American youth and American marriage.[3] But virtually everyone portrayed the system dating replaced as infinitely simpler, sweeter, more innocent, and more graceful. Hardheaded social scientists waxed sentimental about the "horse-and-buggy days," when a young man's offer of a ride home from church was tantamount to a proposal and when young men came calling in the evenings and courtship took place safely within the warm bosom of the family. "The courtship which grew out of the sturdy social roots [of the nineteenth century]," one author wrote, "comes through to us for what it was — a gracious ritual, with clearly defined roles for man and woman, in which everyone knew the measured music and the steps."[4]

Certainly a less idealized version of this model of courtship had existed in America, but it was not this model that dating was supplanting. Although only about 45 percent of Americans lived in urban areas by 1910, few of them were so untouched by the sweeping changes of the late nineteenth century that they could live that dream of rural simplicity. Conventions of courtship at that time were not set by simple yeoman farmers and their families but by the rising middle class, often in imitation of the ways of "society."

By the late nineteenth century a new and relatively coherent social group had come to play an important role in the nation's cultural life.[5] This new middle class, born with and through the rise of national systems of economy, transportation, and communication, was actively creating, controlling, and consuming a national system of culture. National magazines with booming subscription rates promulgated middle-class standards to the white, literate population at large. Women's magazines were especially important in the role of cultural evangelist.[6]

These magazines carried clearly didactic messages to their readership. Unlike general-interest (men's) magazines, which were more likely to contain discussions of issues and events, women's magazines were highly prescriptive, giving advice on both the spiritual and the mundane. But while their advice on higher matters was usually vaguely inspirational, advice on how to look and how to act was extremely explicit.

The conventions of courtship, as set forth in these national magazines and in popular books of etiquette, were an important part of the middle-class code of manners. Conventional courtship centered on "calling," a term that could describe a range of activities. The young man from the neighboring farm who spent the evening sitting on the front porch with the farmer's daughter was paying a call, and so was the "society" man who could judge his prospects by whether or not the card he presented at the front door found the lady of his choice "at home." The middle-class arbiters of culture, however, aped and elaborated the society version of the call. And, as it was promulgated by magazines such as the *Ladies' Home Journal*, with a circulation over one million by 1900, the modified society call was the model for an increasing number of young Americans.

Outside of courtship, this sort of calling was primarily a woman's activity, for women largely controlled social life. Women designated a day or days "at home" to receive callers; on other days they paid or returned calls. The caller would present her card to the maid (common even in moderate-income homes until the World War I era) who answered the door, and would be admitted or turned away with some excuse. The caller who regularly was "not received" quickly learned the limits of her family's social status, and the lady "at home" thus, in some measure, protected herself and her family from the social confusion and pressures engendered by the mobility and expansiveness of late nineteenth-century America. In this system, the husband, though generally determining the family's status, was represented by his wife and was thereby excused from this social-status ritual. Unmarried men, however, were subject to this female-controlled system.

The calling system in courtship, though varying by region and the status of the individuals involved, followed certain general outlines. When a girl reached the proper age or had her first "season" (depending on her family's social level), she became eligible to receive male callers. At first her mother or guardian invited young men to call; in subsequent seasons the young lady had more autonomy and could bestow an invitation to call upon any unmarried man to whom she had been properly introduced at a private dance, dinner, or other "entertainment." Any unmarried man invited to an entertainment owed his hostess (and thus her daughter[s]) a duty call of thanks, but other young men not so honored could be brought to call by friends or relatives of the girl's family, subject to her prior permission. Undesired or undesirable callers, on the other hand, were simply given some excuse and turned away.[7]

The call itself was a complicated event. A myriad of rules governed everything: the proper amount of time between invitation and visit (a fortnight or less); whether or not refreshments should be served (not if one belonged to a fashionable or semi-fashionable circle, but outside of "smart" groups in cities like New York and Boston, girls *might* serve iced drinks with little cakes or tiny cups of coffee or hot chocolate and sandwiches); chaperonage (the first call must be made on daughter and mother, but excessive chaperonage would indicate to the man that his attentions were unwelcome); appropriate topics of conversation (the man's interests, but never too personal); how leave should be taken (on no account should the woman "accompany [her caller] to the door nor stand talking while he struggles into his coat").[8]

Each of these "measured steps," as the mid-twentieth century author nostalgically called them, was a test of suitability, breeding, and background. Advice columns and etiquette books emphasized that these were the manners of any "well-bred" person — and conversely implied that deviations revealed a lack of breeding. However, around the turn of the century, many people who did lack this narrow "breeding" aspired to politeness. Advice columns in women's magazines regularly printed questions from "Country Girl" and "Ignoramus" on the fine points of calling etiquette.[9] Young men must have felt the pressure of girls' expectations, for they wrote to the same advisers with questions about calling. In 1907, *Harper's Bazaar* ran a major article titled "Etiquette for Men," explaining the ins and outs of the calling system.[10] In the first decade of the twentieth century, this rigid system of calling was the convention not only of the "respectable" but also of those who aspired to respectability.

At the same time, however, the new system of dating was emerging. By the mid-1910s, the word *date* had entered the vocabulary of the middle-class public. In 1914, the *Ladies' Home Journal*, a bastion of middle-class respectability, used the term (safely enclosed in quotation marks but with no explanation of its meaning) several times. The word was always spoken by that exotica, the college sorority girl — a character marginal in her exoticness but nevertheless a solid product of the middle class. "One beautiful evening of the spring term," one such article begins, "when I was a college girl of eighteen, the boy whom, because of his popularity in every phase of college life, I had been proud gradually to allow the monopoly of my 'dates,' took me unexpectedly into his arms. As he kissed me impetuously I was glad, from the bottom of my heart, for the training of that mother who had taught me to hold myself aloof from all personal familiarities of boys and men." [11]

Sugarcoated with a tribute to motherhood and virtue, the dates — and the kiss — were unmistakably presented for a middle-class audience. By 1924, ten years later, when the story of the unfortunate young man who went to call on the city girl was current, dating had essentially replaced calling in middle-class culture. The knowing smiles of the story's listeners had probably started with the word *call* — and not every hearer would have been sympathetic to the man's plight. By 1924, he really should have known better.

Dating, that great American middle-class institution, was not at all a product of the middle class. Dating came to the middle class through the upper classes — and from the lower. The first recorded uses of the word *date* in its modern meaning are from lower-class slang. George Ade, the Chicago author who wrote a column titled "Stories of the Streets and of the Town" for the *Chicago Record* and published many slang-filled stories of working-class life, probably introduced the term to literature in 1896. Artie, Ade's street-smart protagonist, asks his unfaithful girlfriend, "I s'pose the other boy's fillin' all my dates?" And in 1899 Ade suggested the power of a girl's charms: "Her Date Book had to be kept on the Double Entry System." Other authors whose imaginations were captured by the city and the variety of its inhabitants — Frank Norris, Upton Sinclair, O. Henry — also were using the term by the first decade of the twentieth century. [12]

The practice of dating was a response of the lower classes to the pressures and opportunities of urban-industrial America, just as calling was a response of the upper strata. The strict conventions of calling enabled the middling and upper classes to protect themselves from some of the intrusions of urban life, to screen out some of the effects of social and geographical mobility in late nineteenth-century America. Those without the money and security to protect themselves from the pressures of urban life or to control the overwhelming opportunities it offered adapted to the new conditions much more directly.

Dating, which to the privileged and protected would seem a system of increased freedom and possibility, stemmed originally from the lack of opportunities. Calling, or even just visiting, was not a practicable system for young people whose families lived crowded into one or two rooms. For even the more established or independent working-class girls, the parlor and the piano often simply didn't exist. [13] Some "factory girls" struggled to find a way to receive callers. The *Ladies' Home Journal* approvingly reported the case of six girls, workers in a box factory, who had formed a club and pooled part of their wages to pay the "janitress of a tenement house" to let them use her front room two evenings a week. It had a piano. One of the girls explained their system: "We ask the boys to come when they like and spend the evening. We haven't any place at home to see them, and I hate seeing them on the street." [14]

Many other working girls, however, couldn't have done this even had they wanted to. They had no extra wages to pool, or they had no notions of middle-class respectability. Some, especially girls of ethnic families, were kept secluded — chaperoned according to the customs of the old country.[15] But many others fled the squalor, drabness, and crowdedness of their homes to seek amusement and intimacy elsewhere. And a "good time" increasingly became identified with public places and commercial amusements, making young women whose wages would not even cover the necessities of life dependent on men's "treats." [16] Still, many poor and working-class couples did not so much escape from the home as they were pushed from it.

These couples courted on the streets, sometimes at cheap dance halls or eventually at the movies. These were not respectable places, and women could enter them only so far as they, themselves, were not considered respectable.[17] Respectable young women did, of course, enter the public world, but their excursions into the public were cushioned. Public courtship of middle-class and upper-class youth was at least *supposed* to be chaperoned; those with money and social position went to private dances with carefully controlled guest lists, to theater parties where they were a private group within the public. As rebels would soon complain, the supervision of society made the private parlor seem almost free by contrast. Women who were not respectable did have relative freedom of action — but the trade-off was not necessarily a happy one for them.[18]

The negative factors were important, but dating rose equally from the possibilities offered by urban life. Privileged youth, as Lewis Erenberg shows in his study of New York nightlife, came to see the possibility of privacy in the anonymous public, in the excitement and freedom the city offered. They looked to lower-class models of freedom — to those beyond the constraints of respectability.[19] As a society girl informed the readers of the *Ladies' Home Journal* in 1914: "Nowadays it is considered 'smart' to go to the low order of dance halls, and not only be a looker-on, but also to dance among all sorts and conditions of men and women. . . . Nowadays when we enter a restaurant and dance place it is hard to know who is who." [20] In 1907, the same magazine had warned unmarried women never to go alone to a "public restaurant" with any man, even a relative. There was no impropriety in the act, the adviser had conceded, but it still "lays [women] open to misunderstanding and to being classed with women of undesirable reputation by the strangers present."[21] Rebellious and adventurous young people sought that confusion, and the gradual loosening of proprieties they engendered helped to change courtship. Young men and women went out into the world *together*, enjoying a new kind of companionship and the intimacy of a new kind of freedom from adult supervision.[22]

The new freedom that led to dating came from other sources as well. Many more serious (and certainly respectable) young women were taking advantage of opportunities to enter the public world — going to college, taking jobs, entering and creating new urban professions. Women who belonged to the public world by day began to demand fuller access to the public world in general. City institutions gradually accommodated them.[23] Though still considered risqué by some, dining out alone with a man or attending the theater with no chaperone did not threaten an unmarried woman's reputation by the start of the twentieth century.

There were still limits, of course, and they persisted for a long while. Between 1904 and 1907, *Ladies' Home Journal* advisers repeatedly insisted that a girl should not "go out" with a young man until he had called at her home.[24] And in the early 1920s, Radcliffe girls were furnished with a list of approved restaurants in which they could dine with a young man.[25] Some were acceptable only before 7:30 P.M.; others, clearly, still posed a threat to reputations. These limits and conditions, however, show that young men and women of courting age were *expected* to go out — the restrictions were not attempts to *stop* dating, only to control it.

Between 1890 and 1925, dating — in practice and in name — had gradually, almost imperceptibly, become a universal custom in America. By the 1930s it had transcended its origins: Middle America associated dating with neither upper-class rebellion nor the urban lower classes. The rise of dating was usually explained, quite simply, by the invention of the automobile. Cars had given youth mobility and privacy, and so had brought about the system.[26] This explanation — perhaps not consciously but definitely not coincidentally — revised history. The automobile certainly contributed to the rise of dating as a *national* practice, especially in rural and suburban areas, but it was simply accelerating and extending a process already well under way. Once its origins were located firmly in Middle America, however, and not in the extremes of urban upper- and lower-class life, dating had become an American institution.

Dating not only transformed the outward modes and conventions of American courtship, it also changed the distribution of control and power in courtship. One change was generational: the dating system lessened parental control and gave young men and women more freedom. The dating system also shifted power from women to men. Calling, either as a simple visit or as the elaborate late nineteenth-century ritual, gave women a large portion of control. First of all, courtship took place within the girl's home — in women's "sphere," as it was called in the nineteenth century — or at entertainments largely devised and presided over by women. Dating moved courtship out of the home and into man's sphere — the world outside the home. Female controls and conventions lost much of their power outside women's sphere. And while many of the conventions of female propriety were restrictive and repressive, they had allowed women (young women and their mothers) a great deal of immediate control over courtship. The transfer of spheres thoroughly undercut that control.

Second, in the calling system, the woman took the initiative. Etiquette books and columns were adamant on that point: it was the "girl's privilege" to ask a young man to call. Furthermore, it was highly improper for the man to take the initiative. In 1909 a young man wrote to the *Ladies' Home Journal* adviser asking, "May I call upon a young woman whom I greatly admire, although she had not given me the permission? Would she be flattered at my eagerness, even to the setting aside of conventions, or would she think me impertinent?" Mrs. Kingsland replied: "I think that you would risk her just displeasure and frustrate your object of finding favor with her." Softening the prohibition, she then suggested an invitation might be secured through a mutual friend.[27] She had been even stricter two years before, insisting that "a man must not go beyond a very evident pleasure in a woman's society, by way of suggestions."[28] Another adviser, "The Lady from Philadelphia," put a more positive light on the situation, noting that "nothing forbids a man to show by his manner that her acquaintance is pleasing to him and thus perhaps suggest that the invitation [to call] would be welcome."[29]

Contrast these strictures with advice on dating etiquette from the 1940s and 1950s: An advice book for men and women warns that "girls who [try] to usurp the right of boys to choose their own dates" will "ruin a good dating career. . . . Fair or not, it is the way of life. From the Stone Age, when men chased and captured their women, comes the yen of a boy to do the pursuing. You will control your impatience, therefore, and respect the time-honored custom of boys to take the first step."[30]

One teen advice book from the 1950s told girls never to take the initiative with a boy, even under some pretext such as asking about homework: "Boys are jealous of their masculine prerogative of taking the initiative."[31] Another said simply: "*Don't ask*," and still another recounted an anecdote about a girl who asked a boy for a date to the Saturday-night dance. He cut her off in mid-sentence and walked away.[32]

Of course, some advisers stressed that women were not without resource. Though barred from taking the initiative, nothing forbade women from using tricks and stratagems, from showing by a friendly manner that they would welcome an invitation for a date.

This absolute reversal of roles almost necessarily accompanied courtship's move from woman's sphere to man's sphere. Although the convention-setters commended the custom of woman's initiative because it allowed greater exclusivity (it might be "difficult for a girl to refuse the permission to call, no matter how unwelcome or unsuitable an acquaintance the man might be"), the custom was based on a broader principle of etiquette.[33] The host or hostess issued any invitation; the guest did not invite himself or herself. An invitation to call was an invitation to visit in a woman's home.

An invitation to go out on a date, on the other hand, was an invitation into man's world — not simply because dating took place in the public sphere (commonly defined as belonging to men), though that was part of it, but because dating moved courtship into the world of the economy. Money — men's money — was at the center of the dating system. Thus, on two counts, men became the hosts and assumed the control that came with that position.

There was some confusion caused by this reversal of initiative, especially during the twenty years or so when going out and calling co-existed as systems. (The unfortunate young man in the apocryphal story, for example, had asked the city girl if he might call on her, so perhaps she was conventionally correct to assume he meant to play the host.) Confusions generally were sorted out around the issue of money. One young woman, "Henrietta L.," wrote to the *Ladies' Home Journal* to inquire whether a girl might "suggest to a friend going to any entertainment or place of amusement where there will be any expense to the young man." The reply: "Never, under any circumstances." The adviser explained that the invitation to go out must "always" come from the man, for he was the one "responsible for the expense."[34] This same adviser insisted that the woman must "always" invite the man to call; clearly she realized that money was the central issue.

The centrality of money in dating had serious implications for courtship. Not only did money shift control and initiative to men by making them the "hosts," it led contemporaries to see dating as a system of exchange best understood through economic analogies or as an economic system pure and simple. Of course, people did recognize in marriage a similar economic dimension — the man undertakes to support his wife in exchange for her filling various roles important to him — but marriage was a permanent relationship. Dating was situational, with no long-term commitments implied, and when a man, in a highly visible ritual, spent money on a woman in public, it seemed much more clearly an economic act.

In fact, the term *date* was associated with the direct economic exchange of prostitution at an early time. A prostitute called "Maimie," in letters written to a middle-class benefactor/friend in the late nineteenth century, described how men made "dates" with her.[35] And a former waitress turned prostitute described the process to the Illinois Senate Committee on Vice this way: "You wait on a man and he smiles at you. You see a chance to get a tip and you smile back. Next day he returns and you try harder than ever to please him. Then right away he wants to make a date, and offer you money and presents if you'll be a good fellow and go out with him."[36] These men, quite clearly, were buying sexual favors — but the occasion of the exchange was called a "date."

Courtship in America had always turned somewhat on money (or background). A poor clerk or stockyards worker would not have called upon the daughter of a well-off family, and men were expected to be economically secure before they married. But in the dating system money entered directly into the relationship between a man and a woman as the symbolic currency of exchange in even casual dating.

Dating, like prostitution, made access to women directly dependent on money. Quite a few men did not hesitate to complain about the going rate of exchange. In a 1925 *Collier's* article, "Why Men Won't Marry," a twenty-four-year-old university graduate exclaimed: "Get Married! Why, I can't even afford to go with any of the sort of girls with whom I would like to associate." He explained: "When I was in college, getting an allowance from home, I used to know lots of nice girls. . . . Now that I am on my own I can't even afford to see them. . . . If I took a girl to the theatre she would have to sit in the gallery, and if we went to supper afterward, it would be at a soda counter, and if we rode home it would have to be in the street cars."[37] As he presents it, the problem is solely financial. The same girls who were glad to "go with" him when he had money would not "see" him when he lacked their price. And "nice girls" cost a lot.

In dating, though, the exchange was less direct and less clear than in prostitution. One author, in 1924, made sense of it this way. In dating, he reasoned, a man is responsible for all expenses. The woman is responsible for nothing — she contributes only her company. Of course, the man contributes his company, too, but since he must "add money to balance the bargain" his company must be worth less than hers. Thus, according to this economic understanding, she is selling her company to him. In his eyes, dating didn't even involve an exchange; it was a direct purchase. The moral "subtleties" of a woman's position in dating, the author concluded, were complicated even further by the fact that young men, "discovering that she must be bought, [like] to buy her when [they happen] to have the money." [38]

Yet another young man, the same year, publicly called a halt to such "promiscuous buying." Writing anonymously (for good reason) in *American Magazine*, the author declared a "one-man buyer's strike." This man estimated that, as a "buyer of feminine companionship" for the previous five years, he had "invested" about $20 a week — a grand total of over $5,000. Finally, he wrote, he had realized that "there is a point at which any commodity — even such a delightful commodity as feminine companionship — costs more than it is worth." [39] The commodity he had bought with his $5,000 had been priced beyond its "real value" and he had had enough. This man said "enough" not out of principle, not because he rejected the implications of the economic model of courtship, but because he felt he wasn't receiving value for money.

In all three of these economic analyses, the men are complaining about the new dating system, lamenting the passing of the mythic good old days when "a man without a quarter in his pocket could call on a girl and not be embarrassed," the days before a woman had to be "bought." [40] In recognizing so clearly the economic model on which dating operated, they also clearly saw that the model was a bad one — in purely economic terms. The exchange was not equitable; the commodity was overpriced. Men were operating at a loss.

Here, however, they didn't understand their model completely. True, the equation (male companionship plus money equals female companionship) was imbalanced. But what men were buying in the dating system was not just female companionship, not just entertainment — but power. Money purchased obligation; money purchased inequality; money purchased control.

The conventions that grew up to govern dating codified women's inequality and ratified men's power. Men asked women out; women were condemned as "aggressive" if they expressed interest in a man too directly. Men paid for everything, but often with the implication that women "owed" sexual favors in return. The dating system required men always to assume control, and women to act as men's dependents.

Yet women were not without power in the system, and they were willing to contest men with their "feminine" power. Much of the public discourse on courtship in twentieth-century America was concerned with this contestation. Thousands of sources chronicled the struggles of, and between, men and women — struggles mediated by the "experts" and arbiters of convention — to create a balance of power, to gain or retain control of the dating system. These struggles, played out most clearly in the fields of sex, science, and etiquette, made ever more explicit the complicated relations between men and women in a changing society.

The Economy of Dating

T he "date" made its transition from lower-class slang to upper-crust rebellion and into middle-class convention with relative ease. To most observers, the gradual change from calling to dating looked like a natural accommodation to the new realities of twentieth-century life. Dating filled a need in an urban society in which not all respectable young women had parlors in their homes and childhood friends infrequently grew up to become husband and wife. Dating quickly became, and remains, the dominant mode of American courtship.

In the early twentieth century, the gloomiest critics feared only that this new system would make it harder for youth to negotiate the true business of courtship: marriage. Poor but ambitious and worthy young men could not attract suitable partners without spending vast sums on entertainment, and every theater ticket and late supper meant less money set aside toward that minimum figure needed to marry and start a family.

The critics were right, but in some ways their criticisms were irrelevant. Dating was not about marriage and families. It wasn't even about love — which is not to say that American youth didn't continue to fall in love, marry, and raise families. But before World War II, long-term commitments lay in the future for youth, clearly demarcated from the dating system. In the public realm, in the shared culture that defined the conventions of dating and gave meaning and coherence to individual experience, dating was not about marriage. Dating was about competition.

Through at least the first two-thirds of the twentieth century, Americans thought of courtship as a system governed by laws of scarcity and abundance, and acted in accordance with that perception. Furthermore, America's system of courtship, as much as any other sphere of national life, mirrored the vicissitudes of economic and social opportunity and demands. In the 1920s, dating provided a new frontier for public competition through consumption, and in the 1930s it accepted competitive energies denied outlet elsewhere. In the post-war years, however, youth looked to courtship for a respite from the demands of a competitive society.

These different attitudes toward the role of competition in court-ship before and after World War II are expressed in two distinct forms of dating. Before the war, American youth prized a promiscuous pop-ularity, demonstrating competitive success through the number and variety of dates they commanded. After the war, youth turned to "go-ing steady," saying that the system provided a measure of security and escape from the pressures of the postwar world. The courtship experi-ence and ideals of those who grew up before the war were profoundly different from those of teenagers in the postwar years, and the differ-ences created much intergenerational conflict. Yet, for all their dis-agreement, both groups understood dating in the same terms: compe-tition, scarcity, abundance. This understanding of dating, as much as the system itself, was an accommodation to modern life.

Shortly after World War II ended, Margaret Mead gave a series of lectures on American courtship rituals. Although the system she de-scribed was already disappearing, she captured the essence of what dating meant in the interwar years. Dating, Mead stressed, was not about sex or adulthood or marriage. Instead, it was a "competitive game," a way for girls and boys to "demonstrate their popularity." This was not a startling revelation to the American public. Americans knew that dating was centered on competition and popularity. These were the terms in which dating was discussed, the vocabulary in which one described a date.[1]

In 1937, in the classic study of American dating, sociologist Willard Waller gave this competitive system a name: "the campus rating com-plex." His study of Penn State detailed a "dating and rating" system based on very clear standards of popularity. To be popular, men needed outward, material signs: an automobile, the right clothing, fra-ternity membership, money. Women's popularity depended on build-ing and maintaining a reputation for popularity. They had to *be seen* with popular men in the "right" places, indignantly turn down requests for dates made at the "last minute" (which could be weeks in advance), and cultivate the impression that they were greatly in demand.[2]

Waller gave academic legitimacy to a practice and a label commonly employed since the early 1920s.[3] The competitive system of rating and dating flourished on college campuses well before Waller's study. It was a product of many long-term trends that had produced an awareness of youth as a discrete and definable experience and had fostered the development of a national youth culture. In the 1920s, youth most extravagantly celebrated their culture (for themselves and for the nation, through the attentions of national newspapers and magazines) on college campuses. While their numbers were relatively small, the doings of college youth carried much symbolic weight with adults and their nonstudent peers, who viewed youth culture sometimes with suspicion, sometimes with envy, almost always with fascination.

As Paula Fass argues in her study of American college youth in the 1920s, "Competition within conformity and conformity in the service of competition were the structuring facts of campus life in the twenties." Competition and conformity, the individual and the group, held each other in a delicate balance. Conformity to peer group standards set the limits of competition — and unleashed the forces of competition within the limits of peer culture. Sports, school spirit, organizational rivalry, social life, and consumption allowed full play of competitive urges. But because youth and its institutions were a separate culture in which one could participate for only a few years, competition was without significant long-term risk. This protected competition was seen as a training ground for the struggles young people would soon face in the world outside college. Moreover, and paradoxically, this competition expressed itself through conformity; conformity was the ultimate sphere of competition. It was a self-contained, self-regulating, self-limiting system.[4]

Fass explores these issues primarily in terms of organizational and institutional competition, but youth's evolving system of courtship also perfectly expressed them. The rating-and-dating system *was* individual competition expressed through conformity. The competition was individual, but in the 1920s success in courtship came to be defined by the peer group. Success was popularity. Popularity was — and could only be — defined and allocated by others.

By the 1930s, the competitive system of courtship was well entrenched. However, though the rating-and-dating system stayed much the same, it was fed from different sources in the Depression years of the 1930s. No longer was competitive youth culture seen as the training ground for success-bound youth. Instead, success in social competition compensated for fears that other avenues of competition were closed off. But that a system based on abundance, consumption, and relative protection from the realities of adult life could persist and grow stronger in the face of a national depression shows how completely it had replaced the older systems of courtship.

No matter how people conducted their private lives, from the mid-1920s to World War II the rating-dating system dominated public discourse on courtship.[5] Waller's model is validated by countless examples from the popular media. College campuses, the peer cultures in which the rating-dating complex originated, offer textbook cases. In *Mademoiselle*'s 1938 college issue, a Smith senior advised incoming freshmen that they must cultivate an "image of popularity" if they wanted dates. "During your first term," she wrote, get "home talent" to ply you with letters, telegrams, invitations. College men will think, "She *must* be attractive if she can rate all that attention."[6] And at Northwestern University in the 1920s, the competitive pressure was so intense that coeds made a pact not to date on certain nights of the week. That way they could preserve some time to study, secure in the knowledge that they were not losing ground in the race for popularity by staying home.[7]

Although Waller did not see it, the technique of image building was not always limited to women. For men, too, nothing succeeded like success. A *Guide Book for Young Men about Town* advised: "It's money in the bank to have lots of girls on the knowing list and the date calendar. . . . It means more popularity for you." As proof, the author looked back to his own college days, recalling how a classmate won the title of "Most Popular Man" at a small coed college by systematically going through the college register and dating every girl in the school who wasn't engaged.[8]

At some schools, the system was particularly blatant. In early 1936, a group of women at the University of Michigan decided to rate the BMOCs (Big Men on Campus) according to their "dating value." Men had to have dated several women even to be considered for the list. Those qualifying were rated either "A — smooth; B — OK; C — pass in a crowd; D — semigoon; or E — spook." As the Damda Phi Data sorority, these women made copies of the rating list and left them around campus. The Michigan *Daily* reported that the lists were being used "quite extensively" by women to check the ratings of potential blind dates.[9] This codification helped women to conform to peer judgments of dating value (and also to gain some kind of power over the most powerful men).

The concept of dating value had nothing to do with the interpersonal experience of a date — whether or not the boy (or girl, for that matter) was fun or charming or brilliant was irrelevant. Instead, the rating looked to others: "pass in a crowd" does not refer to any relationship between the couple, but to public perceptions of success in the popularity competition. Dating a "spook" could set you back, but the C-rater would hold your place, keep you in circulation.

Subtle manifestations of the rating-dating complex reveal the stress on competition even more clearly. In 1935, the Massachusetts *Collegian* (the Massachusetts State College newspaper) ran an editorial against using the library for "datemaking." The editors concluded: "The library is the place for the improvement of the mind and not the social standing of the student."[10] Social standing, not social life: on one word turns the meaning of the dating system. That "standing" probably wasn't even a conscious choice shows how completely people took for granted that dating was primarily concerned with status, competition, and popularity. Dates were markers in this system of exchange. Success — the only goal structurally possible — was to acquire enough popularity to continue to compete.

Popularity was clearly the key — and popularity defined in a very specific way. It was not earned directly through talent, looks, personality, or importance in organizations, but by the way these attributes translated into dates. These dates had to be highly visible, and with many different people, or they didn't count. In the mid-1930s, for instance, an etiquette book for college women compared a Northwestern University organization of campus "widows" (who showed they were faithful to faraway lovers by wearing yellow ribbons around their necks and meeting to read letters and share mementos while others dated) to women who were "pinned" to one man. The author made just one caveat: the widows "stay home all the time, and the pin wearers *at least* have steady dates" (emphasis added).[11] One man was only marginally better than none.

The rating-dating system, and the definition of popularity on which it was based, was not restricted to college campuses. Originally, popular magazines and advice books had described it as a college phenomenon, but during the 1930s, the college campus ceased to be the determining factor. In 1940, a *Woman's Home Companion* article explained the modern dating system (with no mention of college campuses) to its readers: "If you have dates aplenty you are asked everywhere. Dates are the hallmark of personality and popularity. No matter how pretty you may be, how smart your clothes — or your tongue — if you have no dates your rating is low. . . . The modern girl cultivates not one single suitor, but dates, lots of them. . . . Her aim is not a too obvious romance but general popularity."[12]

The tone of the article is unqualified approval. As the popularity-ideal passed from college youth into the culture at large, it lost its aura of difference, its suspectness. For one thing, college youth raised on rating-dating were, by the late 1930s, the ones writing the advice columns for young people. In national magazines, they standardized and perpetuated the competitive dating system.

High school students of the late 1930s and 1940s, then, were raised on rating and dating. Not only did they imitate the conventions of older youth, they were advised by some young columnists, who spoke with distinctly nonparental voices, that these conventions were natural and right. *Senior Scholastic,* a magazine used in high schools all over the United States, began running an advice column in 1936. "Boy Dates Girl," written under the pseudonym Gay Head, quickly became the magazine's most popular feature.[13]

Gay Head's advice always took the competitive system as a given. She assumed that girls would accept any *straightforward* offer of a date if not already "dated" for the evening, and that boys, in trying for the most popular girl imaginably possible, would occasionally overreach themselves. She once warned girls never to brush off any boy, no matter how unappealing, in a rude way, since "he may come in handy for an off-night."[14] An advice column for "sub-debs" in the *Ladies' Home Journal* struck the same note. The columnist advised that shunning blind dates as "public proof" of a slow social life was bad policy. Even if "imperfect," she wrote, blind dates would "help keep you in circulation. They're good press agents. They even add to your collection."[15]

Teenagers had little argument with this advice. Early debates on "going steady" in *Senior Scholastic* (which show that some students, at least, wanted a "single suitor") overwhelmingly rejected the steady-date plan. Negative responses were blunt: "If a girl goes steady she loses her gift of gab; she doesn't need to compete with others of her species" (Chicago); "Going steady is like buying the first car you see — only a car has trade-in value later on" ("Two Boys," Milwaukee); "One is a bore — I want more!" ("A Girl," Lynwood, California). A girl from Greensboro, North Carolina summed it all up:

> Going steady with one date
> Is okay, if that's all you rate.[16]

Rating, dating, popularity, competition: catchwords hammered home, reinforced from all sides until they seemed a natural vocabulary. You had to rate in order to date, to date in order to rate. By successfully maintaining this cycle, you became popular. To stay popular, you competed. There was no end: popularity was a deceptive goal. It was only a transient state, not a trophy that could be won and possessed. You competed to become popular, and being popular allowed you to continue to compete. *Competition* was the key term in the formula — remove it and there was no rating, dating, or popularity.

In the 1930s and 1940s, this competition was enacted, most visibly, on the dance floor. There, success was a dizzying popularity that kept girls whirling from escort to escort. An etiquette book for college girls (1936) told girls to strive to be "once-arounders," to never be left with the same partner for more than one turn around the dance floor. Spending all your dances with the same man, the author advised, was in poor taste unless you were engaged to him.[17]

According to *Mademoiselle* in 1937, some critics were concerned about the system "which rates a party a success if the ratio is seven stags to every girl and which demands that she be the living embodiment of the perpetual motion dream." These critics insisted that girls did not really like the "terrific competition for popularity." But, *Mademoiselle* reported, the girls said "Nuts."[18] The dream of popularity (and the power of its reality) had a firm hold, and it was fed from many sources. A 1940 Carson, Pirie, Scott ad in the *Daily Northwestern* captured the dream and captioned it "The Stag Line Waits . . . For You in Black Velvet with Taffeta."[19]

The dream, as those things go, could very easily become a nightmare. Dance chaperones worried about ways to "translate" wallflowers, and often gave young men a nudge in their direction.[20] But much, much worse than being a wallflower was "getting stuck." At least a wallflower could hide in the ladies' room or pretend to devote herself to an elderly chaperone. Getting stuck was a highly visible catastrophe.

Dancing and cutting in were governed by a strict protocol. The man had to request the dance and was responsible for the woman until she was taken over by another partner. On no account could he leave her stranded on the dance floor or alone on the sidelines. Only she could suggest leaving the dance floor, and then only if she spotted a group of friends to which she could retire. Otherwise, he would have to remain with her there.

Getting stuck meant, quite simply, not getting cut in on. Gradually the woman's smile would grow brittle and desperate; the man would begin casting beseeching looks at possible rescuers. Everyone would notice. This image haunted young women and certainly kept young men from asking girls to dance who had not already and undeniably proven their popularity.

Getting stuck was taken quite seriously as a sign of social failure.

Even getting stuck with one's escort was a disgrace. In a lengthy passage on the subject, Vogue *Etiquette* advised women to suggest leaving the dance floor as soon as getting stuck "seems likely." If the situation got "completely out-of-hand," if there were no groups of friends to join and everyone else was "dancing gaily," it continued, "the best thing to do is go home." [21]

A 1933 advice book told the story of a girl who, upon catching her partner waving a dollar bill behind her back as an inducement to cut in, offered, "Make it five and I'll go home." More seriously, the author added, to be popular at a dance required the "endurance of a Spartan and the training of a Southerner." [22] A college student, writing for *Mademoiselle*, advised, "Keep smiling if it kills you," and a mother, writing in *Harper's* on the accomplishments she expected of her daughter, sandwiched "Face the brutality of stag lines at parties" between passing college board examinations in chemistry, French, and Latin, and being able to change a tire. [23]

This form of "brutality" would change dramatically. By the early 1950s, "cutting in" had almost completely disappeared outside the Deep South. In 1955, a student at Texas Christian University reported, "To cut in is almost an insult." A girl in Green Bay, Wisconsin, said that her parents were "astonished" when they discovered she hadn't danced with anyone but her escort at a formal. "The truth was," she admitted, "that I wasn't aware that we were supposed to." [24]

This 180-degree reversal took place quickly — during the years of World War II — and was so complete by the early 1950s that people under eighteen could be totally unaware of the formerly powerful convention. It signaled not simply a change in dancing etiquette but a complete transformation of the dating system as well. Definitions of social success as promiscuous popularity based on strenuous competition had given way to new definitions, which located success in the security of a dependable escort.

The dimensions of the change were captured in an unexpectedly poignant article in *Woman's Home Companion*. The author, Cameron Shipp, was attempting to explain the new dating and dancing customs to bewildered adults by recounting conversations with "Emmie," a gorgeous, auburn-haired young lady of sixteen, who was, incidentally, his niece. He asked her about her school prom:

> "Have fun? Dance with lots of boys?"
>
> "It was real neat," she told me patiently. "But naturally I didn't dance with lots of boys. I danced with Jim."
>
> "Every dance?"

"Naturally every dance."

"You were stuck?"

Emmie tossed her flaming hair at me in disgust which she quickly tried to hide, being a good kid.

"Not stuck, Uncle Cam," she explained. "Everybody danced every dance with their dates — I mean, see, that you just dance with your date, is all. . . . Anyway, what other way is there?"

Cam, the aging charmer, recalled the other way very well:

It was like this: You fetched a girl to a dance to show her off and give her a good time rather than to hold her in your arms all night while staring longingly at a dozen other bits of fluff you'd like to hold in your arms.

He continued:

You saw that she danced with other guys. It was your responsibility to start her off, present all your friends to her and see that she got cut in on enough to feel popular. That way, a girl might go to a dance where she didn't know a soul to begin with and wind up the belle of the ball.

I saw that happen one night. The girl's name was Susan and she was scared and beautiful. I took her to her first big dance and she almost backed out on me at the last minute, being frightened and all. Suppose no one cut in?

I took care of that. It was a cinch. The Class of '26 took over at once, after three introductions, and that girl hardly got her feet on the floor. They *carried* her around, passing her from one boy to the other.

Thoroughly inspired, he continued:

A girl can't enjoy an experience like that today. This strikes me as a sadness and a shame. At least once, at some dance, a lady of sixteen ought to get a rush, enjoy the triumph and tuck away a warm and tender memory she can smile over when she's a grandmother. And a boy ought to know what it's like to see his girl competed for and appreciated. It makes a man in his teens feel important.

A sadness and a shame or not, the old way was gone. Emmie's friend, at once more savvy and more vulgar, explained the change. "It's like this," she said. "There aren't enough neat guys to go around. . . . A few big wheels. Oh, a girl doesn't demand a big wheel but she doesn't want to bounce around between queaks, does she? You wouldn't want me to go out with a *pimple*, would you?" [25]

Cutting in was a convention originally based on a sociological reality. In a society where men outnumbered women, it had provided an ordered and civilized way to share access to women. It had been a difficult system to maintain for quite a while in the United States, for women were not particularly scarce in most circles that held formal dances. Hostesses of private parties worked very hard to supply the overabundance of men necessary to make a dance successful.

The convention of cutting in finally gave way to demographic realities and practicalities — demonstrating popularity by being a once-arounder was getting more and more difficult. More important, cutting in succumbed to *fears* about what people *saw* as a new reality. After World War II, for the first time, women outnumbered men in the United States. Statistically, there weren't enough "guys," "neat" or otherwise, to go around. The dating system that had valued popularity above all was unsettled by women's concerns about the "new" scarcity of men.

Of course, concern that a scarcity of men could keep many American girls "unwilling virgins" was not born at Pearl Harbor.[26] Farsighted social scientists had raised the problem well before the war-induced shortage was felt. Ernest Groves and William Ogburn, in their 1928 text, *American Marriage and Family Relationships*, devoted an entire chapter to the relation of sex ratio to the percentage of marriages in society. From their highly statistical analysis (let $Mm + Fm = \#s$ of married males + married females) they concluded that the highest percentage of the population marries not when the sex ratio is equal but when men outnumber women by about 120 to 100. Women were, therefore, much more dependent on the supply of men than men were on the supply of women — probably because men had to take the initiative in courtship.[27]

By the 1930s, women had begun to notice a scarcity — not of men *per se*, nor of men to date, but of "marriageable men."[28] The Depression had cut deeply into the stock of men who felt they were financially secure enough to take a wife. But the war years brought scarcity of a different kind — it was palpable and heartfelt. A St. Paul woman cried to the nation (through the medium of *Time* magazine), "I want to talk to a man so bad I could scream."[29] One frank but extremely insensitive young woman told a Gallup pollster that she was making a big sacrifice because of the war: "All my boyfriends have gone overseas."[30] Understandably, British women did not have much sympathy for such complaints ("We over here have been on rations, etc., for years, while the Yanks have never sacrificed a single thing"), and few American women would have been so blunt.[31] Still, it was a hardship. Girls grew up expecting, or at least wanting, to be wined and dined and sought after, to be whirled around the dance floor by a constant succession of eager young men. The departure of 16,354,000 men (including virtually every physically fit male between the ages of eighteen and twenty-six by early 1943) for military service shattered that dream.[32]

Everyone understood that the temporary shortage of men was a trivial problem when America's whole way of life was at stake — and that simply compounded the problem. To complain about lacking dancing partners seemed selfish and unpatriotic when former dancing partners were fighting and dying in foreign lands. But this generation of women had expected to have their years of popularity, of commanding the attention of men. The competitive dating system was the only frame of reference most young women had. There were few models for a society of women, a society in which promiscuous popularity was a scarcer, and less appropriate, commodity.[33]

Public advice on how to deal with the situation varied widely. Some saw the problem as intensified competition. A 1943 *Good Housekeeping* article warned, "Somebody's After Your Man." The author claimed that ever since men "headed up the list of war scarcities," women had become "huntresses" and "hijackers." She offered a typology of "man-stealers" (the Vamp, the Pal, Big Sad Eyes, and the Button-Twister) and some tried-and-true methods for combatting their techniques.[34] Another article in *Good Housekeeping* tried to ease the competitive tension, advising women not to be self-conscious or sorry for themselves if they were an "extra woman" in a group, since "everyone knows there aren't enough men to go around these days."[35]

The hardest hit were those of courting age — especially college girls, who were isolated in an environment that was not at all what it was supposed to be. Many coed campuses were left with enrollments of 75 percent to 90 percent women.[36] On campuses almost bereft of men, women complained about the new social system and schemed to make it better.

At Massachusetts State (soon to become the University of Massachusetts, Amherst), where the ratio of men to women was one to eight (it had been one to five the other way in the "Golden Age" of the 1930s), "morale hit the dirt as dungaree sales soared."[37] Women turned to one another for companionship, forming six sororities (the first in the school's history) between 1941 and 1945. This was not simply a ploy to monopolize the remaining men in Mass State's eleven fraternities, for all were essentially inactive during World War II.[38] At the end of the war, the *Massachusetts Collegian* praised students for having been "generous in sharing the wealth [men]" during hard times.[39] Perhaps emphasizing cooperation instead of competition was easier because women at Massachusetts State had never had a terribly competitive social life. With five men to every woman on campus, there was easily enough male attention to go around. Dates were less valuable when overabundant, and these women didn't have to cut through such an entrenched system of competition for popularity.

Not all universities handled the public dimensions of the problem so gracefully. At Northwestern University, a private university with a fairly wealthy student body and a fairly competitive social life, many students hung on to the competitive ideal. With a one-to-ten male-female ratio by early 1945, Northwestern coeds faced with a dateless Junior Prom set up a date bureau. Even though the women were willing to supply the cars and buy the bids, they got little response. Ellen McConnell, co-head of the date bureau, told the *Daily Northwestern*, "We are simply furious at the men on campus. There must be SOME who want prom dates."[40] Soon after that episode, the *Daily*'s male editor lambasted "spoiled" NU coeds who had pledged to volunteer at hospitals, roll bandages, and do other forms of war work, but who hadn't followed through with it because they still thought only about men and dates.[41]

Northwestern differed from Massachusetts State in another important way during the war years. Even though the *Daily* could reprint an *Esquire* cartoon showing a coed fainted dead away, phone dangling, with the caption "Someone called her for a date" on their "Featuring NU" page, all was not hopeless.[42] There *were* men around. NU, like many other American colleges, had a military training base on its campus. Six thousand trainees passed through Northwestern's camp during the course of the war. Deering Library became an unofficial dating bureau for coeds and navy men. The *Daily* quipped, "To study is to pursue knowledge. To study at Deering is to pursue — period." When the navy semester closed in early November of 1944, several weeks before the Northwestern term ended, women complained about being left with nothing but a "handful of 4-F civilians."[43]

But the navy men were not NU sophomores, competing for the prettiest and most popular coeds. They had the upper hand now, and they knew it. One navy man, Bart R. Swopes, wrote to the *Daily* that he had heard all about NU's pretty girls when he was assigned there, but "I was not overwhelmed. . . . I was confronted with a group of overage females. These, I was told, were 'Northwestern's pretty girls.'"[44]

In this context, McConnell's anger over her failed date bureau makes more sense. The navy men were eligible for that date bureau, but they had not come forward. They were not playing the college game. Many NU women saw themselves as failed competitors. They couldn't get dates even if they advertised for escorts and paid for the dates themselves. What's more, their collective failure was spread across the front page of the college newspaper. Such across-the-board, public failure was even more of a shock than scarcity had been.

Perhaps the snidest argument over the implications of the man shortage arose at Harvard and Radcliffe, where the administrations had combined classes as an expedient measure because the student bodies and faculty were so depleted by the war.[45] Harvard men, now a scarce commodity, took their revenge on Radcliffe women (formerly the scarce ones) in the *Crimson*:

> The almost pathetic eagerness of the girl who gets a date is apt to have a dangerous effect on the tender side of a susceptible male. . . . The adolescent freshman, once thought "cute," is now reckoned a full-fledged college man . . . [Once] the Copley, the Ritz, or, in a pinch, the Statler, was the only place to dine. [Now] a snack at Liggetts, or — in the case of a particularly heavy date — supper at Hayes-Bick, is gratefully accepted by any girl. . . . Women have lost the initiative. . . . Now rules the strong, silent Harvard Man.[46]

The *Radcliffe News* responded in kind, questioning the masculinity of those who remained at Harvard ("We take time out from writing to our MEN overseas to refute the statements from last Friday's ersatz 'Crimson'"). But the kind of evidence the editors marshaled to prove that Radcliffe women were not "panting for dates" is what's surprising. They reported the following "typical statements":

> "Lost the initiative" — said the senior, addressing her wedding invitations between footnoting her thesis. "Lost the initiative?" said the junior, cleaning her wedding ring. "Lost the initiative?" laughed the sophomore, dashing from her several escorts to answer the phone. "Lost the initiative!" murmured the freshman, waiting for the "At Port" wire from her husband.[47]

Three of the four are unconcerned with dining — or with dating, for that matter. In the face of a shortage, Radcliffe's public definition of success shifted. The *Radcliffe News* bragged that Radcliffe still had its competitive edge. Quoting a new report that one of every seven American girls of their generation would not be able to marry, the paper said that Radcliffe girls' prospects "may not be so black." A list of just-married (thirty-two undergraduates and fifty graduate students) and engaged students (lengthy) followed.[48] This bragging was a far cry from the 1938 etiquette book's condescending dismissal of girls who were pinned to just one man.

The conventions of courtship had not shifted from an ideal of wild popularity to one of eighteen-year-old marriage that quickly, nor that uniformly. The return of men to campuses revived the date, though not in its former competitive glory. But, of these three models (Massachusetts State, Northwestern, and Radcliffe), Radcliffe's accommodation to fears of scarcity — its redefinition of success — was increasingly the one adopted by the youth of the nation.[49]

For the problem of scarcity did not disappear with the return of American troops. Even though the formerly men-bereft campuses were suddenly flooded with men taking advantage of the GI Bill, and even though the incredibly high marriage rate seemed to contradict the popular perception of scarcity, popular books and magazines seized upon the "man shortage." Statistics showed that the future happiness of American womanhood was threatened. As early as June 1945, a *New York Times Magazine* article began: "With half the war won, men are coming home to America, but not enough of them." The author quoted the "optimistic view" that approximately 750,000 women who wanted to marry would have to live alone, and warned that psychiatrists all agreed that these women would become "neurotic and frustrated" because women cannot ignore biological laws without "damaging themselves."[50]

Good Housekeeping captioned a photo of a bride and groom descending church steps with: "She got a man, but 6 to 8 million women won't. We're short 1 million bachelors!" The accompanying article began: "MALE SHORTAGE. . . . It's worse than ever." Quoting the now-familiar statistic that "one girl in every seven will have to live alone, whether she likes it or not," the author warned, "Unless you watch your step, this may be you."[51] An advice book for women, *Win Your Man and Keep Him*, was equally blunt: "Baldly stated, many girls of your generation will never marry."[52]

Esquire apprised men of the situation in an article by a regular contributor, J. B. Rice, M.D. Dr. Rice more than half-seriously discussed the possibility of instituting a polygamous marriage system in the United States. The original wife, faced with the choice of half a man or none, would retain economic security, companionship, and "the warm feeling that she still belongs to someone." Many women, he asserted, would rather have "a half interest in a real man than a supposed exclusive on a second-rater."[53] Even the teen magazines raised the issue. *Senior Scholastic* informed its readers that, for the first time, America had a surplus of women.[54]

Reasons given for the male shortage — or the female surplus — were many. Fewer male babies were conceived and born alive, and they had a higher rate of infant mortality than female babies. More adult men held stressful or dangerous jobs than women, and men had a higher rate of fatal disease and accident. The ratio of men to women had always been artificially inflated in America by the great influx of immigrants — the greatest proportion of them men. America was beginning to see the effects of tightened immigration laws. Of course, the war hadn't helped matters.

Most of the alarmist articles nodded toward the immigration explanation and skirted the war-death issue. No one was graceless enough to complain about the 250,000 men who died in the war, thus depriving an equal number of women of lifelong companionship. Instead, most authors pointed to an explanation more in keeping with the competitive system of American courtship: foreign women were stealing American men. By 1946, in spite of red tape, 50,000 American GIs had married English women, and Australian girls had led 10,000 or more up the aisle. French, Belgian, and other foreign women had claimed another 30,000 men who should have been potential husbands for American women.[55]

American women's rivalry with British and French women was strong and often strident. But German women — as one American wrote later — were the "final insult."[56] In response to stories about the many American men who were deserting their girlfriends or wives and families for German "frauleins," women demanded action. In mid-1945, 70 percent of American women under thirty believed American soldiers should not be allowed to date German women. In one U.S. city a group of women organized to pressure army authorities to prevent military men from marrying foreign wives. The army did institute nonfraternization rules for American GIs in Germany. Soldiers caught with German women could be given fines ranging from $65 to $325 or six months' hard labor; officers could be court-martialed and discharged. However, *Life* showed German women luring American men with "seductive" poses and scanty clothing, noting that the GIs greeted German girls with "Goodday, child," since the nonfraternization rules did not apply to children. Within a few months, authorities had eased the ban to allow soldiers to walk with girls in "public places," but not to visit them in their homes or bring them to their own quarters.[57]

As American troops came home, many young women, not surprisingly, desperately wanted everything to return to the way it had been — or the way it should have been. On college campuses, especially, women attempted to erase the *experience* of the war. In public speech, many treated it as an inconvenience that had interrupted the more important matters of life. The Northwestern student handbook for 1945–

46 advised women students: "The etiquette of dating is an art in itself. Each year more men return from the armed forces to campus, so there will be dates."[58] An advertisement for a women's clothing shop serving the University of Texas campus totally denied the reality of war: "That guy, who was someone nice to send your letters to last year, is back in your college life. Vaulted corridors will resound once more to the tread of size twelve brogans. And what a welcome change the boys make in your college life, in your college wardrobe. . . . G.I. (Guy Interest) is the theme song of Goodfriends."[59]

This kind of welcome did not please many returning veterans. College newspapers across the country printed letters criticizing the American coed. One University of Texas veteran, obviously not placated by "Guy Interest," called on his "quick sobering maturity and the sweeping education of war travels" to complain about Texas women. The college girl, he said, expected too much and gave little in return. She "makes no attempt at being a good date or trying to show the boy, who is willing to spend his time, money and efforts in obtaining her company, that she is appreciative."[60] Another former GI suggested that all male students make dates with three women on the same night and then get together for a stag party, standing up all the women at the university. Thereafter, he claimed, the University of Texas would have "the most cowed, trustworthy group of women to be found anywhere in the world outside Moslem India."[61]

Angry exchanges in student newspapers often boiled down to one issue. Veterans claimed that they simply wanted women — not girls. Coeds angrily insisted that they knew what that meant — and publicly said no. But the misunderstandings went deeper than standards of sexual behavior. College men were saying that the American college girl was spoiled, self-centered, that she knew nothing of the realities of life. The girls simply knew that the men were different and that they didn't like it. The ways coeds tried to combat the problem shows the depth of the misunderstanding.

The Women's Student Government Association at Massachusetts State College brought in a "noted beauty consultant," Elizabeth Mac-Donald Osborne of Dorothy Gray Laboratories. Mrs. Osborne told students, "Men who have seen duty in foreign countries may be a little more critical of American women than they were before the war." After her lecture she held four beauty clinics and scheduled individual "check-up conferences."[62]

At Northwestern, the YWCA held a forum: "Toward a better understanding between Veterans and Women Students." Major topics for discussion included "What is it about girls that annoys veterans most?"

and "What about dating? Do women measure up to the expectations of veterans? What are the expectations?" [63]

It turned out that veterans expected things that didn't fit well into the competitive model of courtship. Lieutenant Mike Carter, Eighth Army Air Force, told a *Mademoiselle* interviewer that "being overseas changes things. Those boys have gone through a hell of a lot . . . and they're going to want to come back to somebody more like the old style. I don't care about the bright lights now. I want a pretty solid all-round girl . . . and a sincere one. A boy wants to know where he stands . . . not all this beating around the bush. I'm not looking for the most popular girl on the dance floor now." [64]

American men, silenced during their four-year absence, were now ready to speak. Returning servicemen launched a full-scale public condemnation of the American woman. An *Esquire* article in July 1945 argued that men had the upper hand because of the laws of supply and demand, and because of their war experience, American men knew what they wanted. They had been released from the domination of American women by discovering that they were romantic heroes to the rest of the world's women. After that, how could they return to the "bobby-soxy, chicken-poxy, small-fry-hope-to-die, swooning type of adoration" that was all American girls had to offer? [65] Another *Esquire* article on the same theme provoked 2,200 women to write the author. Many betrayed the depth of their misunderstanding by enclosing photographs as proof, saying, "Not me, I'm cute." [66]

A *New York Times Magazine* article, "The American Woman? Not for this G.I.," was even harsher. American girls couldn't compare to foreign women, wrote Victor Dallaire, a former correspondent for the *Stars and Stripes.* Dallaire said that he'd heard more complaints from American women over the lack of nylons than he had heard from European women over the destruction of their homes and the deaths of their men. Moreover, he declared, the European women really were women. While American girls tried to compete with men, insisting on a "full share of the conversation with their escorts," French girls let their escorts do the talking, seeming to be there for the "sole purpose of being pleasant to the men." Unlike American girls, European girls were interested in "the rather fundamental business of getting married, having children and making the best homes their means or conditions will allow." [67]

Maybe American women weren't as interested in marriage as their European sisters, but they were making an awfully good showing anyway. In 1946, the American marriage rate of 16.4 per 1,000 population was the highest (with the single exception of Hungary) of any record-keeping country in the history of the twentieth century. That rate was up almost 25 percent from the previous record of 13.2 marriages per 1,000 in 1942.[68]

There are several easy explanations for the inflated marriage rate. Wars tend to do that — to make young people want something or someone to hold on to. The Depression was also partly responsible — it had prevented many couples from marrying. Conventional wisdom, dating from the previous century, said that a young man could not expect to marry until he had established himself and was financially able to support a wife and the children that were certain to follow. Between 1930 and 1931, the marriage rate dropped by 5.9 percent, and then another 7.5 percent between 1931 and 1932.[69] In the face of war, couples who had waited so long began to realize they couldn't wait forever, and the improved economy made marriage seem more feasible.

Many commentators dismissed the marriage fever as a temporary state brought on by the *carpe diem* philosophy born of war and turbulence.[70] They expected things would settle down to normal soon — though normal was hard to define after almost twenty years of abnormality. However, things didn't get back to normal, whatever people meant by that word. The marriage rate stayed high (though of course not at record level), and more strikingly, the average age at marriage plummeted. In 1890, the average age at marriage had been 26.1 for men, 22 for women; by 1951 men were marrying at an average age of 22.6, women at 20.4. Of course, this decrease was part of a long-term trend (25.1 for men and 21.6 for women in 1910; 24.3 for men and 21.3 for women in 1930).[71] But a reversal of the trend, one that doesn't show up on the ten-year census figures, made the young marriage ages more significant to contemporary observers. Average age at marriage had shot up drastically during the Depression. By 1939, it was 26.7 for men and 23.3 for women — higher than the 1890 figures.[72] People remembered that situation — if not the statistics then the experience. Late or delayed marriage was their frame of reference. Often, too, they remembered the frustration and anguish delayed marriage caused.

These statistics show a real change in the way young Americans lived. But even more striking is the change in American attitudes toward marriage. Before the war, when discussions of courtship centered around rating, dating, and popularity, marriage had few cheerleaders. It was discussed, certainly, desired and valued, but marriage was thought of as something that would come at the proper time. Marriage was the end of youth; it removed one from youth culture and from the dating system. It was not meant for children, nor for young people. But, as World War II drew to a close, the popular media began to celebrate American marriage — for *youth*. This celebration would last for almost twenty years.

In one sense, the media was simply documenting a trend. Young people were marrying, and in record numbers. By 1959, fully 47 percent of all brides married before they turned nineteen, and the percentage of girls between fourteen and seventeen who were married had jumped one-third since 1940.[73] *Newsweek* reported in 1957 that 16 percent of America's three million college students were married. The total was much higher at some schools — 24 percent at Michigan State, for example, and up to 25 percent at many western, southern, and Big Ten colleges and universities.[74]

Media representations, however, were doing much more than documenting a trend. They fed it and helped create and standardize a new ideal. When *Life* went to the University of Southern California's Delta Delta Delta "pansy breakfast" (honoring the sorority's engaged seniors) and printed glamorous pictures of ten of the forty-eight young women who stepped through the pansy ring, it added fuel to the fire.[75] In 1949, the *Ladies' Home Journal* ran a photo of a young man studying at a ramshackle kitchen table, his even younger wife hanging over his shoulder. It was captioned: "Many young men find that they can do much better work if they get the girl out of their dreams and into their kitchen."[76] Another *LHJ* feature, "How Young America Lives," was all about young married couples.[77] Each such article — and there were many — helped establish the new convention of early marriage. "Campus Romance" (he's twenty-one, she's eighteen, they're getting married) was becoming the new ideal.[78]

This early-marriage ideal was changing the face of college life. The Michigan *Daily* noted in 1957 that "coeds seem to have changed their outlooks and objectives. Whereas women formerly avoided admitting to ulterior motives behind their 'educational' aims, today they freely confess to seeking a 'Mrs.' degree to accompany various diplomas."[79] A survey at Northwestern found that most women were attending college to find a husband. Joanne Sykora, class of 1950, told the *Daily Northwestern*: "My mother told me that if I went to college I might meet a boy who would be able to provide me with things to which I would like to become accustomed."[80] NU's chapter of A E Phi advertised in their sorority newspaper, *Chez E Phi*, for "Husbands for all A E Phi seniors so they will not graduate a disgrace to their sorority."[81]

Mademoiselle, in its self-appointed role as adviser to the sophisticated college woman, offered an article titled, "Pursuit of Learning and the Undaily Male." The author's premise: "It's trying to get an education and a man at the same time that's the number-one problem and strain on any girl." To ease that dilemma, she offered a "Dating Map" of northeastern colleges and her evaluations of colleges across the country. No discussion of academic standards or entrance requirements entered in; for her purposes Radcliffe was the equal of MacMurray College and vice versa. Her sole criterion was the availability of men.[82] *Mademoiselle's* Dating Map looks like an artifact from the dating-and-rating era. It is a graphic display of abundance — of men, of dates, of college interrelationships. But this stress on abundance had a very different purpose. It was a counter to the fear of scarcity. Women went to college for "an education and *a* man" (emphasis mine), not to become once-arounders on the dance floor. The more abundant the men and dates the better one's chance of landing a husband.

The best example of the early-marriage trend and the concomitant shift in the dating system comes from Radcliffe, whose women had no peers when it came to saying what they thought. The change in campus ideals is illustrated wonderfully by the changing content of the winning songs in Radcliffe's annual song competition. The early winners contained the usual women's college sentiments: sisterhood, loyalty to college and class, a sense of mission. The class of 1917 won the 1914–15 competition with this effort:

> Classmates, now we bring together,
> Loyalty and friendship strong,
> That will echo down the ages
> In the spirit of our song.
>
> . . . .
>
> In the battle, may our weapons
> Sword of courage, shield of truth
> Fight for freedom and for honor
> With the daring strength of youth.
> Thus we reach toward high ideals
> Which through knowledge we have seen,
> And fulfill the love we bear thee
> Radcliffe, nineteen-seventeen.[83]

The battle here is clearly not for a man. In fact, only once does a man figure in a Radcliffe song before 1929. The Radcliffe student handbook for 1909 included a song titled "The Only Man." "Once upon a time," it went, a Harvard man "got a card to a Radcliffe tea."

He had faced the Yale rush line
    He'd been captain of the Nine
He was not afraid to dine upon the new Memorial plan
    But he'd never thought to be
At a full fledged Radcliffe tea,
    The only, only, *only*, man.[84]

(He turned and ran.) It's a hostile song, with the women's voices climaxing on that final "only." Its tone is superior, almost threatening. These women don't want men to invade their lives.

By 1929 Radcliffe girls were well into the spirit of flaming youth. The 1929–30 award-wining song traces the college career of "Prue":

Now Prue a flaming junior
Wild oats begins to sow
On every date she stays out late
Her studies are "*de trop*" — oh — oh — OH![85]

And by 1948 Radcliffe women were right in step with the new ideal of early marriage. The winner of the 1947–48 song competition was titled "Radcliffe Mothers."

Oh, we are future mothers of a beauteous cultured race,
Joint education schools us in the role we have to face;
Our homes will be like dorms, room and board instead of rent;
And our husbands will be called Head Resident.

Oh, he will sign me out at night and bring me in by one,
He'll call me his Miss Radcliffe instead of saying "hon,"
And at the wedding ceremony held in Agassiz,
He'll wed me with his class ring and then he'll say to me:

Refrain[86]

The 1953 winner also showed the new emphasis on monogamy. It began, "Harvard men are big and strong and rough and tough and passionate" (this is Radcliffe's song, remember), and ended by enjoining Radcliffe women to "fight — fight — fight" as "long as there are enough men for every girl to trap her own."[87] In fact, the student handbook frequently assured students, there *were* enough men to go around. The 1951–52 *Red Book* advised: "Cambridge is a well-stocked hunting ground. . . . Just remember, no pushing or shoving." The 1957–58 *Red Book* reassured students: "There is no scarcity of men; keep your standards high and enjoy your unique situation as a Radcliffe girl."[88]

The student handbook also tried to counter the convention that not having a steady boyfriend, or dating more than one person, was a failure: "And if Prince Charming doesn't appear at your first sally-forth, don't fret, have a good time!"[89] But the award-winning song for that year, "Those Years of Harvard Men" (to the tune of "Bluetail Fly") undercut that soothing advice. Its refrain went:

> You've found yourself a Harvard man
> You've found yourself a Harvard man
> You've found yourself a Harvard man
> You met at your first Jolly-Up![90]

That some of the most intelligent and talented young women in America would cast themselves in the roles suggested in these songs (roles that were, of course, the same ones most young women publicly espoused) shows how completely the new convention had triumphed among youth. Early marriage, however, unlike rating-and-dating, could not be totally enclosed in the peer culture. It had implications in the outside world, and so required the support of parents and the larger society.

Several women's magazines endorsed early marriage quite directly in articles aimed at parents. These articles, based on the testimony of a range of prominent "experts," argued that early marriage was much healthier for the couple and for society, and that parents should be willing to subsidize their children for the first years of marriage. The criterion of financial independence should no longer hold sway. Dr. William F. Snow, chairman of the American Social Hygiene Association, flatly insisted that youth's "*right* to marry" should not be abridged by requiring financial independence of them. The head of Yale's Division of Psychiatry and Mental Hygiene suggested that boys should marry at around age twenty or twenty-one, and girls at eighteen or nineteen, providing that both were "nonneurotic." His counterpart at Harvard believed that the trend toward earlier marriage was "a sign of greater maturity in youth."[91]

These experts gave different reasons for endorsing the trend. Dr. Snow, for example, stressed that an eighteen-year-old girl would still find it "exhilarating" to scrub floors and do her own washing, that she would be more willing to accept her role in life. Most authors, however, were motivated by concern about sexual mores. One argued that late marriage (with some couples having to wait until they were twenty-three) led to irreparable psychological trauma. Young people, if prevented from marrying, had the choice of sin (and later disappointment because the man would believe "she'd do the same with any man") or continence (leading to frigidity or impotence). An article in the *Woman's Home Companion* made a similar argument, and concluded, "When two people are ready for sexual intercourse at the fully human level they are ready for marriage — and they *should* marry. Not to do so is moral cowardice. And society has no right to stand in their way."[92]

For youth, the new convention had many appealing features. Young marriage did allow them to sidestep some of the problems of the contemporary code of sexual morality. Marriage allowed them to combine a sense of independence with a sense of security. And the *ideal* of marriage — even if not yet attained — was more comfortable than the old ideal of rating-dating and general popularity. This system had a goal. In this system, though the competition might be fierce, one could win.

The convention of early marriage, as conventions do, worked as a cycle: teenagers got married *because* teenagers were getting married. As such, early marriage had a certain self-perpetuating momentum. This convention, originating in the specific circumstances of post-Depression, postwar America, lasted until it was interrupted by new circumstances and by its own consequences in the mid-1960s. Over its twenty-year reign, the ideal was strengthened by the trends that had produced it in the first place.

Scarcity — the fear of scarcity — continued to play an important role. *Collier's* ran a semiserious cartoon feature on "Possible ways to provide more eligible husbands in the marriage market."[93] In 1958, *McCall's* held a brainstorming session and came up with "129 Ways to Get a Husband." One suggestion, "Look in the census reports for places with the most single men. Nevada has 125 males for every 100 females."[94] Advice books, aimed at the soon-to-be-old-maid in her twenties, often included careful statistical analyses of the ratio of men to women in different parts of the country.[95] Increasingly, authors of these books advised women not to be too picky. If you're only "so-so," the argument went, and men are scarce, you'll never get a husband if you wait for your "ideal."[96]

As time passed, scarcity receded from the public consciousness. While fear of scarcity underlay the growing trend toward early marriage, it was rarely used as an explanation of it. Early marriage, instead, came to be seen as the "natural" condition that had been interrupted in the early twentieth century. Scarcity became simply the excuse of those who failed to marry.

Two of the most striking changes in postwar courtship were the increased visibility of teenagers and the ever-earlier ages at which children entered the courtship system. This was partially due to older youth's rejection of society's earlier definition of maturity as financial independence and their unwillingness to delay the emotional and sexual gratification of marriage. As parents and educators acceded to the new system, young teens reaped the benefits — or the consequences — of their elders' actions. If girls were to marry at eighteen and boys at twenty, the preparation for marriage — the shopping around, if you will — had to begin earlier than before.

Experts told parents to help their children become datable, to put children in situations where they would begin to date. After all, they stressed, dating was preparation for the important business of selecting a mate. And, as sociologists said, each boy and girl ideally should know twenty-five to fifty eligible marriage partners before making his or her final decision.[97] The implications are obvious: to be prepared to make that final choice at eighteen, children must begin to prepare as soon as possible. And since the shortage of men would complicate matters for girls, an early start might make the difference between a happy marriage and life as an old maid.

Early dating, in the postwar years, was carried to extremes. Thirteen-year-olds who did not yet date were called "late bloomers," and recommended dates were not just parent- or school-sponsored coed activities to encourage boys and girls to feel comfortable around each other. Instead, they were dances where twelve-year-old girls in their strapless formals were "meticulously padded out," and formal "sit-down" birthday dinners and dances for ten-year-old boys and their dates. They resulted in some not-recommended consequences: the eleven-year-old boy taking his nine-year-old girlfriend to the drive-in movie on the back of his bicycle, the grade school "make-out" parties in suburban homes. A 1961 study by Carlfred B. Broderick, professor of family relations at Pennsylvania State (himself twenty-nine with five children) found that 40 percent of the fifth graders in one local middle-class district were already dating.[98]

This pattern of early dating could not have flourished without parental support (someone had to buy those formals and give those dances). Margaret Mead, in fact, believed that parents were supporting the new courtship patterns in order to gain control over the mate-selection process and influence their children's choice of mate.[99] But not all responsibility rests with the parents. These preteens were increasingly identifying with the youth culture of the period, looking to it for their norms.

This generation of young teens accepted a version of the early-marriage ideal and thought they had good reasons for doing so.

Whether or not the postwar decade was really our "best years," many youth saw their world as troubling and insecure. The Korean War, coming so quickly on the tail of World War II, encouraged their pessimism. The Bomb, the Cold War, the certainty of military service — all, they said, perpetuated that classic wartime desire for something stable in an unstable world.[100]

Just as the conventions of young adult courtship changed, a new teenage culture grew up in the postwar years. At its center was a desire for security — in the form of "going steady." It was not a new custom, but an old custom with a new meaning.

In earlier days going steady had been more like the old-fashioned "keeping steady company." It was a step along the path to marriage, even if many steady couples parted company before they reached their destination.[101] By the early 1950s, going steady had acquired a totally different meaning. It was no longer the way a marriageable couple signaled their deepening intentions. Instead, going steady was something twelve-year-olds could do, something most fifteen-year-olds did. Few steady couples expected to marry each other (especially the twelve-year-olds), but, for the duration, they acted *as if* they were married. Going steady had become a sort of play-marriage, a mimicry of the actual marriage of their slightly older peers.[102]

In the prewar years, high school students had emulated the dating-rating system of their elders, trying, against great odds, to maintain a system of popularity that required automobiles, formal clothing, expensive dates at glamorous night spots. As conventions changed for older youth, the younger segment tried to keep up. But the ideal for those of, say, nineteen or twenty — was to be married. Though plenty of fourteen to seventeen-year-olds followed suit, child marriage was neither financially nor socially practical or possible for most of them. So teen culture developed its more feasible parallel convention.

By 1950, going steady had completely supplanted the dating-rating-complex as the criteria for popularity among youth. In 1955, a University of Wisconsin sociologist conferred a parallel title on the new system: the "going steady complex." He argued in the *Journal of Marriage and Family Living* that scholars and professionals had not yet acknowledged the "prominence of this practice in current adolescent life."[103] But if some social scientists were reluctant to end the reign of Waller's complex, most young Americans were aware of the power of the new system. A popular qualitative study of American teenagers, *Profile of Youth* (1949), reported that in most high schools the "mere fact" of going steady was a sign of popularity "as long as you don't get tied up with an impossible gook."[104] In a 1953 survey, 36.4 percent of

University of Wisconsin undergraduates polled said that the popular students in their high school had gone steady, and another 33.4 said that the popular students often dated the same person. Only 8.7 said popular students "completely played the field." [105] The *Ladies' Home Journal* reported in 1949 that "every high-school student . . . must be prepared to fit into a high-school pattern in which popularity, social acceptance and emotional security are often determined by the single question: does he or she go steady?" [106] And, according to *Cosmopolitan* in 1960, if you didn't go steady, you were "square." [107]

The importance of going steady rose steadily in the postwar years. In 1948, 42 percent of high school students (46 percent of the boys and 39 percent of the girls) approved of going steady in high school, while 35 percent disapproved. By 1959, 59 percent approved (57 percent of the boys and 61 percent of the girls) and another 15 percent thought it was "probably" OK. Another 1959 poll found that 57 percent of American teens were going steady or had gone steady. [108] One boy, in a letter to the dating column in *Senior Scholastic*, complained that everyone in his high school went steady, and that he was called a "playboy" if he tried to date more than one girl. [109]

A description of the contemporary system of courtship in a 1957 textbook, *Modern Courtship and Marriage*, by sociologist E. E. LeMasters, shows how completely the going steady ideal had triumphed. Trying to explain the limited persistence of the old pattern, which he called "random dating," LeMasters wrote: "After all, not everyone can be fortunate enough at any given moment to have a steady boy or girlfriend." He continued: "It is interesting to note how closely this resembles the role of the slum in the modern city: no matter how prosperous the American economy becomes, nor how much people prefer the suburb, the slum continues to exist; not only that, but it also sports a 'no vacancy' sign most of the time. Random dating may not be preferred by modern Americans but some of them have no choice, and for them it is random dating or no dating at all." [110] The ideal of rating and dating was long gone.

The new protocol of going steady was every bit as strict as the old protocol of rating and dating, and the form of going steady in many ways mirrored teenagers' concepts of young marriage. To go steady, the boy gave the girl some visible token (class ring, letter sweater, etc.) or they exchanged identical tokens, often gold or silver friendship rings worn on the third finger of the left hand. Customs varied locally: In Portland, Oregon, steadies favored rings (costing from $17 to 20). In Birmingham, Michigan, the girl wore the boy's ID bracelet, but *never* his letter sweater. In rural Iowa, the couple wore matching corduroy "steady jackets," but in the Far West, any couple wearing matching clothing would be laughed at.[111]

As long as they went steady, the boy had to call the girl a certain number of times a week and take her on a certain number of dates a week (both numbers were subject to local convention, but usually ranged from two to seven). Neither boy nor girl could date anyone else or pay too much attention to anyone of the opposite sex. While either could go out with friends of the same sex, each must always know where the other was and what he or she was doing. Going steady meant a guaranteed date for special events, and it also meant that the girl had to be willing to help her boyfriend save up for the event by budgeting "their" money, even if it meant sitting home together. Going steady also implied greater sexual intimacy — either more necking or "going further."[112]

In spite of the intense monogamy of these steady relationships, teens didn't intend to stay with their steadies forever. A 1950 study of 565 seniors in an eastern suburban high school found that 80 percent had gone steady or were going steady. Out of that number, only eleven said that they expected to marry their steadies.[113] In New Haven, Connecticut, high school girls wore "obit bracelets." Each time they broke up with a boy, they added a disk engraved with his name or initials to the chain. Other steadies spelled out their names on the bumpers of their boyfriends' cars — in *removable* reflector tape. A teen advice book from the mid-1950s advised girls to get a "Puppy Love Anklet." Wearing it on the right ankle meant that you were available; on the left that you were going steady. So temporary was each state, evidently, that the author advised having "Going Steady" engraved on one side, "Ready, Willing 'n Waiting" on the other — just in case the boys couldn't remember the code. All these conventions, cheerfully reported in teen columns in national magazines, show how much teens took it for granted that going steady was a temporary, if intense, arrangement.[114]

Harmless as this system sounds today, however, especially compared to the rigors of rating and dating, going steady precipitated an intense generational battle. Early marriage was one thing, as was early dating. Going steady was another. It flew in the face of parental understandings of the dating system.

Adult reactions to the practice were overwhelmingly negative. Some parents and authorities were confused: one man admiringly recalled a college friend from the 1930s who dated fifty-six different girls in one academic year, and wondered how teens would learn to understand the opposite sex if they only "know" one partner.[115] Others flatly condemned the practice: Reverend James Carey, head of St. Michael's High School in Jersey City, announced that any student "dating one person to the exclusion of all others shall be expelled."[116] Still others tried to deny the whole problem: the author of one marriage textbook insisted that there was no going steady craze. His proof was a 1952 study of 1,600 students at eleven representative U.S. colleges. In the text, he reported that 2 out of 3 of the 1,000 students who weren't engaged or married preferred to date "the field." In the footnotes we learn that, of the total sample of 1,600, 10 percent were married, 15 percent were formally engaged, and 15 percent had "an understanding."[117] In short, only about one-third of this sample sought the old promiscuous popularity. Many simply were past the going steady ideal, and subscribed to the ideal of early marriage.

The generational battle over going steady never quite became a debate. The confrontation was words against actions, adult condemnations against the ever-increasing prevalence of going steady. The fight, in its largely one-sided eloquence, boiled down to two essential issues. The first, not surprisingly, was sex. Adults — parents, advice columnists, educators — believed, with some reason, that the practice of going steady led to increased premarital sex.

Representing the extreme view, a Catholic priest called going steady "a serious occasion of sin" unless marriage was in the "very near future."[118] An advice book for teenage girls, *Joyce Jackson's Guide to Dating*, argued that going steady inevitably led girls to heavy necking and thus to guilt for the rest of their lives. This sequence, the author claimed, resulted from strict dating rules that limited how many people one could date at a time. Better to date strangers, she concluded, than to end up necking with a steady boyfriend.[119]

The implied argument here, that it is sexually safer to date many different people, even strangers, is difficult to support. Adults who advocated this system of insurance must have had very selective memories. In the days of promiscuous popularity, how "far" to go with a date was of great concern to youth. Necking with a never-ending succession of different young men seems much more likely to leave that burden of guilt. And who knew whether that stranger, parked on a dark road, would listen to a firm but polite no?[120] At least a steady boyfriend was less likely to take that road without his girlfriend's consent. Promiscuous dating and going steady held different dangers.

Consent was the difference. A beleaguered system of sexual control based on the resolve of young girls to say no, at least to the final step of actual intercourse, was further breaking down in the new system of going steady.[121] As going steady was a simulated marriage, sexual relationships could and did develop within the protection of its (even short-term) security, monogamy, and, sometimes, its love. Parents thought it was easier for girls to say no to intercourse to the rapid succession of boys who were, at some level, markers for popularity. They were afraid that it was harder to say no to a steady.

The second major issue in the going steady battle came down to a fundamental confrontation between the values of two generations: security versus competition. Fifties' teenagers were trying to do the unthinkable — to factor competition out of the popularity equation. Adults were appalled. To them, going steady, with its extreme rejection of competition in favor of temporary security, represented all the faults of the new generation.[122] Teenagers and some sympathetic scholars tried to explain the new system; adults answered from an entirely different discourse. Both sides built their cases on the concept of competition, and neither side could accept the values that weighted the other's understanding of the term.

For most youth, going steady represented a secure niche in a competitive and uncertain world. Competition was still given, and ultimately inescapable, but going steady provided some respite. The security going steady offered took several forms. First, as psychologists told the public, going steady was "the current teen-age answer to the general anxiety of the times."[123] Teenagers were more likely to describe it as "date security" or "social security." The terms meant two things. Going steady guaranteed one a date to all major functions and for most weekend nights. Going steady also allowed youth to escape the "discomfort" of participating in the "fiercely competitive business of dating" — at least for a while.[124] Some experts concurred with youth. One study of high school dating systems concluded: "Steady dating was found to relieve many students of the emotional and psychological problems involved in the competitive rating-dating pattern."[125]

The security of a steady date grew increasingly important as going steady became a more prevalent convention. According to the *Ladies' Home Journal,* one high school student reported, "At our school, if you don't find someone to go steady with by October, you just don't date that year. Everyone is all tied up."[126] A college student, looking back to high school, stated flatly, "You either went steady or you never went."[127] A steady date was necessary in order to be included in a social life built around couples. Without a steady, you couldn't rate enough even to *participate.* But, as in the convention of early marriage, one could win in this system. A flurry of competition at the beginning of the season and you'd made it for the duration. You didn't want to get stuck with an "impossible gook" or a "queek," but the fact of going steady was almost enough in itself. Once they'd made it, girls didn't have to worry about whether their "stock" was going up or down; boys didn't have to spend lots of money to impress a stream of new faces.[128]

Some adults, perhaps with their own "tender memories" of competitive triumph, couldn't understand the lure of going steady. It seemed so "dull," so "middle-aged," a "dismal boredom-by-the-couple."[129] Critics thought that teenagers just didn't understand what they were missing. Monogamy — even going steady — meant settling down, and settling down didn't allow for once-arounds on the dance floor or the power that came from being in demand. "This is the time in your life for meeting boys — as many as you can," an advice book warned. "In short, now is the only time you'll have to experiment with friendship and romance."[130] Another book's warning was more graphic. The author demonstrated that many boys went steady for "expediency" ("When I'm not going steady, I have to spend a lot of money to make an impression. I can't call up and say I'll be half an hour late.") and felt she'd made her case. "You girls can see it is often more fun to take a chance on single dates. You are too young to let yourselves be taken for granted."[131]

Other adults, perhaps with a clearer understanding that in the "real" world there was no final success, only the ability to continue to compete, attacked the teenage desire for security with no holds barred.[132] As one writer advised boys, "To be sure of anything is to cripple one's powers of growth." She continued, "To have your girl always assured at the end of a telephone line without having to work for her, to beat the other fellows to her, is bound to lessen your powers of personal achievement."[133] As for girls, the argument went, "She's afraid of competition. She isn't sure she can compete for male attention in the open market; 'going steady' frees her from fear of future failures."[134]

The more specific the criticism gets, the more we see how completely the adult criticism of going steady is located in the old norms and conventions — in the old economy of dating. The author of *Joyce Jackson's Guide to Dating* tells the story of "Judith Thompson," a not-especially-attractive girl with family problems, who has been going steady with "Jim" since she was fourteen. Lest we think that poor Judith deserves someone to care for her, or see Jim as a small success in her life, the author stresses that going steady is one more failure for Judith: "Now that Judith is sixteen and old enough to earn money and help herself in other ways to recover from her unfortunate childhood, she has taken on the additionally crippling circumstance of a steady boyfriend. How pathetic. . . . The love and attention of her steady boy-friend are a substitute for other more normal kinds of success." What should Judith be doing? "A good deal of the time she spends going steady with Jim could be used to make herself more attractive so that other boys would ask her for dates." [135]

Another (though less mean-spirited) version of the same critique spelled out the alternative vision of success more clearly. If you didn't have a steady, the author argued, you would spend more time "exploring." With good old "Freddy," there's "no competition and no impression to be made. . . . If you didn't have Freddy, you'd be spending a lot more time in front of the mirror — deciding how to bring out your best features. You'd be poring over fashion magazines and exploring shop windows to find out what the perfect style is for you. Without Freddy, you'd be putting your best foot forward and there wouldn't be an old sneaker on it." [136]

These adult criticisms of the going steady complex are equally strong indictments of the old rating-and-dating system. They clarify the assumptions behind the old system and bring its values into stark focus. There are certainly lots of problems with a system that puts twelve-year-old girls in padded bras, demands semipermanent pairing off at fifteen, and pushes eighteen-year-olds to marry. There are at least as many problems with a system that privileges quantity over quality, that fosters the belief that a man can come to understand women by dating fifty-six different girls in nine months, that prepares youth for a lifetime of monogamous marriage by stressing an ideal of promiscuous popularity.

However, both systems, different as they seem, were based on the same model of scarcity and abundance. Both valued the scarce resource over the plentiful one, and both located power in the control of scarce resources.

In the prewar decades, dates (as persons and as events, and for both men and women) were perceived to be abundant. To scarcer commodity was full participation in the emerging peer culture that centered on consumption. Consumer goods — the automobile, the clothes, the expensive dates, all visible signs of wealth and, significantly, all necessary for men to "rate" — were symbols of success in peer culture. Young men competed for these symbols and used them to compete for status or popularity.

Women, of necessity, took a different tack. Men controlled the money economy and thus access to these symbols of success. Men paid for the expensive dinners and nights on the town; a wealthy woman, according to convention, must accept the level of luxury the man who asked her out provided, just as she would later derive her status from her husband's and accept the level of support he provided. Thus, in this model, women competed for success in peer culture by attracting men who "rated." In this system, a woman became a success by making *herself* a scarce commodity, by fostering such a demand (or perception of such demand) for her dates that she could not meet it. "Men like girls that other men want," the line went. Successful young men competed for a falsely scarce resource — popular young women — and made them into further symbols of success.

The postwar ideals of early marriage and going steady are a profound contrast to rating and dating. Yet going steady, too, centered around concepts of scarcity, abundance, and competition. However, it drew on different definitions of competitive success. Youth culture, more than ever in the 1950s and early 1960s, centered around consumption and consumer goods: cars, clothes, records. But access to this culture was not as restricted as it had been in the 1920s. New technology offered more goods more cheaply. More American families shared in economic prosperity. Teenagers had unprecedented amounts of expendable income, so much that new magazines appeared to advise them on how to participate fully in youth culture — what to buy, what to do, what to like. Furthermore, girls and young women were more able to participate independently in this sphere; they were ever less dependent on men (except fathers) for access to these symbols of success.

The scarce resources were different after the war. Fear of the man shortage (and thus of the boy shortage and of the husband shortage) probably did encourage early marriage, going steady, and parent-sponsored precocious dating. But public discussions of courtship suggest that youth felt another, perhaps more compelling, scarcity in their lives. Competition was overabundant, security and human closeness too scarce. That eighteen-year-old marriage was often a dismal failure and that the twelve-year-old steadies became the sexual revolutionaries of the 1960s does not lessen the value of the sense of human need these young people introduced to the public model of courtship they transformed.

The Worth of a Date

B efore the sexual revolution of the 1960s provided juicier material, *Esquire* was fond of running cartoons featuring a short, elderly, and paunchy millionaire escorting a tall, enormous-breasted young showgirl through opulent settings. The captions didn't really matter. The cartoons worked best subtextually, and all contained variations on the same theme: money and sex; the coupling of wallet and bosom.

It is easy, today, to center on the objectification of woman represented by the showgirl, a caricature stripped to her essentials: legs, breasts, and greed. She is clearly a commodity, purchased by man's wealth. But the man, too, is objectified. His value to her lies only in what he can buy. He is interchangeable with any other well-stuffed wallet. Their relationship is obviously mutually exploitative: the man is as much a commodity to the woman as she is a commodity to him.

The millionaire and the showgirl are a long way from our image of young love, but this mass-produced image can illustrate some of the values inherent in the American dating system. In courtship, no less than in the culture at large, we find America's "culture of consumption" — a way of seeing that encourages the paired acts of consumption and commodification.

The culture of consumption, as Jackson Lears and Richard Wightman Fox describe it in a book of that title, is not simply the system of values underlying a consumer economy or a society "saturated by mass-produced and mass-marketed goods." It is also "an ethic, a standard of living, and a power structure" that centers on consumption, in which "individuals have been invited to seek commodities as keys to personal welfare . . . even to conceive of their own selves as commodities."[1] And, I might add, to transform personal relationships into commodities.

In dating, American young people sought their "personal welfare" through dates (and later through steadies), as commodities that afforded public validation of popularity, of belonging, of success. Whether or not one liked the date (person) the date (event) was valuable, a necessary commodity in youth culture. As commodities, dates (events) were valued differentially by the level of consumption they entailed — in short, by their cost. The date (person) could also become a commodity. In this system, men and women often defined themselves and each other as commodities, the woman valued by the level of consumption she could demand (how much she was "worth"), and the man by the level of consumption he could provide.

The particular form the American dating system took as it emerged in the early twentieth century was determined, in large part, by the new centrality of money in the act of courtship. As "going somewhere" became the thing to do, the man had to spend money to provide entertainment, refreshments, and transportation for the couple. Gradually, as dating became the dominant form of courtship, participants and observers recognized how important money had become. In general, dates had come to be defined by the fact that they cost money. Over and over in the national media, women and men, girls and boys, advisers and experts insisted on this definition of dating. Money was central: a date took place when a couple "went out" and spent money.

All the polls and columns and books on dating in the second third of the twentieth century made abundantly clear that American youth did not consider spending time with a member of the opposite sex the same as dating. In almost all instances, a date centered around an act of consumption: going out for dinner or a Coke, seeing a movie, buying access to some form of entertainment. Of course, the emphasis was not on unbridled consumption. The act had to take place within certain limits and according to many conventions, one of the most important being that the man pay the woman's way.

The "sub-deb" adviser for the *Ladies' Home Journal* shows the extent of these implicit definitions of a date in a 1944 column. She tells the story of a young girl — about fourteen — who is "fed up" because she can't get a date. The girl, as the author describes her, has a good social life — lots of friends, including boys who like her well enough to meet her and sit beside her at the movies. The adviser does not give the obvious moral. Instead of pointing out that this sub-deb should concentrate on enjoying the movie and the boy's company, she approvingly recounts the girl's "plan": she will concentrate on "Pete," the "likeliest one" (note that she does not say "the one she likes best"). "When he sits by me in the movies," the girl says, "I'm going to pretend he paid my way in. I'm going to play-act it's a real date." [2] The only thing lacking, evidently, is knowledge that the boy *paid* for her.

A real girl, Margaret Graves of St. Louis, had a similar opinion on the subject. Writing to *Senior Scholastic* in 1951, she said, "If a girl has to pay her own way [on a date], she might as well go alone or with girl friends." [3] To her, the date was not the event, was not the companionship, was not even being *seen* with the boy. A date meant being paid for. And boys agreed. A *Senior Scholastic* poll on dating found that while 90 percent of the girls questioned would agree to "occasionally," if reluctantly, share expenses, 50 percent of the boys strenuously objected to the idea. "If a boy is financially embarrassed," one boy wrote, "he shouldn't date." [4]

Even those boys and girls who would accept a dutch date now and then were not willing to make the arrangement public. (Significantly, "dutch date" comes from "dutch treat" — originally, it seems, a derogatory term for a false "treat" where the guests end up paying their own way.) It was "embarrassing," American youth insisted almost unanimously, for the girl to be seen paying for herself. If dutch dating was absolutely necessary, the girl should give money to her date ahead of time so it would at least *look* as if he were paying her way. [5]

This concern with being seen is crucial, for it relates to the role of the date in youth culture. As I argued in chapter 2, dates often functioned in youth culture as tools for acquiring popularity — much as did clothes, cars, and other consumer goods. But a date that had no independent content, that was only a marker for popularity, had no meaning if no one knew about it. The date had to be public.

The boy who longed for a date, as Margaret Mead noted in the 1940s, was not longing for a girl, much less for a relationship with a particular girl. [6] He desired to be in the public situation that defined a date: he desired to *have* a date, and he desired for others to see that he had a date. This sort of date, "had" and displayed, is itself a commodity.

The scores of adult advisers who wrote about courtship in twentieth-century America uniformly portrayed dates as commodities. Those who wrote during the period before World War II and for the too-young-to-get-married teens after the war concentrated primarily on how to "get dates." In most of these books and columns, the date appears as an end in itself — a worthwhile goal, a personal triumph. The experience of the date was a secondary concern. Simply *having* the date was a success. As one adviser wrote in 1941: "It makes little difference, really, who dates whom." And the *Seventeen* advice book reassured girls that "any girl can get a date."[7]

Not having dates, conversely, was to fail. The writer of the *Woman's Home Companion* teen column dealt sympathetically with the misery of being dateless on "Date Night": "You wait for the phone to ring . . . but if it does, you're ashamed to be caught at home. You could join the other dateless Dotties at the corner drug, but the whole town would see you."[8] Failure, no less than success, was defined publicly — through the possession or lack of a date.

In the 1950s, a writer for *Mademoiselle* rebelled against these definitions, complaining to his readers that dates had become mere "commodities." The real "date," he said — the man or the woman — was becoming ever less important as an individual.[9] His article was filled with stories of the pathetic deceptions of supposedly archetypal young women — college girls who would turn off their room lights and hide in dark dormitory basements on Friday and Saturday night so that no one would know they were dateless. He offered little hope. If dates were commodities, they obviously were prized commodities.

Of course, some dates were prized more than others. Teen advice books warned girls to be understanding and hospitable to the boy who was occasionally low on funds, but not to let him get in the habit of hanging around their living rooms with no "real" dates in exchange. And real dates, the public culture of dating constantly emphasized, were expensive and flamboyant. While most polls discovered that teens' usual dates were for a movie and a snack, the magazines that conducted these polls frequently described the unusual dates — the "ideal" dates — in loving detail.

In 1938, for example, in a still-depressed economy, *Senior Scholastic* described an ideal teenage date for dinner at the Ritz — a dinner that cost the high school senior hero of the column over $5.50.[10] (Just two years before, the National Resources Committee had found that one-third of American *families* spent $31 or less per year for "leisure."[11])

A 1955 *Look* pictorial celebrated the "first date" of thirteen-year-old Janice Walters of Encino, California. Her escort, also thirteen, brought her an orchid corsage for the formal dinner and dance they attended.[12] And in 1956, *McCall's* chronicled a "Blind Date" to which a local Long Island newspaper treated two "outstanding" high school students. The winners — the girl a varsity cheerleader and the boy president of his high school class — received a "$350 date." They traveled in a chauffeured Cadillac, dined at 21, saw *Plain and Fancy* on Broadway, and danced at the Persian Room. Each also received a $200 "evening wardrobe." This was the stuff of teenage dreams. Of course, the two students went to different high schools, and while they said they enjoyed the date, they probably wouldn't ever see each other again.[13]

While almost no one outside of magazine contests had $350 dates, the ideal was widespread. In 1963, *Mademoiselle* surveyed two hundred young women (most of whom would have been in high school at the time of that celebrated date). Although the majority of these women said they didn't "need" expensive dates, most described their "ideal" date as beginning with cocktails, then dinner at an "elegant" restaurant, attending the theater or a concert, and then dancing.[14]

The first generation of daters had complained about the new costs of courtship, but by the 1940s "the high cost of dating" was a cliché. The phrase cropped up frequently in *Senior Scholastic*'s advice column, and male students, responsible for meeting those costs, wrote to complain about the conditions the phrase described. Even simple movie dates were expensive, they said, especially when followed by the virtually obligatory soda or sundae. In a 1953 "Jam Session" on the high cost of dating, a boy from Newcastle, Pennsylvania, reported that the average movie date at his high school ran roughly $2.50 ("If you're lucky"): $1.50 for the movie, $.25 for popcorn, $.75 for sundaes or milk shakes and the jukebox — and transportation was extra. An English class at Rushville High School in Illinois "thoroughly discussed the problem" and concluded that an "average date" usually cost a boy $5.25: $3 for a car, $1.25 for a "show," and $1 for "eats."[15]

If these "usual," "average," or "ordinary" dates seemed expensive to youth, the cost of special dates was astronomical. The high school prom, the biggest social event of the year, represented the "ideal" date to most students. Proms were, of course, something more than special dates. They were a kind of rite of passage that transformed boys and girls into young men and women; they were occasions for magical extravagance. They required elegant evening attire and transportation, and included postprom entertainment at the fanciest night spot the area offered.

Such extravagance was costly — and, indeed, expense was a critical part of the experience. It seemed, as one critic of the system wrote sarcastically in 1956, as if a sixteen-year-old boy who was going steady — and thus was obliged to take his girlfriend to "every stated teenage function" — had "more obligations than an unemployed father of eight with the mortgage clawing at the roof and also a bank loan due."[16] In 1949, the *Ladies' Home Journal* reported, teens at Manhattan high schools estimated that each couple spent at least $100 each on prom expenses. For the boy, the tux rental cost $10, and then there were the dance bid, carfare or gas, and late-night entertainment at "class nighteries" at an average cost of between $25 and $35. A corsage for his date was mandatory, and for seven out of ten boys the corsage was a $7 orchid.[17] Median family income in 1949 was $2,739.

Girls didn't get off cheaply either. The same *LHJ* article estimated that most girls spent between $15 and $45 on a formal (depending on whether or not they made it themselves) and then another $5 to $10 on "high heeled 'naked slippers'" and evening bag.[18] When a *Senior Scholastic* poll asked "Are High School Proms Getting Too Expensive?" (1950), Carma Riley from Royal Oak, Michigan, pled the girls' case: "Boys are always complaining and with just cause of the great expense proms involve, but do they ever think of the many formals we girls must buy?"[19] In fact, a 1957 Purdue Youth Poll found that high school girls *did* spend significantly more on proms than their male counterparts.[20]

The results of this Purdue poll clearly show the high cost of proms for high school students — both boys and girls. While few matched the Manhattan extravagances reported by the *Ladies' Home Journal* in 1949, the average student spent a considerable portion of his or her father's income on promming. In 1957, when median family income was $4,353, 42 percent of the boys and 72 percent of the girls who went to proms spent over $15 on each prom they attended. Boys from families with lower incomes and from rural areas were more likely to spend over $30 than their wealthier peers.[21]

Proms offered high school students not only a taste of the "ideal" extravagant dates otherwise largely denied them (at least until they were older) but also a forum for social competition. The first level of competition was simply rating a bid or getting a date; the next was getting the "right" date. Beyond these basics, proms stressed competition through material goods. With all (who qualified) brought together, it was easy to compare dresses, to see who rated an orchid and who just a gardenia, to rank postprom destinations and modes of transportation. The pressure could be intense, and during the Depression years of the 1930s, Chicago high school principals frequently cancelled school proms because they feared the many students who couldn't afford them would be "psychologically wounded" by that failure.[22]

In college, the pressure was more consistent. College students didn't have to contend with only one prom or ideal date a year, but with a whole succession of extravagant events. College football weekends were glamorized by a wide range of national magazines as one dizzy succession of brunches and lunches and dances and dinners — at a cost to men, *Good Housekeeping* estimated in 1953, of about $83 a weekend.[23] *Mademoiselle*, in its 1954 college issue, showed the pressure for expensive dates by defining "*Quiet Evening* (kwī-et év-ning) n." as "Any nocturnal date that results in a heightened feeling of well being and costs less than $5."[24] The previous year *Good Housekeeping* had published results of an informal survey of the cost of college "big" dates. Average outlays for one date ranged from a low of $25 in Boston and Dallas to a high of $35 in St. Louis. Paducah, Kentucky, with a population of 35,000, came in just about average at $30.[25]

On campus, dances were an important part of college life. The University of Michigan's *Daily*, in 1924, estimated that Michigan students spent upward of $80,000 a year for dances, including Friday-and Saturday-night informals at the student union, eighty fraternity formals a year (for which the fraternities spent $15 a person), and universitywide events such as the J-Hop (at $10 per couple). Michigan, however, ceded the "conference championship in 'fussing'" to the University of Wisconsin, whose students reportedly were spending over $100,000 a year on dances.[26]

College dances had long offered opportunities for extravagance and display. As early as 1904, the *Daily Northwestern* reported on controversy at the University of Nebraska: men who did "lots of 'fussing'" were complaining that coeds were spoiled by the custom of hiring "hacks" for informal dances, and threatened to boycott if women wouldn't agree to walk the four blocks to the dance.[27] In the 1930s the President's Council at Ohio State reported that some fraternities were spending $1,000 per formal.[28]

Even in the midst of such abundance, universitywide proms were still the big social events of the season — at least for those students who could afford them. In a front-page article, the University of Massachusetts newspaper interrupted its report on the "joyous memories of that three-day holiday" (the 1926 Junior Prom) to note: "Those who are unfortunate enough not to be able to take it in, can only stand and look in from the outside at the glittering lights." "Unfortunate," of course, meant that they couldn't afford to go. In fact, only about thirty-four couples attended that year's prom; of those, only one man was not a fraternity member. Although the school was coed, only eight of the women present attended U. Mass. The *Collegian* specified that the low attendance was due to the prom's high cost, but never criticized that fact.[29]

By the late 1930s, Northwestern's student newspaper was carrying on a crusade for less expensive formals. "Mr. Average Student": the

Daily announced in 1939, "Your bill for the next all-university formal will run something like this:

Ticket	$4
Corsage	$2
Food and Drink	$2
Transportation and Parking	$1
Cleaning and Pressing	$1
Tipping and Hatchecking	.50
Misc.	.50
	$11.00"

These figures were approved by the Interfraternity Ball co-chairmen as a "low estimate," and the *Daily* complained that such expense put all-university dances out of the range of most students.[30]

The *Daily*'s call for cheaper formals was met the next day with the announcement that ticket prices would be reduced from $4 to $3, that a "tax" would be levied on corsages to discourage them, and that free hat- and coat-checking would be provided.[31] At least one student was annoyed by all this haggling over cost, and insisted that luxury was the point of proms. In a letter to the editor, which the *Daily* ran under the headline "Public Be Damned," he or she wrote: "1) The good thing about our formals is their exclusiveness; 2) Only those who can afford this luxury should be able to attend. Why let people come who won't be able to take advantage of this when they are out of school? 3) Gym informals cater to the social life of the masses of the students. Let us who have 'better tastes' have our formals and let those who like gym dances have their informals."[32]

No other student was willing to add his or her voice to this anti-democratic diatribe, but the same issues surfaced in a much more specific and long-running debate. The *Daily* had suggested eliminating corsages at proms as a way to scale down men's prom expenses. One woman, speaking for many, objected. A "very large gardenia" costs only $.75, she wrote — "no price to quibble over." If forced to choose, she argued, she'd rather have the large gardenia than a "Coke date": "You can buy yourself cokes, but it's rather awkward to buy yourself flowers."[33] A subsequent poll found that 67 percent of Northwestern students (65 percent of the men and 69 percent of the women) opposed the corsage ban.[34]

Northwestern's Interhouse Ball that year found a compromise of sorts. Gardenias were sold at the door for $.25, and all other corsages had to be checked. The dance committee announced in advance: "In order to assure every man that he will not be embarrassed by others having bought corsages, we will enforce this rule. Nothing but single gardenias will be permitted on the dance floor."[35] Ten years later, in 1949, with prom bids going for $5.50, the struggle was still going on. Prom chairmen requested that men not buy corsages for their dates, but recognized continuing competitive pressure by noting that the policy would "have a bad effect unless all men cooperate."[36]

Flowers, both in college and outside, exemplify the dating system's emphasis on competing through consumption. Almost every description of a "big date," from the 1920s through the 1950s, features the kind of corsage the girl or woman wears, and sample budgets for major dates allot anywhere from $2 to $10 for corsages.[37] These flowers were not private gifts — cut flowers for the woman's dressing table — but public symbols. They said, for the man, "See what I can afford," and for the woman, "See how much I'm worth." The girl who said she could buy her own Cokes understood that in the dating competition the companionship of a Coke date couldn't match the symbolic importance of flowers on a big date.

Like dates, the flowers were necessary commodities in and of themselves, but were valued according to their cost. In popular magazine articles from the 1930s through the 1950s, popular girls insisted on — and got — orchids. A southern girl frankly explained in *Esquire* that she liked orchids best: "I like to think that he paid five dollars apiece for them."[38] She liked everybody else to know that, too.

In quite literal terms, women gauged their own value in dating by how much money men spent on them. *Mademoiselle*, in 1963, described women who "assess themselves as if they were stock issues (as a twenty-five-dollar date, or a fifty-dollar date)."[39] In this system, that the man pay for the date was crucial. Beyond that, the more he spent — publicly — the better. By rating visibly expensive dates — orchids, good seats at the theater, dinners at elegant restaurants — women publicly demonstrated how much they were worth in the dating system.

Orchids were expensive. So were proms, football weekends, and dinners at the Ritz. The high value accorded such expensive dates directly influenced the way women evaluated men as dates. The nominal equivalence works nicely here: if ideal date (event) is expensive, the ideal date (person) is a man who can afford them. The man and the event are equivalent, jointly valued and evaluated in economic terms.

Public sources that characterized dates economically (as in "$350 date") applied the same criterion to men. The favorite designation for a good date was "free spender."[40]

A 1941 deodorant ad in *Esquire* directly paralleled the values of date (event) and date (person) for men's benefit: "The dinner was marvelous. The theatre tickets were premium ducats!" and "Young Bob had a million-dollar smile and his dad had a million dollars." Even so, "Betty" walked out on these ideal "dates" because Bob hadn't used Mum.[41] Some things, the ad suggested, were too much to bear at any price.

While bad hygiene might ruin even the most expensive date, boys and men were cautioned from all sides that the better the dates they provided the better they would seem as dates. *Senior Scholastic* told boys not to "expect to make an impression with nothing but your Casanovan charm," and proposed "Selling Point — Number One" on a date: "Select your entertainment carefully."[42] *Good Housekeeping*, in 1953, noted that "today it would be social suicide for [a boy] to cut corners on a big date."[43]

Advice books warned women against "free loaders," and insisted that they could judge how serious a man was by how much he spent on them.[44] A high school girl stated her own economic criterion very clearly in 1930, saying, "I know I don't give many second dates to boys unless they can take me to keen places. Some of the fellows I'd like to go with can't afford it, and I just don't go with them, that's all."[45] The same sentiment echoes through the decades, from the teenage girls who said in 1949 that their "ideal" date spent between $5 and $10 and didn't "look worried at prices," to the 1959 poll in which 67 percent of the girls said they'd be more likely to go out with a boy if he had a car, to the 1970s cheerleader who insisted that "if a guy can't afford to pay for me on a date, then he can't afford to go out with me period."[46]

In 1950, Gay Head, the *Senior Scholastic* dating advisor, wrote a column that seems to have been intended to downplay some of the emphasis on money in dating. Stressing that good character and good grooming were important qualities, she also wrote: "[Girls] like a boy who is earning some of his own dating money. They *dislike* feeling that they're dating his father's wallet."[47] The implication was, of course, that girls would rather date the boy's own wallet.

While Gay Head's phrasing might have been untrue to her intentions in this case, the same point was made less explicitly throughout the discourse on dating. Because dates were evaluated in economic terms, it followed logically that men had to be evaluated by the quality of the dates they were able to provide. The public conventions of dating, insofar as they placed money at the center of the dating system, symbolically transformed men into no more than wallets. Just as countless sources told men that they could evaluate women on the size of their breasts, others told women to evaluate men on the thickness of their wallets. The public culture of dating portrayed men, no less than women, as interchangeable commodities. Still, the language that betrays the commodification of men in dating is relatively subtle, for the process itself is obscured by the power that men's control of money gave them in the dating system. Women, on the other hand, are spoken of directly as commodities purchased by men's money. Both the words used to describe women in courtship and the advice given to men about women clearly reflect this commercial relationship.

Since dating is a public act, much of the public discussion of courtship for men deals with the "type" of girl with whom one should be seen and how much it will cost to be seen with her. In the 1940s, the *Daily Northwestern* ran a column reviewing Chicago's night spots. The reviewer cautioned men to gauge their dates' worth carefully. "If she's blonde and simply gorgeous," he advised, "take her to the luxurious green and gold *Empire Room* at the Palmer House," where (he warned) it will cost $3 weeknights and $3.50 on Saturday (formal attire optional).[48]

When *Senior Scholastic* asked readers in a 1941 poll how much a "usual date" should cost, several high school boys based their answers on how much the girl was "worth." Burton J. Hoffman of Philadelphia was adamant: "Any chicken has to be a Lana Turner or a Hedy La Marr to rate more than a buck seventy-five or two bucks for a usual date."[49] (If it offered any consolation to the girls who didn't quite measure up, Burton's figures were quite generous by contemporary standards.)

The question of women's monetary worth also came up frequently in advice literature. One late-1940s book for men suggested techniques for winning various "types" of women. For the "prom queen" (which the author considered an overpriced commodity), one must "spend money like water. You don't win prom princesses," he said, "you buy them — like show horses."[50]

The show horse analogy wasn't bad. Public sources, over and over, emphasized that women should be evaluated as if they were show animals. Women's value as dates — so far as they had individual value — lay in the public impression they made, in how the possession of them made men look. In an article co-authored by Gloria Steinem, *Esquire* apprised the "student prince" of necessary techniques, suggest-

ing, "If your date is very good-looking, exploit it. Meet her at your
dorm and take her to college places. If your date is not very good-
looking, tell your friends you are having an affair with a married
woman and take her to the movies."[51] The "it" in the first sentence is a
bit awkward. Perhaps even this junior-Machiavelli had trouble coming out with "exploit her." But for clarity of expression, we can most
profitably turn to Cornell University, where men called a girl who was
right to be seen with a "fixture."[52]

The language describing women as commodities is most consistently pronounced in men's magazines such as *Esquire* and, later,
Playboy — just as language traditionally grew more explicit in the
sanctuary of men's clubs or locker rooms. A 1963 *Cosmopolitan* article complained that the message of such magazines was, "Women are
nice to have around when necessary; an accessory for the well-dressed
bachelor."[53] The writer's indignation here is not totally appropriate.
Certainly some of the more strident articles were written with tongue
in cheek; many were intended to satirize or caricature. But much satire
and humor works by building on existing tensions and situations,
playing out their implications to "ridiculous" extremes. In tracing a
way of seeing through a culture, these mass-marketed extremes help to
define the system's perimeters.

Esquire, the "spectacularly successful" men's magazine that pre-
miered in 1933, offered a guide to consumption through both advertisements and articles.[54] Women fit very neatly into that format. In
post–World War II America, when many American men complained
publicly that American women were greedy and that men had to
spend entirely too much money to satisfy their dates, *Esquire* defused
this challenge to the consumer ethic. *Esquire* aired similar changes in
its pages, but at the same time shifted away from the troublesome ac-
cusation that women somehow controlled or demanded men's expen-
diture of money. In *Esquire*'s world, men did not spend money to
satisfy women, nor even "for" women. They spent money "on" them,
as they spent money on wine and clothes and cars and travel. Women
— beautiful women — were part of the good life, an essential, though
costly, accessory for the *Esquire* man.

Esquire consistently portrayed women as commodities. Its pinup
girls are one example; mass-produced images, glossy and perfect, a
different one each month. These women demand nothing; they are objects presented for men's pleasure. The same argument, however, can
be made about centuries of erotic art and/or pornography. *Esquire*'s
textual descriptions of women and prescriptions for male action re-
garding women are much richer sources.

For example, in 1948 *Esquire* presented a "new kind of guide" to vacation spots. A handy reference chart gave all the pertinent information:

AT: (location)

YOU'LL MEET: (kind of girls)

TALK ABOUT:

AMUSE HER BY:

IT'LL COST YOU:

Defending the added expense of travel, the author wrote: "Far be it from us to imply that the Three Tetons, for example, are less impressive in contour than the blond on the clubhouse porch. And yet there is a certain satisfaction in seeing them artistically superimposed one on the other."[55] Just part of the landscape; an important (but costly) amenity to consider in selecting the right vacation spot.

Esquire's fashion section, a catalog of clothes and accessories for the *Esquire* man, frequently included women in the accessory category. In the "Man, Mode and Manners" section of the February 1945 issue, a fashion photo shows the male model buying flowers. The caption: "The flowers for the lady in question are just another expression of his good taste." As was the lady, evidently. According to a 1951 article, "A beautiful woman with an orchid to match is one of the real pleasures of life."[56]

Playboy, which Hugh Hefner began after leaving his job in *Esquire's* promotion department in the early 1950s, was not essentially different in its commoditization of women, though its language was a bit more strident.[57] One issue of *Playboy* contained a "coloring book" full of line drawings of the amenities of life for the aspiring playboy to color in. One page shows three voluptuous women. The coloring instructions read: "Make one of the girls a blonde. Make one of the girls a brunette. Make one of the girls a redhead. It does not matter which is which. The girls' haircolors are interchangeable. So are the girls."[58]

The coloring book's action takes place mainly in the playboy's "pad," which is full of all sorts of expensive furnishings to color: stereo speakers, modern furniture, art objects, a "playmate" with a "strapless 39-D brassiere." They're all the same, except the furnishings will be around longer. The girl, as the coloring instructions say quite explicitly, is to be used and discarded.[59]

Margaret Mead, searching for a way to describe American courtship in the 1940s, came up with an apt simile. "He takes her out," she wrote, "like he takes out his new car, but more impersonally, because the car is his for good but the girl is his only for the evening."[60] In fact, the equation of women and cars was common in mid-century American culture. Both were property, both expensive; cars and women came in different styles or models, and both could be judged on performance. The woman he escorted, just as the car he drove, publicly defined both a man's taste and his means.

In 1951, *Time* magazine prepared a special feature on the "Younger Generation," including youth's attitudes toward premarital and extramarital sex. A paratrooper at Fort Bragg told a *Time* correspondent: "Before the property is yours, I don't see why anybody can't use it." But his "buddy" added: "After marriage, some guy taking my wife would be like taking my car and putting on a few extra miles. It might improve through use, but I like to drive my own." The equation of wife and car passed without comment in the resulting story, but *Time*'s compiler-author seemed to feel the latter comment was reassuring, showing that youth had not abandoned traditional morality altogether.[61]

Earlier that same year *Esquire* had slickly conflated the appeal of women and cars in its "*Esquire* Girl, 1951 Model" feature. The text read:

> You understand, of course, that anyone touching an exhibit in motion does so at his own risk. The guarantee is just what you see with your eyes, gentlemen. Don't ask us about trade-in value, speed, miles per gallon, upholstery, or how long the job will retain the charm of its marvelous lines and the smoothness of its velvety finish.
>
> You now have the 1951 model before you; available in twelve body types, all with substantially the same superb chassis, the finest combination of everything that biology and industry can devise for entertainment, education, inspiration and insomnia.[62]

The pseudo-sales pitch does note that "upkeep and operation cost" for the 1951 model is "slightly stupendous."[63] In fact, these models and others like them cost American women much more than they cost men.

The "ideal" beauty, in twentieth-century America, was a clearer standard than ever before in history, and it was an ideal held up to and available to a much greater percentage of the population — both men and women — than ever before. Hollywood film stars usually embodied the ideal, which was presented to the nation through the movies and reinforced by magazine photographs and articles, advertisements, models, and pinup girls. The man who had observed in 1922 that it was becoming almost impossible to tell the difference between the well-off small-town girl, the shop girl, and the city girl was clearly a poor observer.[64] A multitude of clues remained. But he was right in that increasingly in the twentieth century all three subscribed to the same basic ideals of beauty, as set forth in the national media, and that all three had recourse to the same mass-produced products in their attempts to attain that ideal.

"With the constant example before us of Hollywood perfection," a 1950 husband-hunting manual explained, "our standards of physical appearance have become extraordinarily high." The author insisted, "If you are not gifted with a perfect figure and flawless skin, there is only one solution for you. You must apply yourself relentlessly to the task of making nature over so that you can take your place without self-consciousness in the race for a husband."[65]

And American women spared little effort or expense in the task of making nature over. In 1956, *Life* magazine reported to its better than six million readers, American women spent $1.3 billion on cosmetics and toiletries; $660 million on "beauty treatments," $400 million on soap and "electric devices," and $65 million on reducing. The grand total ($2,425,000,000), the article pointed out, was two times the total defense budget of Italy.[66]

Expenditures on beauty had been climbing steadily throughout the century. The figures quoted in popular magazines are not directly comparable, but do give a sense of scale. In 1942, for example, the *LHJ* reported that American girls spent close to $800 million a year on "keeping beautiful." In 1940, *Esquire* complained that American women had spent $7 million on "charm schools" in 1939, and claimed that "Europe could live happily ever after" on the amount American women spent every year on clothes. In 1930, the American cosmetics industry did a volume of $180 million, and the United States boasted forty thousand beauty parlors, up from five thousand in 1920.[67] Consumption was central to the quest for beauty.

In 1963, a teenage girl wrote to *Seventeen* for advice: "After dating one boy for six months, I have begun to wonder about many things. I don't want to lose him. I don't want to become an 'old thing' to him. Should I attempt different hairdos, etc.? Would this keep him as attentive and alert as he was on first dates?"[68]

This letter was written — and answered — quite seriously. Where did this girl get the idea she could enhance her relationship with her boyfriend by changing her hairstyle? Well . . . everywhere. She was literally parroting what countless sources — advertisers, advisers, "experts," even her peers — had been telling her since she could remember: the "right" appearance is critical. For example, when *Senior Scho-*

lastic's teen dating adviser asked rhetorically, "Why do some people click and others not?" the correct answer was "Personality." In the column below the question, however, she talked about appearance, just as if it were the same as — or determined — personality.[69] And the *Ladies' Home Journal* "sub-deb" adviser cautioned her readers: "It takes extra care in dressing and making up the raw material you were blessed with to do its best selling job for that personality of yours." [70]

The author of a women's advice book published in 1943 worried that her readers might take offense at its inordinate emphasis on appearance. That, she cautioned, would betray an unrealistic attitude. Appearance is crucial, she said, and the contemporary stress on a few narrowly defined "types" of beauty could easily be turned to any woman's advantage. "Everyone can become a type that's in the current physical fashion," she wrote, "if they have the courage to make themselves into that type." [71]

The same kind of advice about "types" was offered to teenagers. In a heavily didactic *Senior Scholastic* advice column masquerading as a story, a pair of rich sisters seek help from "Jerry," the heroine of the tale. Their appeal is: "We want you to tell us what's *wrong* with us — clothes, hair, face — everything. Here we are, with everything most girls want, but without the very thing most girls *have* — popularity." Jerry, who has never liked either girl before, doesn't even mention personality or how they treat others. Instead, she promises them popularity through a "remake." They should "stick to type," she advises, and wear clothes that suit that type. Her most concrete piece of advice is to buy a girdle.[72] This story has two morals. First, appearance is the key to successful personal relations, and second, the right appearance is a matter of skillful consumption.

America's public culture, since at least the 1920s, constantly reiterated this same message: women should compete for men by consuming, for the race goes not to the good, not to the merely pretty, but to the most skillful consumer. "It cuts through competition like a rapier," promised a 1940s perfume ad. Whether the competition was for dates or for a husband, women were not without resource. As one husband-hunting manual noted in 1950, "The modern world has given you a billion-dollar cosmetic industry, diet experts, specialized stylists and brand-new psychological knowledge; all to storm the barricades of bachelorhood." [73] Another reassured women: "Science has placed the magic of Cinderella into the hands of today's women. . . . All that is necessary for the aspirant to beauty is to select the proper cosmetic for the proper occasion." [74]

Of course, all these reassurances had a dark side. Since (theoretically) any woman willing to invest the necessary time and money could be beautiful, a woman had "no excuse" for not being attractive.[75] And in a world governed by such reasoning, the competition was always escalating. Women understood that they were competing with not only the real women in their immediate sphere but also with the "ideal" women of screen and magazine; film actresses and models on whom no expense had been spared and no skill withheld to enhance their beauty.

The "types" these models and actresses represented, the media told women, were proven successful. They *were* ideal beauty; they were what men liked. Naturally, the average woman couldn't best Marilyn Monroe or Dorothy Lamour in a one-to-one competition. But, as advertisers and advisers stressed, she could imitate them. By becoming as much *like* one of these ideal types as possible, a woman could take advantage of men's desire for these unattainable ideals of beauty.

For almost twenty-five years, from the sweater girls of World War II well into the 1960s, one ideal of beauty dominated America's national culture. At the very least, one could say that America — or American men — had a love affair with the bosom. Less charitable observers called it a fetish.[76]

"Never before in history," a pre-"Cosmo-girl" *Cosmo* article complained, "has the average man been so incessantly bombarded with hoopla about one type of female beauty — the long-legged, big-bosomed, Jayne Mansfield-Anita Ekberg style."[77] From the sweater-girl pinups of the World War II era to *Playboy*'s nude centerfolds, men's magazines focused on women's breasts. They were full of photos of disproportionately developed mammary glands that, through some feat of engineering, were made to stand straight out to full forty-two inch circumference with no visible means of support. In the late 1950s, *Playboy* featured the continuing "adventures" of Miss June Wilkenson (43–22–36), whom they called "The Bosom." In "The Bosom in Hollywood," Miss Wilkenson's adventure is to walk down the street, breasts encased in conical bra and preceding the rest of her body like the prow of a battleship, or perhaps the fins of a Cadillac in reverse.[78] Evidently that was enough of an adventure for the males who watched.

Quite a few plausible and implausible explanations have been advanced for this obsession with breasts. Whatever the psychological origin, however, the equivalency of breast size and desirability meshes neatly with the commoditization of courtship. Big breasts, in the popular conception, signaled that a woman was "expensive." Cartoons used this shorthand frequently, and even letters to the editor in men's magazines joined the words *big-bosomed* and *expensive* to describe the contemporary ideal.[79] By dating women with big bosoms, men showed that they could afford the expense, could command such abundance.

Furthermore, breast size was easily and palpably quantified. It removed the subjectivity of most other evaluations of a woman's "worth." A thirty-eight-inch chest was "better" (more prestigious) than a thirty-two-inch chest, making it easier for men to compare women, and so to measure their own attainments in the competitive world of dating. Thus, a man's date becomes not "Lucy," not a "nice girl" or a "pretty girl," but "a 39-D" or perhaps a "playmate" in a "strapless 39-D brassiere." (The addition of bra cup size to measurement lends a sense of three-dimensionality; it makes the measurement more precise.)

Most American women were not 39-Ds, especially in conjunction with the relatively slim hips and waist necessary to make breasts appear startlingly large. In a culture that regarded being small-busted as a defect, a culture that insisted that "the glamour men . . . most frequently go to the girls who have what it takes to keep a strapless evening dress in a vertical position," this "inadequacy" clearly presented a problem.[80]

Not an insurmountable problem, however. American women imitated the ideal; they went about the task of making nature over with a little help from the garment industry. In its 1951 catalog, Sears offered twenty-two kinds of falsies — rubber cones in white or fleshtone, some equipped with nipples. It's hard to say how many women, as *Esquire* put it in 1941, were moved to "sport a gadget in addition / To keep abreast of competition," but a poll at the University of Wisconsin in 1960 found that most coeds wanted bigger busts, and a college student told a *Ladies' Home Journal* forum in 1956 that teenage girls worried that they would "have to wear falsies in order to look right."[81]

A male seal of approval for the falsie came in an *Esquire* article titled "Beauty and the Bust" (which appropriately enough appeared in a feature issue on cars): "The female bust is with us more opulently and more openly than ever before in our history. Unlike other revolutionary changes in feminine fashion, it has not cruelly excluded women whose contours do not conform to its dictates. In fact, the new fashion made the invention of the falsie possible and inevitable, and gave the flat-breasted an artificial chance for equality."[82] In other words, women insufficiently endowed by nature could resort to technological artifice; they could compete by consuming.[83]

And just as women consumed so they could compete, they competed so they could consume. The heroine of a 1955 *Ladies' Home Journal* story explained the process this way:

> And I'm going to tell you a secret now. It's about girls and how they dress and how they do their hair. Men always think these things are frivolous matters. Nothing could be further from the truth. The girl in the red dress with the plunging neckline may be only shopping for a washing machine as she tangos so sensually upon the dance floor. She may know very well that it takes this dress to get that fellow to let her wash those clothes in that washing machine he's going to buy her when they are married.[84]

She could have explained that the girl in the red dress was shopping for a husband — that she was really demure or serious but that it took such frivolousness, such overstated sexuality, to attract men. Instead she jumped a few steps. Attracting men and getting a husband were just steps along the way. A husband was necessary, the base of the pyramid on which she would pile washer-dryers and refrigerator-freezers and sterling and fine china. He would buy them for her; he would justify her possession of them. In this vision the man is not only an interchangeable commodity, he is ultimately less important than the other commodities he makes possible.

Many advertisements went just as far with this scenario. Ads for beauty products portrayed them as weapons for getting a man ("I'm another bride thanking Camay for helping me to a Lovely Skin") — but even in these cases the man himself was often superseded by the material goods he brought.[85] In the Pond's series ("She's ENGAGED! She's Lovely! She uses Ponds!"), the ads featured real women such as Virginia Masterson, "daughter of one of Chicago's old families." Instead of picturing the brides-to-be with their fiancés, the ads showed close-up enlargements of their engagement rings.[86]

The importance attached to engagement rings, bridal showers, wedding gifts, and extravagant weddings and receptions emphasizes the crucial place of consumption in the culmination of courtship. The wedding business was big business. In 1960, for example, when the median American family income was $4,970, the "average" wedding cost $3,300. The bride and groom received an average of $1,003 worth of gifts. The average bride spent $243.29 for her trousseau and the average groom spent $398.79 for an engagement ring (more than for the average honeymoon at $361).[87] *Look*, in 1957, did a four-page, ten-photo spread on "Double Wedding . . . double glamour," an un-average wedding with six hundred guests, twelve bridesmaids, fourteen ushers, and three bridal consultants. Each bride received six hundred-plus presents, which were displayed in a separate building and guarded at night.[88] *U.S. News and World Report* estimated that newlyweds were worth $23 billion to the U.S. economy. An advice book for women summed it up: "Merchandise plus Marriage equals our economy."[89]

In a very real sense that bald statement was true. Marriage allowed young men and women to enter fully into society, to take their places as adults in the social and economic structure of America. In a culture that centered around consumption, taking one's place meant establishing a new unit of consumption. Receiving and buying goods gave young men and women a sense of belonging to the culture, a personal sense of meaning. The act of consuming gave them a joint interest that cemented the relationship between bride and groom.

Within such a culture, it was only appropriate that this ritual of initiation privileged the act of consuming. Here, marriage became, in an additional sense, the culmination of courtship. For while the theme of consumption in courtship is tangled, this much is clear: courtship was, for most young Americans in this era, the time when they began active consumption of America's visible plenty. In their courtship, youth defined themselves through *acts* of consumption and in *terms* of consumption. Thus they celebrated their lives and their loves.

Sex Control

Youth born in the first four decades of the twentieth century had sexual experiences fundamentally different from the experiences of their nineteenth-century counterparts. Of course, the sexual *activities* of youth were not totally different; as many excellent histories have shown, American Victorians were neither antisexual nor asexual. Nineteenth-century youth played kissing games that rivaled twentieth-century versions, engaged couples indulged in what their grandchildren would call "heavy petting," and rates of premarital intercourse did not change drastically at the beginning of the new century.[1] What changed were not sexual acts so much as what those acts meant — how they were perceived, what symbolic freight they carried. Individual sexual expression changed less than the context for that expression. The new context for and understandings of sex, however, profoundly changed how youth experienced sex. In the twentieth century, sex and sexuality increasingly entered the public sphere and became part of the very definition of youth.

Nineteenth-century Americans had participated in the creation of a public discourse on sex — proscribing, regulating, categorizing. But this discourse was not a discourse of youth. Youth, as we understand the term, hadn't yet come into being. And as discussions touched on young unmarried people of the "respectable" classes, they usually equated sex with body, prescribing cures for the solitary sexual act of masturbation, not for heterosexual union.

The twentieth-century discourse on sex centered around youth and their heterosexual premarital experience. While many condemned the linkage of youth and sex, a celebratory current began to gain strength by the 1920s. Some of the more accepting attitudes toward sex stemmed from the doctrines of popular Freudianism, which seemed to insist that a freer expression of sexuality was necessary for mental health. But the celebration also came from another source: many Americans were fascinated with "youth" — young men and women who defined themselves, as *youth*, partly through public sexuality and sexual experimentation.

Public discourse absorbed both currents, the condemnatory and the celebratory, and new sexual conventions grew in the tension between old and new, between the sexual proscriptions of authorities, who sought to control sexual expression, and the sexual prescriptions of youth, who placed sexuality at the center of youth culture. In forging the new conventions and in living with them, the meaning of youth's sexual experience was transformed.

The crucial element in this transformation was the rise of a national youth culture. Firmly in place by the 1920s, this new and visible phenomenon was produced in part by new associations of boys and girls (and men and women) in coed high schools, colleges, and the workplace. In the late nineteenth and early twentieth centuries, youth were segregated increasingly by age and decreasingly by gender. Groups of young men and women came together in an intimacy of common experience, sometimes with relative freedom from the supervision of family and traditional community, and formed tight peer cultures. These local groups contributed to a revolution in the way youth defined themselves.[2]

By the 1920s, when more and more youth had access to peer cultures and national media were helping to create a *national* peer culture, "youth" had become the transcendent definitional category, the encompassing category — defined in opposition to age — that overrode the more traditional oppositional category of gender. In other words, young people thought the divisions between men and women were less important than the division between young and old. This allegiance of youth (boys and girls together) threatened the authority of adults. Sex quickly became the key issue in the struggle that ensued.[3]

While the decline in the power the family exerted over its young, the freedoms offered by the city, the surge in the number of young people attending high school, and the flow of young women into offices all helped produce the new youth culture in the twentieth century, local youth cultures had begun to develop earlier on college campuses. Authorities had not missed their implications. Horace Mann, in his presidential inaugural address at Antioch in 1853, warned of the "dangers" of men's and women's "association together, *without supervision*" that coeducational colleges allowed.[4] In 1915, the Dean of

Women at the University of Wisconsin lamented the "tidal wave of ir-responsible joyousness" that had come to college campuses in the 1890s with the influx of youth who believed "college life" was "more fun for your money." She warned that the problem of "inexperienced, unrestrained young men and women thrown together socially without adequate guidance" was critical, and that something must be done to control the students.[5]

Control, however, was difficult. The peer cultures had their own norms and conventions, and where peer cultures were strong, they could undermine the conventions and norms offered by authorities. At Northwestern, for example, in 1904, the Dean of Women told coeds in chapel: "I have heard . . . that some young women allow men to touch them, to hold their hands! . . . My dear girls, never in-dulge in such frivolous actions." The *Northwestern* put her advice in perspective with the headline "Alas, that Co-eds Should Spoon."[6]

While peer cultures developed earlier and stronger at colleges, dis-crepancies between the conventions of youth and adults were also be-coming plain in the larger society. The adviser for the *Ladies' Home Journal* complained in 1907 that she was "plied with queries from ap-parently respectable youths as to how soon after the first meeting a man should feel free to kiss a girl" and asked by girls what to do about "this or that young man [who] had showed his devotion by affection-ate demonstrations." It was beginning to seem, she said, that young men and women between about fifteen and twenty "expected" hand-holding and kissing. The adviser, who believed a couple should "by no means" hold hands until betrothed, lamented this state of society, but in so doing, she confirmed the strength of new conventions to her one-million-plus readers.[7]

As youth culture grew in strength and had its existence ratified by the attention of national media, the oppositions between it and the larger culture were made more explicit. Sex, to most contemporaries, seemed the central issue in the opposition. Youth's attitudes about sex and their sexual practices seemed to directly oppose conventional morality and the values of (older) authority — and youth meant them to.[8] The tension surrounding sex is not surprising — all societies regulate sex and sexuality in some way, and any change in sexual norms creates tension.

But the generation born between 1900 and 1910 was growing up as old sexual conventions crumbled in the face of new understandings of sexuality and new ways of life. Because of the new ways of life — more freedom for women, the automobile, the possibilities for anonymity in the urban landscape — these young people had more real freedom than respectable youth had had before — in the span of adult memory, any-way.[9] New sexual norms were emerging with these changes. And because of new understandings of sexuality, including popular Freud-ian theory, the resexualization of women in popular and scholarly thought, and more public acknowledgment that sex could be for pleasure as well as for procreation, young men and women grew up with slightly different ideas about the role sex played in life. But in creating "youth," young people pushed the gradual change in norms one step further. Sex became the central public symbol of youth culture, a fundamental part of the definition that separated youth from age.

"Petting" and "necking" were the major conventions youth contrib-uted to courtship in the years between World War I and the sexual revolution of the 1960s. (A significant percentage of young people had premarital intercourse during this period, but it did not become "conventional" behavior among youth until the mid-1960s.) In 1922, the *Ann Arbor Times News* argued that "snuggle-pupping" (a briefly popular term for petting) was nothing new: "Years ago it was called 'spooning,' later 'fussing,' then 'petting.'"[10] The author, though he sounds like an eminently sensible man, turned out to be wrong. He assumed that "petting" was just a new term for the light lovemaking celebrated in the popular songs about courtship of the late nineteenth century. (Another writer in the 1920s defined the "petting party" as "a party devoted to hugging."[11]) By the 1930s, petting would have a more exact definition — one that was a long way beyond spooning and hugging.

While the "technical language of the science" varied in different parts of the United States, necking was generally accepted to mean ca-resses above the neck and petting caresses below. A 1950s marriage text offered a more exact distinction. In necking, stimulation is from the "neck up," and the "main areas" of sexual stimulation remain cov-ered by clothing. The neck, lips, and ears are "utilized extensively as sexual objects." Petting, on the other hand, "includes literally every caress known to married couples but does not include complete sexual intercourse."[12]

Of course, as sexual acts go, neither petting nor necking was new. Their new significance lay in their naming, in their rise to convention-ality, and in their symbolic importance to youth. Petting was no longer on the fringes of courtship — something couples did in absolute privacy, not knowing how many others were doing the same. It was no longer what boys and young men did with lower-class girls — ex-ploiting them to save respectable girls from sexual pressure.[13] Sex was accepted by youth, male and female. Necking and petting were public conventions, expected elements in any romantic relationship between a boy and a girl. As Floyd Dell explained in *Parents* magazine in 1931, when a girl pets, "she is acting according to the code of her own adolescent world, she feels behind her the approval of her own age group, and she is serenely sure that she is all right."[14]

By 1952, a marriage text noted that necking and petting were *"customary"* for young Americans, a basic part of the subculture of youth. The author continued: "A girl in modern society may neck whether she personally enjoys it or not. She wishes to be a member of the dating group, and this is one of the requirements for membership. It is certainly well known that many young people smoke or drink for this reason, so why should it be so difficult to see that they engage in mild sexual contact for the same reason?"[15]

Both explanations, though twenty years apart, emphasize the same point: petting and necking were part of the definition of youth culture.

The continuing normalization of sex came partly through the dating system. Dating meant, in practice, that young people had many partners — and these were all potential necking or petting partners. New norms were reinforced gradually as youth encountered similar expectations of sexual behavior from many different people. By 1957, a girl could write to *Seventeen*'s advice columnist about these peer conventions, saying, "I've noticed that every boy I've gone out with wants to kiss me on the first date."[16]

Necking and petting were integral parts of the dating system, and to participate in the system, one had to meet its requirements. Furthermore, the dating system promoted sexual experimentation not only through the privacy it offered but also through the sense of obligation it fostered. Dating was an unequal relationship: the man paid for everything and the woman was thus indebted to him. According to many, boys and men were entitled to sexual favors as payment for that debt; the more money the man spent, the more petting the woman owed him. One boy, answering the question "Does a girl have to pet in order to be popular?" wrote: "When a boy takes a girl out and spends $1.20 on her (like I did the other night) he expects a little petting in return (which I didn't get)."[17]

New sexual norms were also reinforced in the public arena, through the mass media. Sexual experience in the twentieth century was laid open to public view as never before in history. Hundreds of articles were written about sexual mores, and sex was studied and reported on by a multitude of experts and pollsters. Many of these public reports, especially the polls and questionnaires so popular in the 1930s through the 1950s, measured sexual activity less than they measured sexual attitudes. And as many researchers admitted, respondents' answers often correlated more closely to what they thought they should say than to what they really thought or did or knew.[18] It's difficult to say which set of conventions exerted more pressure on respondents in any given poll — desire to live up to the conventions set forth by authority, or desire to conform to peer conventions. Nonetheless, these polls and reports have great historical value simply because they were public. They helped establish and normalize conventions by providing youth with a national frame of reference for their private sexual acts.[19]

The polls told young people in 1938, for example, that 88 percent of American women believed most youth petted. Polls told them that in 1939 41.7 percent of high school girls dated boys who expected a good-night kiss, that in 1949 81 percent of U.S. high school students believed it was all right to neck or pet, that in 1950 51 percent of high school boys believed in kissing on the first date.[20] In 1966, *Look* told teens that 45 percent of them believed it was OK for a boy and girl to "live together" if they were in love.[21] College students more often got their normative figures from textbooks. In the 1950s they were told that 93 percent of them agreed that necking was appropriate when going steady and that 87 percent of junior and senior women in one 1946 study thought premarital intercourse was justified if the couple were in love.[22]

How closely these figures mirrored behavior is unclear. It isn't likely that 51 percent of American high school boys kissed on the first date or that 87 percent of college upperclasswomen had premarital intercourse — one group probably couldn't, the other probably wouldn't. (Although *Mademoiselle*, in the 1950s, insinuatingly featured wedding gowns that weren't "strictly" white: "a layer of white over a layer of blue to make the color slightly mysterious."[23]) Nevertheless, the results of these and similar oft-quoted polls ratified youth's sexual experience — they showed youth how strong their conventions were. And, to some extent, by bringing sex into the public eye, polls and studies removed it from the realm of the private and made it more of a normative measure of how well one conformed to the peer group.

Faced with youth's public rejection of conventions of sexual control (whether or not they rejected them in private), parents and authorities attempted to regain control of young people's sexuality. Several generations of parents were involved here, and most of them had, at one time, been "youth" themselves. However, youthful experience didn't usually translate into later tolerance. The official line against sex, drawn heavily from nineteenth-century understandings, remained remarkably consistent for the first two-thirds of the twentieth century.

Authorities tried to control sexual experimentation in many different ways. Popular magazines, while printing the results of polls and surveys that showed heavy petting (and even premarital intercourse) to be common, heavily "interpreted" these results for readers. The controversial 1953 Kinsey Report, *Sexual Behavior in the Human Female*, was not ignored by popular magazines. But *Time*, in its cover story "5,940 Women," warned of the "dangerous . . . idea that there is morality in numbers." The *Ladies' Home Journal* ran a story under the blurb "The facts of behavior as reported . . . are not to be interpreted as moral or social justification for individual acts." And *Look* ran a page of outraged letters to the editor that included the following: "I resent the implication that the findings of Dr. Kinsey . . . are in any sense scientific. Any sampling of 5,940 women of the barroom, dance hall type . . . cannot represent the mental, moral, or spiritual integrity of American womanhood."[24]

Yet preserving the "moral integrity" of American womanhood seemed to be a monumental task. One expert told parents they'd better begin at birth if they wanted to keep their daughter from becoming a "petter." She advised them not to love the baby "too much"; to "practice the control you are going to teach her . . . in all your family life." Too much affection could create an "excessive appetite for love" and make her "hungry for physical demonstrations of affection" in later life.[25]

Other experts, in the tradition of Jane Addams, insisted that young people drifted into sexual experimentation because they lacked opportunities for wholesome recreation. The Chicago Board of Education accepted this reasoning in the first decade of the century. When it learned of a report that six hundred Chicago public high school students had been treated for venereal disease in the twenty-three months prior to the study, the board suppressed the information and appropriated $10,000 for nine social centers to combat the problem.[26] During World War II, many authorities advocated similar measures to combat sexual delinquency and Victory girls who so casually paired off with soldiers.[27]

Yet another approach attempted to defuse the subject of sex. *Parents* magazine, in the 1930s, advised parents to deal with the question of petting "dispassionately as being much more a matter of etiquette than morals."[28] Early twentieth-century coed high schools set up departments of Manners and Morals, closely linking the two.[29] Advice books were masterful at this approach. Cushioned by the fine points of dating etiquette (Where do you place your purse when dining in a restaurant?) were strong proscriptions against necking, petting, and intercourse.

One of the most effective ways in which authorities controlled sex was by limiting youth's privacy. Parents of high schoolers (usually the girls' parents) circumscribed the private time available to their children on dates by requiring dates be to verifiable destinations or supervised events and by controlling curfews. One magazine suggested parents set curfews at the time the date's main event ended, plus forty-five minutes for the couple to get something to eat.[30] Many parents used some version of this formula. If everything in town closed at 11:30 P.M., they reasoned, what *were* couples going to do if allowed a 12:30 curfew? Of course, couples could buy some private time by forgoing the customary snack or by skipping the movie (and getting a plot summary from a friend as insurance), but that was not so likely to happen on a casual date.

Double or group dates also limited sexual privacy. By restricting access to the family car, thus strongly encouraging couples to double up, parents insured a certain amount of peer chaperonage. Petting and necking would still go on, but weren't as likely to get out of hand with another couple in the front seat. Finally, parents used the classic technique of supervised privacy. Just as, in years past, girls had received serious callers in the parlor with parents discreetly chaperoning from another room, twentieth-century parents encouraged teenagers to have their "private time" at home, where knowledge of an adult presence in the house would usually limit sexual experimentation.

All of these techniques were also used, *in loco parentis*, by colleges and universities, where the struggle between students and authorities over the right to privacy is much better documented. In the main, universities regulated student conduct by regulating women students, combining various systems of parietals, penalties, and personal evaluations.

Parietals in American colleges began as strict and simple codes and became increasingly lenient and complicated as time went on. In 1915, for example, at the University of Wisconsin, the rules for women's dormitories said simply that men could be received on Saturday, Sunday, and holiday afternoons and until 10:00 nightly, and that "business calls" of ten minutes would be permitted at other times. The regulations devoted an equal amount of space to spelling out quiet hours, requiring that bedroom slippers be worn after 10:00 P.M.[31]

The number and complexity of rules built up year by year. By 1962, at the University of Michigan, the official student handbook devoted nine of its fifteen pages to rules for women. The length was necessary because the system was so complicated. Curfews varied from night to night, were stricter for underclasswomen, and were mediated by varying numbers of A.L.P.s (Automatic Late Permissions) for which some events qualified and others did not. The system of penalties for lateness shows how carefully student behavior was monitored. Penalties began when a student had eleven "late minutes" — but late minutes could be accumulated one at a time throughout the semester.[32]

Rules in the earliest years of the twentieth century were less specific and elaborate, not because they were lenient or unimportant, but because authorities assumed many things did not *need* to be said. They generally assumed that young women would not receive callers if not suitably chaperoned, that respectable and serious women students would not wander around until all hours of the night with young men. They were not always right. But as patterns of permissible behavior in society at large changed, and as the character of student bodies also changed, these assumptions were ever less well founded. The multiplying system of rules and the finer distinctions they entailed show how beleaguered the old assumptions were. Authorities now had to tell students that they must behave according to the "social standards of reputable places of entertainment and . . . homes," and they had to craft a myriad of rules to make sure that students did.[33]

As the years passed, students were subject to more and more detailed rules, governing a greater range of activities. At the University of Michigan, in the 1920s, a humor columnist cataloged the "tragic incidents," the "moans and discords" of serenades — a ritual in which fraternity men paid tribute to the lady love of one of the brothers — and in his punchline, speculated that the administration might be forced to regulate serenading to prevent "serious injuries." By 1962, the student handbook listed almost a page of regulations governing serenades.[34] At Northwestern, the first regulation of serenades appeared in the student handbook of 1951–52. Serenades could be held only on Monday evenings before 9:00 P.M. and had to be registered in advance with the Student Affairs Calendar Office.[35]

In another unpopular move at the University of Michigan, the dean's office announced in 1947 that any "mixed" group (of more than two people) listening to the Michigan-Northwestern football game on the radio must have registered as a "party" before noon the preceding Thursday and must have secured the requisite number of approved chaperones. Students recognized this new rule as a further incursion into their privacy. The *Daily* ran an editorial titled "Cloister or College?"[36] The spontaneity of contact between the sexes was being eroded, and with it many of the possibilities for sexual privacy.

The search for privacy was an important part of dates on college campuses — and privacy was not easy to come by, especially in cold climates. The refuge offered by dormitory lounges and date rooms was not especially secure. At the University of Michigan in the 1950s, women students fought with their resident head over the use of Stockwell House lounge. Under pressure, girls passed a resolution against "petting or lying on the couches" in the lounge, but the following semester the house director said the problem of "over-amorous couples" persisted and proposed setting up a "lounge patrol." Students, in a counterproposal, suggested setting up an alternate "visitors' room" where students "could feel free to take grandmothers and great aunts."[37]

At Radcliffe, the student handbook reminded women that dormitory sitting rooms were not "private parlors. You're on display," it warned, "so act accordingly."[38] And, in 1947, following Dean Mildred P. Sherman's announcement that "the process of saying goodnight has degenerated," students under pressure resolved to exclude men from the Radcliffe dormitories after 10:00 P.M. on weekdays. In response, Harvard men threatened:

> The cold stone steps outside the Houses
> Have not the atmosphere which rouses
> The feelings waked by well-filled blouses
> > (line censored — Ed.)
>
> If we can't make the clock stand still
> We'll go to Wheaton — Damn — We will![39]

Other students looked for privacy elsewhere. In 1937, *Pulse,* a student magazine at the University of Chicago, listed nine "tried and true" necking places on campus. While these spots were safe from official eyes, the authors warned that they weren't likely to be completely private. Instead, *Pulse* recommended the automobile "whenever possible."[40] Cars were generally considered the best and most private option for sexual privacy. A short story in *Mademoiselle* describes "college-girl cars with boxes of tissues and clean seat covers that were parked in the lot behind the dormitories" where the student couple made love.[41] But many colleges and universities had regulations against students having cars. In 1963, students at a midwestern university launched a campaign against this restriction. One male student told the *New York Times Magazine* that the issue wasn't transportation but privacy: "We wouldn't care if the cars had no wheels, just so long as they had doors."[42]

Outside college, though subject to none of the institutional regulation and official scrutiny students bore, courting couples also relied on the automobile for sexual privacy. Some municipalities tried to prevent couples from taking advantage of the dangerously excessive privacy cars offered by making a form of supervised privacy available. One police chief in New Jersey allowed parking at night in the county parks. Patrol cars protected "courting" couples, but the couples were required to leave their car lights on and to park legally. In Atlanta in 1953 the city council tried to ban parking between sundown and sunup in Piedmont Park, the traditional Atlanta "parking" place. The order drew national attention, and after someone pointed out that there were advantages in having a specific parking place where group controls operated and possibly limited sex, the council unanimously rescinded the order.[43] Couples were going to park anyway, and as parents chaperoning from the next room had realized long ago, it was better to retain at least some control over their sexual expression.[44]

Most of the controls exerted by authorities and institutions did not deal directly with sex. The elaborate systems of rules did not control sex itself, but instead regulated the times and places and circumstances in which young people could express their sexual desires. As controls, these rules were effective only because they made sex logistically difficult.

Underlying these regulatory systems was a more fundamental and more effective system of control. A complex ideological system, based on historically and culturally produced understandings of male and female roles and of systems of value and exchange, opposed the developing youth culture.[45] It denied that the unity of "youth" could or should overcome the opposition of gender and insisted that sex could not be liberated from that opposition. The basic tenets of this system were used in very dogmatic and unself-conscious forms to defend against the pairing of youth and sex. What were presented as the "laws of nature" of this system filled the advice books and columns through which society tried to control young people's sexual experience.

While the regulatory systems attempted to control sex by controlling women, this ideological system made women, themselves, the controllers of sex. By its logic, women, according to their nature and in their own self-interest, must enforce sexual limits. In order for women to set the sexual limits in courtship, however, their partners had to allow them that power. The system took for granted that men would naturally want some form of sexual activity (and, according to convention, "for gallantry's sake a man [was] not in a position to withdraw from petting even should he very much want to").[46] In order to control and limit sexual expression, the woman had to have absolute veto power over her male partner. Woman's "no" always had to cancel man's "yes," and her "no" had to be as natural and assumed as his "yes."

Many men, however, refused to give up their share of sexual control or to take their share of sexual responsibility. Sometimes man's rejection of woman's veto power was brutal — what a more enlightened generation would recognize as rape. Other times the struggle for sexual control simply meant that a fourteen-year-old boy got his face slapped for kissing a girl (whom he liked very much and who liked him equally) on their first date.

However, if men refused to allow women the power to control their mutual sexual experience, this system of sexual control could not function. Experience offered plenty of evidence that that was the case, but instead of recognizing that the equation was fundamentally unbalanced, the arbiters of convention juggled the terms.

The convention that sexual limit setting was women's responsibility became an If-Then statement. *If* virtuous women imposed limits on sex, *then* men would accept those limits. If the system were valid, failures of "then" could only result from failures of "if." Therefore, in order to maintain belief in the validity of this system of sexual control, one had to believe that men would *always* submit to the limits set by virtuous women. By the logic of the system all unsanctioned sexual acts were the woman's fault: either she had not set limits or she was not truly virtuous.

In the late nineteenth century, this line of reasoning, however unappealing, may have held for (unengaged) young men and women who felt themselves bound by the conventions of respectable society (leaving, of course, the "unvirtuous" lower-class woman fair game). In the twentieth century, the logic of this system became increasingly difficult to sustain, and was tortured to ugly extremes in unselfconscious attempts to preserve traditional control over youth's sexuality.

The progression began benignly enough. In 1905, the *Ladies' Home Journal's* "Lady from Philadelphia" received a letter from "Sadie," asking what to do "when a man persists in holding your hand in spite of all that you can say." Her answer: "No man, who is fit to be welcomed in your home, would refuse to release your hand if you asked him as if you meant it."[47] Her advice is the formula that persisted for decades, but with one important difference. Here, the man's liberties are not necessarily the woman's fault. If the woman is truly virtuous, and the man does not comply with her wishes, it is because he is not "fit to be welcomed in [her] home." That conditional term soon disappeared.

By 1914, the author of a later *LHJ* advice column, "Girls' 'Affairs,'" largely ignored men's possible role. A girl wrote from a coed college asking what to do about boys who refused to date girls who didn't allow "privileges." The adviser, Mrs. Parks, replied: "I think that girls are largely responsible for the attitude of boys in this matter; for if, whenever fun merged into familiarity, the girls would instantly check such conduct, the boys would soon learn what to expect whenever they dared transgress the barrier of a self-respecting manner." [48]

A *Woman's Home Companion* columnist gave the rule a more personal reading in 1919. She told the story of a girl (not a "cheap type") who fell in love with a young man. He came to see her often, and she eventually allowed him "liberties" (kissing), even though they were not engaged. Soon he left her. By permitting him liberties, the author explained, the girl had caused him to "[fail] his own better self," and he quickly began "to tire of the girl who [was] the cause of his turning in disgust against himself." This author was trying to prove by example that the laws of convention (in this case, that a girl must not allow a man "the slightest liberty" until they were engaged) paralleled the "big unchanging laws of human nature and of love." [49] As far as kissing between unengaged couples, she was fighting a battle already lost. But the assumption on which she rested her case — that control was the girl's responsibility and lapses her fault — was gaining power steadily.

These examples, obsessed with the proprieties of hand-holding and kissing (though perhaps representing less acceptable liberties), show how far the official conventions of control were from the peer conventions of behavior. They sound as if the advisers were trying to preserve a lost world. However, the same assumptions of women's responsibility appear in later discussions that frankly acknowledged the contemporary patterns of youth's sexual relations.

In the late 1930s, professors at Vassar put together a marriage text based on lectures they gave in their highly praised marriage course. The chapter on sexual experience argued for legalized abortion and said that a student's decision about where to draw the line in premarital sexual experience was an individual moral decision best reached through personal counseling. The editor of this text, however, still believed that this individual moral decision was the woman's alone. If sex got out of hand, he claimed in the book, it was the woman's responsibility: she had "allowed [the man] too great liberties." [50]

Even more directly, a 1945 male-authored husband-hunting man-

ual for women, in a chapter titled "Courtship, Lovemaking and Petting," advised: "Remember that the average man will go as far as you
let him go. A man is only as bad as the woman he is with."[51] *Senior
Scholastic*, in a 1946 "Boy Dates Girl" column on necking, flatly
stated: "No boy — no matter whether he's Head of the Wolfpack —
will persist in affectionate intentions, if he gets a *positively negative*
response."[52] And *Datebook*'s 1960 guide to teen dating told girls there
was no need to even *have* to say no. Simply "act like a lady," the
author insisted, "and you'll be treated like one."[53]

Acting like a lady, the "if" term, was clearly the key. Many "ladies,"
however, still found themselves in difficult situations. The convention
of woman's responsibility absorbed this seeming contradiction. If the
man took sexual advantage (which, in very early days, might mean
only hand-holding but might extend to rape), or even tried to do so, the
woman must not have *really* been a lady. She must have, somehow,
invited or encouraged him.

Women's behavior was increasingly suspect. A woman or girl
could *seem* to be respectable, even think herself so, but at the same
time give off subtle signals that she was really "cheap." In 1916,
Woman's Home Companion ran an article on the convention that it
was the girl's fault if a man took liberties. The woman author was
arguing that men should not be "chameleons," "cheap with a cheap
type of woman and dignified and respectful with the dignified." Even
as she called for men to accept some responsibility for their sexual behavior, however, she completely accepted that the transgressions were
the girls' fault. Giving three examples of situations in which men took
liberties (the third was of a well-educated, proper girl who, when a
man laid an "affectionate hand" on her shoulder at their office, "put
him in his place"), she concluded: "Again, there is hardly a girl of fine
ideals, I believe, who reads this, who will not have the tendency to
think that in the behavior of these three girls whom I have cited, even
the last one, there must have been something a little bit wrong, a little
bit inviting, a tiny bit free and easy, or surely the men would never
have gone so far."[54] The author had no quarrel with that opinion; she
simply wanted the men to resist women's failings.

If even the respectable young woman in the office of the example
above was at fault, then proper behavior clearly wasn't enough. It
seemed that unless a woman had an absolute inner purity (which
would unfailingly be detected by men) she was "cheap" and thus fair
game.

More and more, women's guilt was presumed. In the 1950s, when a
girl student asked the social director of the University of Illinois Stu-

dent Union how to tactfully manage the situation when boys tried to "see just how much liberty they can take with me" on dates, the director automatically assumed it was the girl's fault that such situations even arose. "You may have a reputation for being a necker," she answered, "so that men expect you to be one."[55] A very highly regarded marriage text took the same approach. The author criticized girls who were shocked when a boy got "fresh." Instead, he believed, the girl should analyze her own behavior and tighten up her standards. He wrote: "It is time for the girl to ask herself, 'What did I do to make him think he could get by with it?'"[56]

There were few limits to this line of reasoning. At the University of Michigan in 1947, a sophomore man was driving a nineteen-year-old coed home from a local party when he pulled onto a side road and parked. He dragged her into the back seat, threatened her, then struck her until she was dazed, and raped her. The police arrested him the following morning. The university indefinitely suspended the man — *and* the woman. The administration's reason: her "conduct" was a credit neither to herself nor to the university.[57] Here presumption of woman's guilt did not stop with popular understandings. It underlay institutional decisions — even the legal system. The man was charged only with assault, and was brought to trial in a system that required rape victims to establish their own sexual innocence.

Of course, it was not an easy task to establish sexual innocence in a culture that generally accepted the maxim "It isn't what the girl does, it's just the way she does it."[58] Circumspect behavior was not enough to prove innocence; underlying a proper demeanor could always be something a "tiny bit free and easy." In a *Cosmopolitan* article, "Do Women Provoke Sex Attack?" (1960), the author answered with a definite yes but said the provocation was not always conscious. Rape was often the result of a woman's "subconscious urges" and "fantasies," he wrote. Rape occurred because of the "combinations of two complementary neuroses — an unconscious predisposition on the part of the victim and a different but equally neurotic frame of mind on the part of the attacker."[59]

According to this reasoning, since some women were subconsciously predisposed to be raped, rape was not usually the man's fault. The author of the *Cosmo* article directly linked rape to the "petting practices" of women: "Small wonder, that, in many such cases, a young man's desires are aroused past the point of no return and, when the girl resists, he seeks gratification by force."[60] An expert on sex crimes, Dr. Richard Hoffmann, warned women "never [to] do anything to provoke an attack." Many rapists are absolutely harmless until somehow freed from their inhibitions or sexually aroused, he claimed, but often it took only a glimpse of a "scantily clad" woman to trigger them. "And the way some girls run around on the streets today," Dr. Hoffmann concluded, "is practically asking for it."[61]

Not only did subscribers to this system often excuse men — even violent rapists — from responsibility for their acts, many authorities and "experts" directly encouraged boys and men to sexually exploit women. Their encouragement encompassed a wide range of behavior. While writers of teen advice columns when they assumed that boys were "within their rights" to "try all the girls out," meant only necking, there was no logical reason why such advice should be so restricted.[62] Other experts pushed it further.

One of the most direct advocates of man's sexual aggression was a psychologist, Dr. Albert Ellis. Whether or not Dr. Ellis's "first-hand . . . -lips, -tongue, and -genitalia" sex research was enthusiastically endorsed by the entire psychological profession, he was able to present an impressive list of credentials to the purchasers of his best-selling book, *Sex and the Single Man* (1963).[63] Among other qualifications listed in the book are: B.A. from CCNY, M.A. and Ph.D. from Columbia (clinical psychology), teaching positions at Rutgers and NYU, chief psychologist at the New Jersey Department of Institutions and Agencies, past-president of the American Psychological Association's Division of Consulting Psychology, past-president of the Society for the Scientific Study of Sex, Chairman of the National Council on Family Relation's Marriage Counseling Section, associate editor of *Marriage and Family Living, International Journal of Sexology,* and *Advances in Sex Research,* and author of twenty-two books and monographs.[64]

Ellis, using the classic scientific journal article form (Steckel, 1923, notes the case), established that men could not remain sexually abstinent without physical or psychological "impairment of health."[65] He then advised men how to satisfy their sexual needs. Ellis favored "calm, consistent, forceful depropagandization" of women — because it yielded a more generalized result: "The girl that you persuade to think well of sex relations today will usually be a more willing bedmate for some other fellow tomorrow."[66] However, he did not discourage physical persuasion. From the first time you make a pass at a girl, he advised, "try to go as far as you can possibly go with her sexually." He then described proper technique in great detail:

> You should in a while be pressing her as closely to you as possible, and vigorously kneading your fingertips to every possible square inch of her ex-

posed surfaces. In the meantime, you should be using your caressing hands to loosen her clothing and to get as much of her body bare as quickly as you can. Deftness and speed often pay off in this regard: since, once you have fully bared a woman's breasts, or taken off her skirt, or removed her undergarments, it is unlikely that she is immediately going to get up and cover herself again. Feeling that she has been sort of unmasked, and that you are still continuing passionately to kiss and caress her, she frequently accepts the inevitable at this point . . . [take off more of her clothes] . . . and do it firmly, vigorously, in spite of some resistance on her part. Show her that you are determined to have her as nude as possible, even though you are not going literally to rip the clothes off her back and begin to rape her.[67]

As extreme as it sounds on paper, this pattern of aggression and limited force confronting stubborn resistance was taken for granted by many advisers. "Dear Abby," in "Blue Jean Biology," portrayed all boys as potential wolves verging on rapists. She advised meeting male force with violence: a "stereophonic slap" ought to discourage any "mad lover." And, if he really likes you, she reassured girls, "a slap won't anger him. He'll respect you."[68] This conventional pattern did merge into behavior: a study of male aggression on a university campus found that over half of the coeds questioned were offended by a date's behavior (necking, petting, or attempted intercourse, sometimes with violence) at least once during the school year.[69]

This system of sexual control had another set of logical consequences. In trying to live up to society's expectations of "virtue," girls and women were likely to build very strong barriers against sexuality. The more "virtuous" the woman (and these, of course, were defined as the most desirable to marry) the stronger her resistance. Contemporary observers recognized the potential problem. A 1938 marriage manual, *Preparing for Marriage*, advised husbands-to-be that they might have to allow several days "for the unconscious resistance of the bride to dissolve." The author explained: "She has all her life been taught that the one thing she must not do is surrender to any man, and she cannot, in every case, cast off the effects of this teaching in a moment, even in the arms of her husband."[70]

Ironically, for this, too, women were blamed. An influential book, *Modern Woman: The Lost Sex*, in 1947 attacked manuals that warned men to be gentle with their brides on the wedding night. By demanding such treatment, the authors argued, women were robbing men of their masculinity. They lamented: "We live today in the era of the apologetic bridegroom, successor to the sturdier rapist of a bygone day." (Of course, the authors explained, old-fashioned forceful bride-grooms were not truly rapists; either the rape was the bride's fantasy or the man was merely a little "rude" or drunk.)[71]

Even advisers who explicitly blamed women for men's sexual advances criticized women who were sexually cold. The same sociologist who was fed up with girls who blamed boys for sexual aggression instead of asking themselves what they had done to provoke it, wrote: "The person who is over-inhibited, excessively prudish, or unresponsive to the extent that he or she cannot or will not tolerate overt expressions of affection from a member of the opposite sex has just as great a problem as the person who aggressively goes as far as possible in petting on all dates."[72]

Datebook, the teen advice guide that told girls they could avoid male sexual aggression by simply acting like ladies, was more direct. One girl, asking for advice, wrote: "I'm a nice girl. . . . I never let a boy kiss me on the first date and seldom neck and certainly never pet. Some boys say I'm frigid and I guess I do freeze up. But how else can I keep from getting a reputation like some girls I know?" The author, "reading between the lines," dismissed the girl's fear for her reputation as a cover for her real problem: "If you find the courage to look a little deeper," he wrote, "you may find fear and even disgust reactions related to sex." And, he continued, although petting is "unwise and risky," it is not "dirty." He advised her to seek counseling and to stop following "rigid rules" on dates.[73] The course of acceptable behavior had become almost impossibly narrow.

It seems that this system of sexual politics masquerading as morality would have broken down under its own weight, since women really were in a no-win situation. However, it was increasingly buttressed by a closely related argument based on a sexual economy that equated value with woman's virtue (the former system's "if" term).[74] The economic argument was very clear. Though a woman might get short-term gains (dates, popularity) through sex, "free" kisses and sex were "cheap" and men did not value them highly. On the other hand, if a woman maintained her virtue (making sex a scarce commodity) her value to men would rise, and she would realize a long-term gain greatly exceeding her "cheap" sisters' one-time bonanza.

The economic principles and analogies of the argument were not masked by moral language — or even by neutral language. It is worth quoting some of the contemporary language used in the argument to give a sense of its accumulated weight. From a 1950s marriage text: "Kisses, like other good things in life, are valued in proportion to their scarcity"; "Kisses freely given are cheap and valueless" (teen advice book, 1954); "A girl who passes out kisses like candy is putting a pretty low price tag on her affections" (*Senior Scholastic*, 1949); "Petting is a commodity in which there will never be a shortage. It's the usual girl, the average one, who permits it. It is the rare one who doesn't. Knowing this, why not make yourself a collector's item, rather than a bargain-counter article?" (women's advice book, 1937); "Any man is apt to place a higher value on a girl who holds herself worthy of courtship" (women's advice book, 1950); "Who wants second-hand goods?" (*Senior Scholastic*, 1945); "Petting and cuddling have the same cheapening effect as that produced on merchandise which has through constant handling become faded and rumpled, smudged or frayed and thrown out on the bargain counter in a marked-down lot" (Emily Post, 1937); "Since she values herself cheaply, she finds few boys or men who cherish her" (teen advice book, 1965); "The boys find her easy to afford. She doesn't put a high value on herself. . . . Your clothes can cost a lot, yet you'll look cheap with that toss of the head. . . . Too many pokes and shoves, too many late hours lower your value. Reprice your line. Limit the supply of yourself, your time and interest. Make yourself scarce and watch your value go up" (*LHJ* teen advice column, 1942).[75] All of these make the same point: a long-term investment in virtue will yield higher returns.

The long-term investment, according to these arbiters of convention, paid off in two ways. The first, most direct payoff was a continuing relationship and eventual marriage. If, as this argument presumed, the laws of supply and demand applied perfectly to the American sexual economy, the "price" of sex would rise in accordance with its scarcity. A 1948 advice book for men and women put it bluntly: sex was "something a man should pay for." The author's suggested selling price was, of course, a high one: marriage.[76] Another author told women to say no to sex to elicit a proposal of marriage. Conversely, though, he warned, women who allowed premarital intercourse could not demand this high price. As he put it, in the classic formulation, "Why should a person buy something that he can get for nothing."[77] Yet another author warned women to demand more than a down payment before delivering: "The engagement ring is no substitute for the wedding ring . . . even the most frugal man is capable of forfeiting his deposit."[78]

The second payoff was less direct but more fundamental. According to this line of reasoning, limiting "free" premarital sex was the only way to preserve a woman's status in society. Since (in this system) a woman's value is based on her virtue (which is, after all, only her creation of a scarcity of a commodity — heterosexual sex — that only she can supply to men) she must maintain that scarcity to maintain her value. A 1932 article in *Parents* magazine made this argument very clearly in terms of "racial woman": "In other countries women are bought and sold in the marketplace as other commodities that satisfy men's appetites." American women, the author argued, could maintain their present position only by keeping the "respect" of men — by not indulging in petting and premarital sex. "The girl who holds herself cheap," he warned, "will force herself back into the marketplace." [79]

Other advisers warned that "free" sex was destroying centuries of "painstakingly built-up safeguards" against men's polygamous nature. [80] The new freedoms, they argued, destroyed the only security women had, and would end by returning all women to "slavery to male whims." [81] After all, one asserted, "in a permissive culture, a girl becomes easy prey to any male strong enough to take her." [82]

This argument provided a further rationale for maintaining the inequitable systems of control. For their collective good, women must continue to define their value in terms of virtue (sexual scarcity). Therefore, the woman who rejected "virtue" was not gaining sexual power or equality with men but was breaking the sexual "trust" and so threatening the precarious position of woman in society. Here, very clearly, we see how the threats of personal (secondhand goods) and collective (slavery) devaluation reinforced the "incentives" of marriage and value that this system of control offered women.

In the face of such threats and the divisions between men and women they fostered and confirmed, youth's symbolic claiming of sex is all the more striking. In fact, young people's sexual experience was governed by both sets of conventions: the peer conventions that were insistently prescriptive, establishing petting, necking, and the "right" sexual attitudes as essential criteria for belonging to youth culture; and the official conventions of adult culture and authority, which were dogmatically proscriptive. The two sets of conflicting conventions were both public, both seemingly "universal," and both extremely explicit. Both systems were strong, and together they shaped the behavior of youth — creating *felt* conventions that existed in the tension between the conventions of youth and of age/authority. Caught between the insistence that youth, by definition, petted, and the equally strong insistence that petting was wrong, the individual decision to pet remained a symbolic commitment as well as an erotic one.

Opposite page:
Source: Purple Parrot (Northwestern University Magazine), January 1927.
Reprinted courtesy of Northwestern University.

IT'S A GREY LIFE IF YOU DON'T WEEK-END

NOTHING ODD ABOUT THIS

Source: Courtesy Northwestern University Archives. Photograph by James L. Bixby.

Opposite page:
Source: Purple Parrot (Northwestern University Magazine), March 1941.
Reprinted courtesy of Northwestern University.

Build up Your Stag Line...
with TANGEE Red-Red

You will discover that girls who know the secret of how to win friends and influence people are boosters for Tangee RED-RED Lipstick.

RED-RED's new and startling shade blends with the new fashion colors, accents the whiteness of your teeth. RED-RED's pure cream base helps prevent chapping and relieves that dry, "drawn" feeling.

Try Tangee RED-RED . . . and the matching rouge, too!

TANGEE
Red-Red
REALLY STAYS ON!

Source: Courtesy
Northwestern University
Archives. Photograph by
James L. Bixby.

Opposite page:
Source: Advertisement
entitled "How to Become
Some Man's Dream Girl — for
Keeps," from *Woman's Home
Companion,* May 1941.
Reprinted courtesy of
Chesebrough-Pond's, Inc.

Putting him in a Mood for *Matrimony*

WRONG

to get huffy or possessive when he smiles at another female. You have to give a man *some* rope, or what's he going to hang himself with?

RIGHT

to make mighty sure that no other girl can make you look faded! That's where your complexion casts the deciding vote. When he looks at you, let him see a complexion that radiates the loving care you give it with Pond's every night. The Other Woman menace will vanish into limbo.

3

Opposite page:
Source: Purple Parrot (Northwestern University Magazine), February 1943.
Reprinted courtesy of Northwestern University.

THIS IS WORTH FIGHTING FOR

*These girls didn't win—but they stand high in the
ranks of Northwestern Glamour Girls and should go
far in the future.*

Poignant, p o i s e d Margaruite
Bunge, one of the brighter star-
lets of Northwestern's alluring
creatures. Unknown a few weeks
ago her name is now on the tip
of everyone's tongue. We don't
have to explain why—look at
this picture.

B. J. Allen is a compact, lush
bit of femininity. Her dark hair
and fair skin attract the average,
red-blooded male. She recently
caused some talk by dating both
Perry Winsberg and Sig Hanson.

Jane Munson, smooth, sultry
manikin, has been enamouring
men long before she attained
her recent fame. Her svelte figure and enticing mien were suf-
fice to bring her into the lime-
light. Alas, for the rest of
mankind, her heart is the private
property of the U. S. Navy.

This Contest,

different from most of the publicity contests at Northwestern, is one with real
meaning. At this time when most Northwestern men are preparing to go out
and fight for their country, a contest of this kind is very apropos. The
SYLLABUS deserves much credit for illustrating the kind of girls men fight and
die for. This democratic contest represents the American ideal—liberty, these
girls, especially Nancy Berthold, represent the American way of life. This is
indeed worth fighting for.

Source: Courtesy Northwestern University Archives. Photograph by James L. Bixby.

Opposite page:
Source: Courtesy Northwestern University Archives. Photograph by James L. Bixby.

Source: Recensio, 1951, Miami University yearbook, Oxford, Ohio.

Source: Recensio, 1951, Miami University yearbook, Oxford, Ohio.

Pall Mall Presents~
GIRL WATCHER'S GUIDE

WHITE-COATED LAB-LOON

CAMPUS TYPE II

Don't let this girl's costume fool you. She's not really a mad scientist. She's a girl—a real, live girl. It's just that she has to prove something—to herself and to her family.

She has to prove that she has a brain and that, if she ever has to compete with men on their own terms, she can do it—and win. But she really doesn't want to compete with men. In her heart she wants to *attract* men and eventually, marry one. The girl watcher should not let this situation disturb him, however.

If the girl is watchable, she should be watched, no matter what her motives or ambitions may be. The same thing is true of a cigarette. If it's smokeable, it should be smoked—and Pall Mall is the most smokeable of all!

Pall Mall's <u>natural</u> mildness is so good to your taste!

So smooth, so satisfying, so downright smokeable!

© A.T. Co. Product of *The American Tobacco Company*
"Tobacco is our middle name"

Source: American Tobacco Company advertisement from *Daily Northwestern,* October 24, 1962.

The Etiquette of
Masculinity and Femininity

"*G*ood etiquette, for a man, is whatever makes a woman feel more like a woman, without making her feel weakminded. . . . Good etiquette, for a woman, is whatever makes a man feel more like a man, without making him feel more harassed and put upon than he normally does anyway," explained a book of contemporary manners in 1959.[1]

Unraveling this somewhat odd definition of etiquette forces us to encounter some of the fundamental issues of mid-twentieth-century America. It raises questions of identity, and of how identity is created and defined in modern society. It announces the fragility of even the fundamental identity of gender (for why else would a man need to "feel more like a man"?) and at the same time expresses doubts about contemporary sex roles ("weakminded" and "harassed"). In the midst of such complicated uncertainties, the partial solution this definition offers — etiquette — is peculiarly revealing. By *conforming* to a set of rules, it claims, men and women can mitigate uncertainty and acquire a stronger feeling of gender identity.

Fears about the fragility of gender in twentieth-century America stemmed from the slowly developing belief that masculinity, as opposed to maleness, and femininity, as opposed to femaleness — were not states of being declared by God or by nature, but were changing codes of behavior produced by culturally and historically specific forces. A gender system that was culturally constructed, as opposed to innate and absolute, seemed more vulnerable.

Many observers argued that the gradual breakdown of barriers between men's and women's behaviors was undermining masculinity and femininity. Because women no longer knew "how to act like women," critics said, men were "confused about how to be men" (or vice versa).[2] According to this understanding of gender, masculinity and femininity were defined by one another: since they were not absolutes, each was definable only through its contrast with the other. "In our culture," an expert on the subject wrote in *Colliers* (1952), "we teach little boys not so much that it is important to behave like a human rather than an animal, as that it is important to behave like a man and not like a woman."[3]

Mid-twentieth-century masculinity and femininity, as defined through opposition to one another, translate readily into "traditional" sex roles. Masculine men are powerful, dominant, aggressive, and ambitious; they are at home in the "world" and provide for their wives and children. Feminine women are dependent, submissive, nurturing, and belong in the home. These definitions, however, did not mesh well with changing social realities, which often merged men's and women's "spheres." In compensation, perhaps, American society increasingly became obsessed with defining "masculine" and "feminine" behaviors — acts that demonstrated and reinforced a "traditional" difference between men and women. Nowhere is this obsession clearer than in the etiquette that governed relations between the sexes — especially the courtship of youth.

The etiquette of masculinity and femininity, as I have dubbed it, dominated American manners from the 1930s well into the 1960s. It was created by the convergence of several intellectual and social trends, the most important being the crumbling of the concept and (limited) reality of the nineteenth-century "separate spheres" of activity, ability, and nature for the sexes, along with an increasing sense that masculinity and femininity were fragile commodities. They came to be seen not as natural traits, proceeding causally, masculinity from maleness, femininity from femaleness, but as identities that must be acquired, earned, and constantly demonstrated.[4] Etiquette, and especially etiquette governing relations between the sexes, told men "how" to be men and women "how" to be women. It also provided a way to demonstrate to others, through conforming to gender-appropriate behavior, that one *was* a man, or one *was* a woman.

The etiquette of masculinity and femininity was an elaborate code that played a key role in the courtship rituals of youth and in the struggles of young American men and women for self-definition. But before we look at the complexities of the code, we must look in more detail at the conditions that produced it and at how contemporaries perceived the confusions reflected in the definition of etiquette above.

"A good deal of pleasure went out of life when anatomy ceased to be a sufficient definition of one's sex," wrote Elizabeth Hardwick in *Mademoiselle* in 1958.[5] Her terms are not totally clear — the current sociology of gender would define sex as anatomically determined, as opposed to gender (or sex roles), which is not. Sex (male or female) is a descriptive label based on biological attributes, while gender (masculinity or femininity) is an "achieved status," a function of socialization. *Masculinity* and *femininity* refer to a cluster of traits that are "socially prescribed and individually learned." But since gender is culturally produced, not innate, definitions of gender are changeable.[6] Thus, in a culture in which the roles played by men and women are changing, in which women may take on traditionally masculine roles or vice versa, anatomy may very well *not* seem a sufficient definition of gender.

Sociological precision aside, Hardwick is making a distinction between sex and gender, and suggesting that the causal distance between the two is widening. In the second third of the twentieth century, people were increasingly aware of this distinction — that a female was not necessarily feminine and a male was not necessarily masculine. This was a relatively new understanding of gender.

In early eighteenth-century America, as in England and on the Continent, there was a relatively low degree of gender awareness. As Peter Stearns explains, preindustrial society "set definite standards of gender. . . . There was indeed no sense of evolution in gender relationships — they seemed fixed, by God and by history."[7] Based on contemporary understandings of the Bible, most people believed that men and women had unalterable God-given roles. The relation of women to men was frequently explained on the model of the Great Chain of Being, with woman appearing as a sort of inferior man, with similar but lesser abilities and qualities. Toward the end of the eighteenth century, understandings of gender shifted, sharply, to stress the *difference* between men and women. Much was written on the meanings of manhood and womanhood, meanings that were generally illustrated in "metaphors of separation."[8] According to the theorists, because of woman's God-given "innate sexual essence," she had a "uniquely feminine" nature and was weaker in her character, mind, and body than man.[9]

Nineteenth-century Americans were increasingly concerned with difference in gender, and elaborated the concept of difference into a theory of separate spheres for each sex. Men were "by nature" thus and women "by nature" so. By mid-century, women's nature no longer was defined as the oversexual embodiment of evil and tempta-

tion previously culled from the Bible, but as the natural seat of good-
ness and morality. Men's complementary nature was more aggressive,
action oriented, intellectual, and sexual. In both men and women,
gender-appropriate behavior was deemed natural — innate — even if it
sometimes had to be fostered.[10] Thus, women who deviated from
nature's prescriptions were called "unnatural," and "third sex."

In the nineteenth century, belief in women's *God-given* inferiority
gradually faded under the combined and sometimes contradictory
pressures of Evangelical Protestantism, the identification of women
with religion and morality, the increasingly differentiated spheres of
activity that came with urbanization and industrialization, and vocif-
erous movements for reform, including women's rights. But as the
biblical theories lost power, a new understanding bolstered the related
concept of natural difference. Darwin's theory of evolution and
natural selection proposed that specialization was the goal of evolution, and thus evolution naturally produced sharply defined different
functions for men and women.[11] Innatism, the belief in natural
difference between men and women (and thus in a close causal connection between sex and gender) received a second theoretical lease on
life.

This same period, however, saw the beginnings of concern about
how natural masculinity and femininity really were. Experience
seemed to undercut the theory of innatism. From the Civil War on, a
literature of concern about masculinity grew. By the late nineteenth
century, guidebooks increasingly defined masculine behavior for their
readers, and the word *sissy* had entered the common vocabulary. TR's
strenuous life centered around a concept of masculinity, as did new organizations such as the Boy Scouts.[12]

This crisis of masculinity in American society, like the one that
would follow in the twentieth century, was blamed largely on women.
In this case, critics noted that women, naturally weaker, passive, un-
worldly, and moral, dominated the home and had virtually sole
charge of raising their sons. The model most often held up to boys of
"respectable" families was that of "Christian Gentleman." Woman's
authority and her stress on a perfect morality and gentility not deemed
natural to man, both contemporaries and historians explain, may
have either undercut the boys' developing masculinity or driven them
to feel they must prove their masculinity because they could not match
their mothers' moral standards.[13] Whether this psychological explanation holds or not, there was a growing concern within the culture that
masculinity was threatened, and even if innate, could still be destroyed.

The behavior of women in the late nineteenth and early twentieth centuries also challenged the theories of innate femininity. Women began, in large numbers, to do things for which they were, by "nature," unfit. They completed college courses, enjoyed physical exercise, entered the workplace as "respectable" women had not done before. Critics saw the new woman of the 1890s as "crowding the masculine domain." [14] Though some prominent women who stepped into the masculine (public) domain, such as Jane Addams, explained that they were acting within their proper roles as guardians of the home, women's extension of liberty went beyond that explanation. Many commentators thought that women's rejection of their natural sphere threatened their femininity, even their womanhood. Late nineteenth-century critics of women reformers and proponents of equal rights labeled them "sexless beings," and insisted that the only way in which a woman could achieve equality was to "unsex" herself. [15] This unsexing, near to impossible in the vocabulary of innatism, seemed more and more possible when looking at women's increasing freedom of action in the new century.

The perception of the fragility of gender, based on experience, was buttressed in the twentieth century, ironically, by yet another theory of innatism. Although Freud's assertion that anatomy determines destiny does, in a much more sophisticated fashion, locate gender in nature (and through popular interpretations contributed to the retreat to traditional womanhood in American after World War II), his belief that individuals must *attain* a mature sexual identity had equally important popular consequences. To go very quickly over complicated territory, Freudian theory presupposes an "original bisexuality" in humans. [16] Freud combined evolutionary theory, contemporary endocrinology, and embryological discoveries (that the embryo at first has both male and female genitalia) to conclude that in the asexual stage of evolution the embryo is masculine. Thus, he concluded, each person is masculine-oriented until puberty — a girl is a "little man" until her sex glands begin to function. [17]

While the girl *will* become a woman, for the developmental pattern of mind, body, and character is biologically predetermined, she must confront and overcome two crises in order to attain "normal femininity." The first, the castration complex, in which she discovers herself to be "incomplete," begins her psychological journey from her original "masculine phase." The second crisis, the Oedipal complex, in which the girl transfers her affection from her mother to her father, completes her journey to biologically indicated femininity.

However — and this was the crucial point to many mid-twentieth-

century popularizers — an incomplete resolution to either of the two
crises could prevent the girl from attaining normal femininity and
could instead lead to frigidity or *masculinity*. The masculine woman,
instead of accepting her new passivity at puberty, emphasized the
characteristics of her prepubescent masculine stage. Helen Deutsch, a
disciple of Freud's, believed that masculine women stressed their intellectual and physical development while "neurotically" avoiding feminine qualities.[18]

Freudian theory — or rather, popular Freudianism — combined with
discoveries in endocrinology and embryology, provided the basis for
scholarly and popular understandings of the relationship between sex
and gender. The hard sciences proved that each sex had the hormones
of the other in its makeup, and psychoanalysis showed that the development of "normal femininity" was not automatic but could be de-
feated by various developmental crises. Popular theorists applied this
understanding of gender's fragility to both sexes. A well-respected
marriage educator, Lawrence Frank, told his colleagues in 1939 that
marriage courses in high schools must help students come to terms
with their sex roles. Since "every individual is bisexual," he explained,
"it is evident that the adolescent during the high school years is still in
the process of differentiating as the man or woman who will be only
partly male or partly female."[19]

The marriage educators, accepting that gender must be fostered, attempted to help students understand what normal masculinity and
femininity were, and to acquire those traits. Much of their texts and
their courses was spent defining the differences between masculine
men and feminine women. Educator Paul Popenoe believed that the
most important task of marriage education was to teach students this
proper difference, and arranged his 1944 University of Southern California marriage course around the six basic differences between men
and women.[20] Henry Bowman's 1942 text, *Marriage for Moderns*,
began with a twenty-six-page chapter inventorying and "proving" the
differences between the sexes.[21] E. E. LeMasters, in his 1957 text,
analyzed male and female subcultures, ending by stressing that one
"must accept the way of life of [one's] *own sex*" and especially warning
against women who, as psychiatrists had found, "reject their roles as
women and unconsciously (or consciously) wish they were men."[22]

While educators were trying to teach students normal masculinity
and femininity, cultural spokespeople were lamenting the fragility of
gender identity. "Maleness in America is not absolutely defined, it has
to be kept and re-earned every day," wrote Margaret Mead in the
mid-1940s.[23] In 1958, Arthur Schlesinger, Jr., wrote in *Esquire* that

"today men are more and more conscious of maleness not as a fact but as a problem. The way [*sic*] by which American men affirm their masculinity are uncertain and obscure."[24] In 1962, Norman Mailer told American men that "masculinity is not something one is born with, but something one gains. . . . [And] in American life, there is a certain built-in tendency to destroy masculinity in American men."[25]

These comments all have to do with masculinity, for mid-century fears about gender identity coalesced around the much-publicized "Crisis of American Masculinity." From World War II through the 1960s, America was deluged with articles claiming that boys and men, as never before in history, were "confused about what they should and should not do to fulfill their masculine roles."[26]

There were two related schools of thought about the crisis, and they were strikingly similar. Both looked to the "breakdown of rigid barriers that hitherto separated [men and women] in their activities and responsibilities,"[27] both located responsibility for the crisis directly or indirectly with women, and both pointed to increased rates of mental illness and homosexuality among men as a result of the crisis.

One explanatory vision described a Sunday afternoon suburban scene: the "captive male" burning leaves. "It is a comfortable, relaxed scene," the author declared, "even if the women do look like keepers of a prosperous zoo and the men like so many domesticated animals inside of it." The point of the article is that these leaf burners have been robbed of the "deep and perfectly normal masculine drives" (attractions to violence, obscenity, pornography, polygamy, and adventure) that were "permitted" them during the war, and that total inhibition of masculine drives will have grave consequences. "For even the quietest Sunday gardener or the most efficient man in a gray flannel suit may have his indestructible dream of greatness and adventure," the author wrote. "This dream may make him a stranger to his wife and family; more often than not it makes him ill at ease in a world that robs him of his chance at heroism. He wonders, seeing this gap between his dream and his daily life — is he even a man."[28]

Writing in the *New York Times Magazine* in 1957, another commentator worried about the broader implications of curbing "masculinity": "If the feminine instinct for security, social responsibility and comfort is allowed to stifle the rather uncomfortable but necessary masculine instinct for risk and creative originality, our culture is threatened with sterility and our society with decay."[29]

These writers — while perhaps going a bit overboard on the "perfectly normal" desires for violence, obscenity, pornography, and polygamy — were responding to real changes in male roles. Since the

mid-nineteenth century, American masculinity had been defined in relation to an industrial capitalist society.[30] A man was to be aggressive,
an independent entrepreneur, doing battle daily in the rough-and-
tumble world of the economy in order to provide for his wife and
children and to maintain the moral haven of his home. While this understanding had little basis in the realities of men's lives in twentieth-
century America, it was a deeply ingrained understanding that was
not easily dismissed.

In the postwar era, Americans were coming to grips with changes
in their economy and society that, they feared, had rendered "traditional" masculinity obsolete and threatened the vitality of American
culture. In the world of the corporation, the "organization," men
needed different qualities to succeed. Teamwork, conformity, cooperation, the "social ethic" — these were functional behaviors for corpo-
rate success. But they were traditional *feminine* behaviors — the an-
tithesis of aggressive masculinity. To continue to provide well for his
family, many feared, a man would have to act like a woman.

A second change in the structure of the American economy and society compounded the threat to traditional masculinity: the fundamental masculine role of provider was being undermined. Before
World War II, Americans assumed that if a woman took a job it
meant that her husband had failed as a provider (and thus as a man).
Confession-style articles detailing the misguided attempts of married
women to hold paying jobs were staple fare in women's magazines
during this period. These articles dealt not only with the woman's
awakening to the error of her ways but also with her husband's attempts to deal with this public challenge to his masculinity. These articles usually dealt with families or couples who were economically
secure without the wife's income. In fact, a very low percentage of
married women worked outside the home (12 percent in 1930, for example), and the overwhelming majority of them did so from absolute
economic necessity.[31]

However, during and after World War II, despite the powerful
ideology of the happy homemaker, more and more women — married
women — worked outside the home. In 1940, married women com-
prised only one-third of the total number of working women; within
ten years the proportion of married women workers leaped to 52 percent.[32] Dual incomes were increasingly necessary — not to survive, but
to live the good life, to partake in the new and seemingly limitless material abundance that America offered. Even though working wives
undeniably retained primary responsibility for housework and child-
care, women's ventures into the economy upset a model of sex roles

based on the man-as-provider model. The economic basis for male dominance seemed to be crumbling, if only slightly.

The second (and dominant) explanation for the crisis of masculinity looked to women's entry into the economy and to related changes in women's role. Criticism was not limited to married women workers. Critics argued a larger point, charging that women were robbing men of their masculinity by adopting masculine (aggressive) roles. A 1957 marriage textbook spent most of the chapter on the "subculture of the male" discussing the problem of women trying to intrude into the male subculture.[33] The *Playboy* panel on "The Womanization of America" lamented the "sex-obliterating aspects of togetherness."[34] Psychologists explained that male homosexuality was increasing because men were scared out of heterosexuality by the demands aggressive women placed on them — demands intensified because "men can define their masculinity through their sexual role alone as the occupational, social, and even sartorial space between the sexes narrows."[35] *Esquire* ran frequent articles devoted to the recovery of male dominance in America. Their author, J. B. Rice, felt that ours was a "sick society," whose cure lay in reorienting male and female roles. "Civilization has given us knowledge, but it has robbed us of the wisdom of the jungle," he wrote. "We must rediscover the art of dominating as the lion dominates the lioness — without force usually, without harshness usually, without faltering always."[36]

As these explanations demonstrate, the crisis of American femininity is not ignored here. It is simply submerged, unnamed. But all agreed that the fragility of gender was the root of the trouble. The necessary barriers had broken down and women were exercising too much power — whether by stifling masculinity or by assuming masculine traits themselves. Since power defined masculinity, women's appropriation of power threatened proper gender relations.

"Crisis of masculinity be damned," *Esquire* proclaimed in 1962, "the problem is the crisis of femininity."[37] The women's magazines concurred, in a roundabout way: masculinity and femininity were mutually defining, they said. "A woman adjusts her femininity in direct ratio to the masculinity she encounters in life" was a *Cosmo* dictum.[38] *Mademoiselle* joined in: "It's a sad, difficult business, for the girls have lost much of their own femininity in the course of their liberation, and they know it. For femininity is a gift a woman receives in larger measure from a man who feels himself to be a man — and, of course, vice versa."[39]

So, while men suffered through their crisis, entreated to once again be *men* and not "stuffed tigers," experts set out programs of recovery for women.[40] Women, they said, must make an effort to regain their femininity — in part to rescue men, in part for their own sakes. Women must *study* femininity, and so learn to make their men masculine again. The proposals for "appropriate" education for women in the 1950s were part of this movement, but so were much explicit advice and hidden persuasion.[41]

Both masculinity and femininity, seen as fragile, seemed to rest in externals, not in the depths of one's being. Most of the attempts to foster femininity focused on such externals — traits one could simulate, products one could buy. In 1960, when *Mademoiselle* profiled graduate student women, the (male) author described them as "sexless" — not because of their intellect or ambition, but because they were poor and forfeited the perfumes, clothes, and other products that made a woman feminine.[42] In 1946, *Woman's Home Companion* marriage adviser Dr. Clifford Adams offered a quiz, "How Feminine Are You to Men?" for girls who "wonder whether their femininity measures up to the men's standards." The first question asked, "Do you prefer to wear your nails without any tint?" Other questions checked on hidden urges for careers in medicine, law, or journalism, a preference for slacks over dresses, and a "natural" feeling when talking to men about business or world affairs.[43] The proper "feminine" answers are easy to figure out, and the quiz offered implicit advice on how at least to *seem* feminine.

If women's fragile femininity was portrayed as turning on tricks and stratagems both of attitude and appearance, prescriptions for masculinity were no less concerned with externals. From a quiz, "How Masculine Are You?" in *Nation's Business* in 1950, American men learned that it was masculine to prefer sports to music and not to cry at sad movies.[44] In a 1959 issue of *Cosmopolitan*, actor Oscar Homolka explained to American men and women that men should refuse to do "chores in the home which make him feel less of a man."[45]

Homolka was not alone in his fear that "women's work" had unmanning effects. *Senior Scholastic* included this letter in the winners of a 1944 essay contest, "What's Your Biggest Problem?" This high school boy wrote:

> My Biggest Problem is trying to be a part-time maid and schoolboy at the same time. I can't say that I find either part difficult, but the problem is can I do the things required of me as a maid and still have time to study and grow to manhood? The blows my pride suffers when I am supposed to do a girl's task are really painful. . . . It is just that I can picture myself years older working in the kitchen while my wife goes off to her job, for she will be sure to learn of my horrible past!"[46]

The boy's parents were both doing war work at Boeing, and his only tasks were to keep an eye on his two younger brothers after school and to do the breakfast and dinner dishes. In contrast, after World War I, the *Woman's Home Companion* had celebrated "Housewifely Husbands" who, when the war took their wives from the home into jobs, "raised the slogan, 'Let the men do the work.'" The article featured a picture of the governor of Arizona knitting, and in no way suggested that such tasks were demasculinizing.[47] By the post–World War II years, however, masculinity seemed so embattled, shored up only through strict compliance to gender-appropriate *behaviors*, that simply performing an act deemed feminine could threaten a man's belief in his own masculinity.

More and more, the popular answer to the problem of masculinity was apartness — a retreat into a separate masculine world. A 1961 *Cosmopolitan* article peeked into "Man's Private World" at the men's-only clubs and poker games the author identified as symptoms of "man's struggle to retain his masculine identity."[48] Vance Packard, in an article on advertisers ("The Manipulators") reported that men had "special enthusiasm" for products such as cigars, which were still exclusively male. According to Packard, a New York ad agency asked a sample of men if they would be interested in a (nonexistent) product that would permanently remove whiskers. Men responded with an almost unanimous no — for whiskers are "one symbol of manliness women couldn't affect even if they wanted to."[49]

Most such struggles, however, took place in the freer world of fantasy. While women might be able to simulate "femininity," men could not really escape the culture of togetherness, since they shared space and responsibility with women in almost every sphere of their lives. Historian of masculinity Joe Dubbert notes the popularity of television programs such as "Daniel Boone," "Bonanza," and "Gunsmoke" in the 1960s, the Davy Crockett fad of the 1950s — all revealing a "heroic past" when "men were men and proved it."[50] *True* magazine, a macho-escape magazine for men, was selling 2-million-plus copies a month in the mid-1960s, and its editorial director attributed *True*'s sales to its stimulation of "masculine ego."[51]

But the guru of separateness was Hugh Hefner. *Playboy* centered around the "problem of male identity," Hefner said, and its editorial policy stressed that men and women should have "*separate* identities." *Playboy* devoted its pages to helping men develop a masculine identity in a world where sex roles were confused, where men were smothered by "togetherness" with women.[52] In offering masculine identity, *Playboy* did offer a vision of escape from oppressive responsibility, as Barbara Erenreich suggests in *The Hearts of Men,* and also offered the frontier of consumption to replace other lost masculine frontiers.[53] But *Playboy* also offered men a world apart — not a world without women, but a masculine world in which men were dominant and women approachable girl-next-door centerfolds or "bunnies." As one panelist on a New York radio talk show explained the *Playboy* philosophy to his listeners, Hefner was trying to "restore the balance" in American society: "In the *Playboy* context, man begins to reassert his masculinity. Even if it has to be contrived out of Chicago by Hugh Hefner, it needs help from someplace." And Hefner endorsed this as "the heart of the matter."[54]

The crisis of masculinity — and the sense of the frailty of a masculinity and femininity *only* culturally constructed — did not seem to many observers to offer new possibilities. Most of them looked backward, hoping somehow to recover or reinforce "traditional" rigid codes. There were critics of this response — modest heroes in their own way. Arthur Schlesinger, Jr., endorsed separateness as a partial solution in his 1958 article on the crisis of masculinity, but concluded:

> The achievement of identity, the conquest of a sense of self — these will do infinitely more to restore American masculinity than all the hormones in the test tubes of our scientists. "Whoso would be a *man,*" said Emerson, "must be a nonconformist," and if it is the present writer who adds the italics, nonetheless one feels that no injustice is done to Emerson's intention. How can masculinity, femininity, or anything else survive in a homogenized society, which seeks steadily and benignly to eradicate all differences between the individuals who compose it?[55]

And Betty Freidan, ever more down-to-earth, looked forward from 1960 to the day when "their mothers' fulfillment makes girls so sure they want to be feminine that they no longer have to look like Marilyn Monroe to prove it, and makes boys so unafraid of women that they don't have to worry about their masculinity."[56]

But these voices, late in the crisis, provided no solutions. At best they named a problem that was larger than any of its symptoms. In the meantime, neither women's declaration of unilateral femininity nor men's apartness (real or fantasized) was enough. Men and women, in the face of the crisis, still had lives to build — *together.*

The belief that, simply put, masculinity and femininity were not innate characteristics, were not natural accompaniments of maleness or femaleness but were threatened by modern civilization and so had to be won or confirmed daily through strict compliance with the conventions defining them, had major implications in the courtship of youth. At the same time that young men and women were gaining new freedoms, especially in their relations with one another, they were turning their attention more and more to the rules of etiquette and to the voices of conventional authority. They were not concerned with thank-you notes, forms of address, or table settings for formal dinners. They wanted to know the rules governing relations between the sexes, the rules that would tell them how to be masculine or how to be feminine.

From the number of books published on the subject and the amount of space it took up in popular magazines, such questions of etiquette seem to have been deemed extraordinarily interesting to young people from the 1930s through the 1960s. And judging by what youth themselves said — and did — about etiquette, it *was* important to them. A *Senior Scholastic* poll in the 1930s found that 90.6 percent of a sample of 4,495 girls said they did not think it at all "silly" for a boy to "help" them out of a car.[57] When the Flint, Michigan, Y began programs for young men and women during the Depression, leaders found little interest in arts-and-crafts classes, but enrolled 188 boys and 187 girls in a course on etiquette in boy-girl relationships.[58] Students responding to *Senior Scholastic*'s poll, "The Kind of a Boy that Girls Like" (and vice versa) rated "knowledge of proper etiquette" one of the most important qualities (girls put it before "pleasing personality").[59] On the college level, sections on "Poise," "Savoir-faire," "Men and Dates," "Do's and Don'ts," — all concerned with etiquette — increasingly appeared in college handbooks, including those produced by student staffs.[60] And as the new teen and junior-teen markets opened up in the years following World War II, a flood of magazines and etiquette-advice books appeared to answer the questions that seemed crucial to pubescent girls.

Etiquette columns had been a staple of popular women's magazines for decades, and advice books addressed to youth were nothing new. But the etiquette columns and books that appeared in the second third of the twentieth century were different. Authors and advisers conflated etiquette with a broader category of advice, and justified their answers in new terms. Instead of presenting the rules of conventional usage and correct behavior as signs of breeding, as most earlier American etiquette books had, these advisers explained the rules of etiquette in the language of gender.

When a culture insisted, as this one did, that insofar as a man was feminine or a woman masculine, to that extent he or she was "repulsive" to the opposite sex, and when it also defined adherence to etiquette as an important way to demonstrate masculinity or femininity, it added great weight to an otherwise arcane field.[61] Rules clothed in the language of gender seemed not merely records of convention but matters of great significance. In this world, etiquette was more concerned with roles than with politeness, and, as young people learned from many sources, these prescribed roles could be transgressed only at great risk to one's masculinity or femininity.

In general, throughout this literature, masculinity translated into "dominance" and femininity into "submission." These traits were acted out in various rituals and customs of etiquette, through which the woman demonstrated her need for protection and the man his ability to protect her. Some of these customs had their origins in the past, once having been necessary services for women hampered by dozens of yards of fabric and tight stays or hobbled by tight skirts and bustles.[62] Most such assistance was patently unnecessary in the mid-twentieth century, but the rituals had begun serving different purposes.

In this scheme, the young man who did not assist his date from the car was not being discourteous in ignoring her need for assistance; he was "unmanly" because he was not *demonstrating* his control and protection. The woman who, on a date, opened the car door and exited unassisted was not performing a difficult feat; instead, she was being "aggressive" and unfeminine by preempting the male role. By performing a role properly masculine, no matter how trivial, women heard from all sides, they were threatening the man's dominance and thus his very masculinity.

When this "preemption" took place in a sphere more directly related to women's changing roles, it seemed even more threatening. Dutch dating was probably the most condemned such breach of etiquette. Because, by convention, men paid for dates (and dates in general had to be paid for), the centrality of men's money in dating conferred power — and control of the date — upon men. When women paid their own ways on dates, men lost that extra power. They were no longer the provider, no longer in control. Beyond that, women's handling of money forcibly reminded men of women's entrance into the economy, encroaching upon a man's world and even attempting to compete with him, to challenge his control. Dutch dating, both symbolically and literally, threatened to undermine the whole system of courtship that had grown up in modern America.

The advice and etiquette books almost universally condemned the practice, and graphically depicted the dangers of going dutch:

> [Dutch dating] sounds wonderful, but almost always it flops. Boys usually like the system at first, but after a few dates in which they play second

fiddle, they begin to feel like sissified heels and their eyes begin to wander to the glamour girls (not gold diggers) who make them toe the mark.

In the beginning the girl feels important and useful, but about the third date she begins to feel she is not out with a masterful, masculine boy, but a real Caspar Milktoast. Can she idolize this sort of boy? No! Emphatically no! Soon she's looking down her nose at him and admiring the fellow who will date her half as much but will take the lead in everything. (1954 teen advice book)[63]

Masculinity and femininity were definitely the issue. *Co-ediquette*, a 1936 etiquette book for college students, warned, "Dutch treats have not worked. Too much independence on a girl's part subtracts from a man's feeling of importance if he takes her out and can do nothing for her. . . . The man unconsciously resents her masculine assumption of initiative."[64] A 1948 advice book aimed at the "young man about town" said flatly that any man who allows a girl to pay for her own entertainment "deserves to lose her respect," and the 1954 classic, *How to Be a Woman*, advised: "It's custom for him to pay the way, and it helps him feel masculine to do so."[65] The most horrifying vision was summoned by a Phillip Morris ad in the *Massachusetts Collegian* in 1955. The ad's hero was seeking a girl who could "appreciate the equity of Dutch treat" — and he found her. "Today," the ad copy read, "Finster goes everywhere and shares expenses fifty-fifty with Mary Alice Hematoma, a lovely three-legged girl with sideburns."[66] Three "legs"?

By and large, youth agreed with the advisers. A *Senior Scholastic* poll of 4,557 girls and 4,177 boys in 1939 found that 65.2 percent of the girls and 71.5 percent of the boys objected to dutch dates.[67] Of the 10,000 students responding to the 1948 Purdue opinion poll, 37 percent thought that dutch dating was "OK," but approval dropped to 25 percent in 1957.[68] More significantly, the language that young people used to condemn dutch dating was identical to the language of the advisers. *Senior Scholastic*, in "jam sessions" on dutch dating in the 1940s and 1950s, printed dozens of letters about dutch dating and its threat to masculinity. A girl from Spokane, Washington, wrote: "I can't picture any normal girl even suggesting she pay her own way. Isn't it true that a boy feels more like a man if a girl's dependent on him?" Gene Frizelle, from Missouri, summed up the boy's perspective in a 1951 letter. He disliked dutch dating because "paying the girl's way gives me a responsible and important feeling. It makes me feel superior to my date."[69]

While dutch dating drew the strongest language from critics, they portrayed a fairly wide range of other situations as proving grounds for masculinity and femininity. Etiquette books and advice columns went into minute detail about the behaviors proper for men and women: where each should walk or sit; which should take the initiative in a given situation. The myriad of rules carefully defined male and female roles. Etiquette said that men should always be in charge when escorting a woman, and as the dominant figure who is able, in his strength, to offer courtesies to the weaker sex, should demonstrate his control through a series of protective acts. As the *Esquire* book of etiquette of 1953 phrased it: "When she's with you, etiquette renders her helpless. You're It." [70] A teen advice book from the same era advised boys to try for "that masterful approach" and treat girls like "fairy princesses on feather pillows." [71]

Such protection and mastery, incidentally, robbed women of their autonomy and their power of public speech. "DON'T tell the waiter what you want," began an etiquette book chapter titled "A Model Girl About Town . . . As Outlined by a Normal Young Man." "Tell *me* and I will do the ordering." [72] A "world-famous psychologist," having studied 10,000 men at a Harvard lab, set forth a list of don'ts for women in 1941. Point 8 was: never give an order on a date, be it to a waiter or a cabdriver. [73] Getting to the heart of the matter, men complained to a *Mademoiselle* writer in 1938 about "strong-minded" women who "almost unconsciously" took charge and ordered in restaurants. [74]

Women, these rules made clear, were to constantly demonstrate their submission and need of protection, avoiding acts they could perform perfectly well but that became "aggressive" in the company of a man. "The most flattering thing you can do for your escort," a woman's advice book proclaimed, "is to take it for granted that he is taking care of you; then let him do it." [75] For example, the social director of the University of Illinois student union explained, a woman should not ever open a door for herself while with a man, for such aggressive behavior might cause him to give up all the other courtesies also. Besides, if the woman opened the door, her escort would have to pass through the door she had opened, and "no man enjoys walking through a door a girl has opened for him." [76]

Women, then, were to avoid aggressive behavior — do nothing that would challenge men's control and so undermine their masculinity. For a woman to ask a man for a date was inexcusably aggressive, and he could justifiably, according to some authorities, simply cut her off in mid-sentence and walk away. [77] But many lesser signs of independence were also intolerable. "Don't smoke when your escort doesn't," the University of Maryland etiquette manual told girls. "[It] makes him feel ineffectual." [78] In a 1959 *Ladies' Home Journal* article titled, "How Lovable Are You?" male critics attacked the "overly competent" girls who insisted on carrying their own packages or sliding in their own chairs at the table. [79]

Even a woman's intelligence, insofar as it challenged masculine dominance, was discussed in terms of etiquette. Just as women were to cultivate "feminine" traits of physical dependence, they also were to act mentally dependent. One 1960s etiquette book for boys, *Male Manners,* approvingly related the story of a girl who found herself the only female in a high school science class. In trying to avoid the "helpless female role," the author said, she made the mistake of trying to act just like the male students (in other words, like a capable and intelligent science student). These boys, however, "gallant" to the man, set her straight by keeping a score card on which they gave her demerits every time she said or did anything "unfeminine." [80]

While most advisers rejected the "play dumb" routine, they stressed that showing intellectual superiority could "injure the masculine ego." [81] A 1940s advice book dismissed the old adage about men not liking brainy women and proposed an intellectual partnership. But the very next paragraph began: "Warning! . . . Be careful not to seem smarter than your man. It's one thing to be almost as smart, but to be or seem smarter — that is tabu." [82] Another such book advised "intellectual women" to seek highly intelligent men, and then to "go gay, in a deep way. He'll know it's only an act. But, you'll soon become the little woman to be pooh-poohed, patronized and wed." [83]

The average man, social scientists reported, wanted to marry a woman of lesser intelligence than himself — and did so. [84] But men were willing to accept intellectual dominance as conferred by etiquette when it didn't exist in reality. As Shaker Heights high school senior and "ideal" teenager Jim Brown admitted in his 1949 *Ladies' Home Journal* profile, "I don't mind if a girl knows more than I do . . . I just like her to act like she knows a little less." [85]

The whole catalog of rules governing relations between the sexes was, of course, a charade. As an "expert" explained in a 1951 *Collier's* article, "Women are faced with a choice of either *being* submissive and weak, or giving the appearance of being so." [86] Women, by and large, were perfectly capable of opening doors, telling waiters what they wanted to eat, and even of paying their own way on dates. Men, on the other hand, were sometimes broke, shy, unsure how to handle situations, or simply tired of taking all the responsibility. Advice and etiquette books, moreover, readily admitted these points. But maintaining the norms, acting "as if" the men were dominant and therefore

masculine and the women were submissive and therefore feminine, remained their crucial message — a message American men and women
accepted.

The reasons why men and women accepted these definitions of
masculinity and femininity, and resorted to an acknowledged charade
to prove they fit these definitions, are many and complicated. A few,
however, stand out. This system derived its power from a combina-
tion of fears. Massive changes and dislocations were taking place in
American society, and had been taking place for a long time. Modern
life was having a profound effect on the roles played by the sexes —
collapsing the "separate spheres" formerly decreed by a woman's re-
productive function and her inability to control it, and further established in the early stages of industrialization, as production moved
from the home and paved the way for the very concept of separate
spheres. The change was compounded by public awareness. Twentieth-century Americans were deluged with mass-media reports and
expert analyses of their changing society. Never before was such a
large percentage of the population *aware* of the magnitude of change
in the values and institutions of their society.

Furthermore, men in twentieth-century America really did worry
about women invading their territory, and women worried about the
consequences of that invasion. If men and women performed the same
tasks, exhibited the same traits, what would differentiate them? What
would happen to a society of "de-masculinized" men and "de-
feminized" women? Some of the loudest voices of protest sought a
return to the past as they imagined it — when men were men and
women were submissive. Others were concerned, in more thoughtful
and complicated ways, with questions of alienation and loss of identity in modern America.

These fears, both the gut-level reactions and the more thoughtful
analyses, tied into other sets of fears. The Great Depression of the
1930s, while delaying new marriages and putting strain on existing
ones, had undermined men's confidence that they were able to fulfill
the masculine role of provider.[87] This fear intensified during World
War II, when pictures of women competently filling "male" jobs had
male workers chanting in cadence: "Women-women-women-what's
going to happen after the war? Will men ever get their jobs back?"[88]
They might well have been asking: Will men ever get their masculinity
back?

Women also confronted a new fear after World War II. For the first
time in American history, there were more women than men. Experts
warned young women in dozens of magazine and newspaper articles

that a significant portion of women in their age group would never marry because of the sexual imbalance. Women overreacted to the warnings, and the "scarcity" of men became a commonplace justification for all sorts of acts. At the same time, American men were berating American women for being "unfeminine" in contrast with their European sisters (and 90,000 American servicemen had married foreign brides by 1946).[89] Men, being "scarce," were in a strong position in courtship, and many said, flatly and publicly, that they wanted submissive, feminine women. If "femininity" would provide the edge in the race for a husband, many women declared themselves willing to play along.

At the same time, playing the roles of "masculine" and "feminine" offered advantages to both men and women. When the charade did work — when the man was dominant-yet-gentle in his control and the woman felt like a "fairy princess," it was just like the movies. A natural and graceful compliance with the etiquette of masculinity and femininity could smooth the early stages of courtship by providing both participants with clearly defined roles to play. Perfect etiquette could make a date with an unattractive stranger bearable, as both retreated into carefully prescribed roles; it could make the first dates with an interesting partner seem ideal. In a time of rapid change and confused sex roles, there was satisfaction in the clearly defined roles etiquette offered. And on a more practical level, men — and boys — got the satisfaction of feeling "manly" and in control, and women had countless "free" dinners, movies, and dances while being released from all (except sexual) responsibility during the date.

The etiquette of masculinity and femininity had one final major role in American courtship. It provided both sexes with a tool in the struggle for power within the courtship system. Increasingly in twentieth-century America, especially during the period between 1940 and 1965, women charged men with effeminacy and men charged women with masculinity. The tone was uniformly strident and hostile, and when not refuting the charges, men blamed their loss of masculinity on women's lack of femininity — and vice versa. All these charges, endorsed and reinforced by advisers, experts, and hundreds of magazine articles and books, play a key role in understanding the balance of power in the courtship system.

To men's advantage, the etiquette of femininity and masculinity could serve to enforce continued male dominance in courtship. By charging women who did not defer to them, according to the prescriptions of etiquette, with "masculinity" (and thus with being unattractive and undatable), men could make women's submissiveness (femininity) a prerequisite for participating in the dating system. Since boys and men asked for the date, they could exclude "unfeminine" girls and so maintain control.

This exclusion was officially sanctioned by advice and etiquette books and articles, including many authored by women, which expressed no tolerance for female "aggressiveness," as they tended to label any deviation from the etiquette of femininity of the day. The author of a 1950s teen advice book answered the question "Why do boys drop girls?" by condemning female aggressiveness or any "masculine" assumption of initiative. "The desirable boys," she instructed, "resent this buddy-buddy relationship and go in search of a feminine girl they can master, protect, and teach. They want a girl who makes them feel like a MAN!"[90]

The same book told boys how to handle the situation if they got stuck on a date with an aggressive girl. "A little strategy and a lot of humor will see you through the evening," the author advised. Her sample strategy (here for handling a girl who took the initiative in showing affection) went like this: "When you stop in front of the movie, sit still. After a few seconds she'll say, 'Well? Let's go.' Look surprised again. Then say, 'I thought you were going to go around and help me out.' Laugh and open the door for her. As you do, comment, 'I thought it was my night to be wooed.'"

Her final piece of advice: "Next time try another girl."[91] (The problem here is that the author assumes the girl won't be so aggressive as to have immediately opened her own door and gotten out of the car.) Many other books offered men the same message: don't treat female aggressiveness seriously, as a true threat to your masculinity, but instead recognize that it is the woman's problem, that she lacks femininity. Most suggested embarrassing the woman into seeing the error of her ways, and excluding her from dates in the future.

Women's use of gender etiquette was less direct, as were most of women's routes to power and control in courtship. One way women could employ gender etiquette to challenge men was by conforming to the etiquette absolutely. Women could become *so* feminine and submissive that men felt inadequate because they could not possibly be masculine enough to meet all the demands created by absolute submission.[92] A man was certain to fail somewhere — to be slow in opening a door, to neglect some nicety of behavior, to be indecisive — and thus lay himself open to charges of effeminacy or un-masculinity. Even the most conscientious men could run into trouble if their manners seemed too studied, formal, or soft. The key to masculine etiquette, which demanded that men "protect [women] in word, thought and deed from

[him]self and herself and events"[93] simply *because* men were stronger and could therefore *afford* to give women the advantage, was that element of controlled power. Impeccable manners without dominance were not masculine.

While magazine articles compared the masculinity of the average American man unfavorably with that of movie stars such as Clark Gable, most advice books recognized that such raw attractiveness and graceful power could not be taught, and so concentrated on the rudiments. *Male Manners,* a 1960s advice book for teenage boys, repeatedly stressed that girls wanted their boys "masculine" and "strong and protective." As a lesson to the young men, the author told the story of a girl who decided to "sit it out" when her dinner date did not help her out of the car. She waited a full fifteen minutes until he came back out of the restaurant to see what had happened to her.[94] By exaggerating her feminine submissiveness to the point of refusing to transgress feminine etiquette even when left for so long, she made her point that the boy lacked masculine protectiveness. The author of this text made no recommendation about future dates — we do not know if the girl was supposed to foster his masculinity through continued ultrafemininity or whether she should try another boy next time.

In another path to power, gender etiquette offered women an excuse for assuming larger shares of control in courtship and in other spheres of American life. We don't *want* to be aggressive and masculine, women cried from the pages of popular men's and women's magazines, but we have no choice. Our men have defaulted, they are inadequate, unmasculine, so we have been forced to assume control.[95] Some of the critics must have felt a nostalgia for the good old days of the clear-cut sex role, but the complaints served another purpose as well. The constant judging of men — which by the 1950s had gained international attention as the American crisis of masculinity — did undercut men's control and make them wonder if they really were inadequate. Women's complaints showed men that they would be constantly judged against a cultural ideal of dominance they could not possibly match, and that every time they failed women could use that failure to attack their fundamental identity as *men.*

The struggle for control in courtship was played out in an essentially conservative system. Through rigid behavioral codes and definitions, Americans attempted to reclaim a past when gender offered a more stable definition and place in the world. Even though the etiquette of masculinity and femininity offered women a path to power within the dating system, it more importantly expressed fundamental fears about the amount of power women were gaining in society. The etiquette of gender sought to draw a line between "public" lives (where barriers between men and women were breaking down in the worlds of work and education) and "private" relationships. Although the "public" and the "private" were ultimately inseparable, the etiquette of gender served as a barrier against new definitions and behaviors. It was a cushion against change.

Scientific Truth . . . and Love

*T*he themes of courtship I have chosen to examine — control, competition, consumption, the sexual economy, and etiquette and gender — emerged from a changing landscape of American life. They have their roots in sweeping forces, in all the -isms that fall under the mantle of modernization, that produced both radical and subtle displacements in the existing systems of American courtship and yielded new sets of governing conventions.

Yet these forces were not unchecked or unchanneled, and these conventions were not transparent reflections of changing social reality. The social forces were mediated by other factors and actors; the conventions were *produced.*

The production of convention, and the giving to it of coherency and legitimacy, fell in large part to a new group of men and women in twentieth-century America. The new arbiters of convention were academics — social scientists in the main — who sought to bring youth's experience in courtship and marriage under the authority of educators and experts, and looked to formal institutions of education to prepare youth for marriage. As the founders and adherents of the marriage education movement that flourished on college and university campuses from the 1930s through the mid-1960s, these "experts" dedicated themselves to improving American courtship and marriage. They hoped to provide students with a practical and "functional" education, solidly based on scientific research and directed toward "an ultimate goal of changed conduct" and of producing "happier, more wholesome lives."[1]

In their quest, these experts and academics came to wield great cultural authority. Hundreds of thousands of students passed through their classrooms and read their textbooks. Popularized versions of their scientific expertise reached the general population through mass-circulation magazines, often in the form of articles or advice columns written by the marriage experts themselves. For several generations of American youth, the marriage educators defined normative behavior and acted as the arbiters of courtship conventions.

The roles of such powerful figures cannot pass unexamined: the concerns and understandings that structured their research, their teaching and writing, provide a crucial context for understanding the conventions of courtship.

In 1952, one of the most prominent and respected members of the marriage-education movement, University of Chicago sociologist Ernest Burgess, explained the genesis of American courtship and marriage to a meeting of the American Council of Learned Societies. The "massive" changes in American attitudes toward courtship and marriage since World War I were, he said, a "mass reaction of people to the changed conditions of life resulting from the transition from a rural to an urban society and from the increased personal and ideational mobility due to the automobile and to the new mass media of communication."[2] Burgess, however, was not simply explaining a phenomenon. This paper, and his whole career, was suffused with an urgency to *do* something about these dislocations.

Ernest Burgess, like many social scientists of his generation, was concerned about the implications of the changes that had taken place as America moved into the twentieth century. He looked back to a time when he believed the family was "self-sufficient . . . surrounded by the protection of the kinship group, the church, the school and the neighborhood." He contrasted this stable and secure family with the twentieth-century family, a "unit of interacting members subject collectively and individually to the pressures and strains, stimulations and frustrations, protections and risks of life in the 'Great Society.'"[3] It seemed clear to him that American family life had been undermined.

In 1946, when Burgess published this comparison, many agreed that the American family was at risk. From the beginning of the twentieth century, Americans had worried that the "new freedoms in manners and morals" brought about by urban life would imperil traditional morality and marriage.[4] Then the Great Depression had prevented or delayed many new marriages while putting economic and psychological strain on existing ones. Between 1930 and 1932, the marriage rate fell 13.5 percent, and average age at marriage rose significantly during the decade.[5] Next the tumult of the 1940s war years brought the greatest marriage boom in American history, followed by an unprecedented rise in the divorce rate. Many social commentators worried not only that marriage was unstable but also that youth lacked appropriate models for learning about proper courtship and family life. They believed the health of the family was in jeopardy — and with it the health of America itself.

But to Burgess, the urgency of the situation also presented an opportunity. He ended his paper to the ACLS with a call to action. American adaptations to modern life had, he said, thus far been "essentially a folk phenomena [*sic*] rather than a result of foresight and planning by the intelligentsia." But now, he concluded, "evidence is growing . . . to indicate the possibilities of more planning in the future."[6] Burgess believed that as old forms of courtship and marriage disintegrated and were supplanted by clearly dysfunctional new forms, the need for rational "planning" by "experts" would become apparent to all. Burgess and his colleagues in marriage education hoped to bring about the day when these experts, armed with social science research of the highest caliber, would school youth in the most functional and successful forms of courtship and family life.

The marriage experts, by and large, used the concept of appropriate authority to justify intervening in family life. "Parents," as one marriage expert wrote, "because of the rapid and sweeping social changes in our society, no longer feel completely adequate to help their sons and daughters resolve all the problems of courtship and marriage." He, and others, explained that at one time parents and grandparents, the church and the community, had been adequate to school the young in the ways of the world. But in the twentieth century, change was too great a force. Each generation lived a different life from its elders. Folk wisdom had little role in an urban and technological society.[7]

The answer to the problem, they declared, was a type of authority in keeping with the demands of modern society. The modern age demanded scientific techniques, not folk wisdom. Scientific knowledge was "essential to happy married life and family experience."[8] As Burgess told his students at the University of Chicago, "Only through research can the necessary basis of fact be found for any practical program to meet the problems of the changing American family."[9]

The solution these experts proposed further removed the education of youth from the family and community. In keeping with the general trend in twentieth-century sociology (the discipline-of-origin for a majority of marriage educators), they looked to science, adopting scientific techniques and translating experience into scientific models.[10]

"Necessary" scientific knowledge became increasingly inaccessible to lay people — not only because the experts relied upon the language and techniques (often heavily quantitative) of professional social science but also because of the simple volume of research on courtship and marriage.

As the years went by, quantitative methods were refined and the data piled up. Between 1945 and 1954, there were 1,034 research publications on courtship and marriage.[11] As the author of a 1950s marriage textbook explained, youth needed to study courtship and marriage in an organized high school or college course because only a "professionally trained person can deal adequately with the mass of research material being published in our society on courtship, marriage, child rearing, and family relationships."[12] In short, the professionals had declared themselves the new arbiters of convention and morality, translators and preachers of their own "science of family living."

Ernest Burgess spoke with certainty when he told that assembly of his colleagues in 1952 that "research findings" had replaced "moral and religious sanctions on sexual behavior." Even clergymen, he said, looked to the scientists for answers.[13] To a large extent, Burgess's claim was true. Many influential Americans shared the professionals' faith in science as the proper guiding force for their new society.[14] Many young people felt that traditional rules had little to do with the lives they led and wanted to believe, as an *American Magazine* article said in 1937: "Chances for happiness in marriage may be raised to something approaching a sure bet if courtship and marriage are studied as a science."[15] The marriage education movement had been produced by a crisis in American life, but it was riding the larger tide of American faith in science, in planning, and in the possibilities of the future.

Marriage educators captured this sense of crisis and opportunity in the intellectual justification they offered for their new field. They explained that just as the family had moved from a producing to a consuming "unit" economically, so had it moved from producing to consuming in the education of its young in moral and practical matters. As an article in *Marriage and Family Living* argued:

> If the family no longer does what it used to do, may we still assume that it can educate its members for family life? . . . Most persons agree that . . . community planning is preferable to letting communities grow like Topsy. . . . We need a similar perspective relative to marriage and the family. Preparation for marriage and family life may no longer be left to chance or blind hope. There is need for guidance, training, and planning in the area as

nearly universally available as resources, courage, and insight can make it.[16]

Obviously, it is very different to plan for love and marriage than to regulate city growth through zoning and tax codes. However, while this analogy may sound facile, it is key to understanding the marriage-education movement. The author's call on planning for legitimacy and authority — not on education or counseling or the reinvestment of authority in the extended family — places the marriage education movement in its proper context.

Those social scientists who set themselves up as experts, as planners, were as much a product of the transformation of American culture as the new mores they hoped to "adjust." They were part of a much larger twentieth-century movement toward centralized power, a movement that sought to control the chaotic forces of modernization by vesting power in a new class of experts and professionals. These marriage experts shared with other experts and reformers, from the progressive era on, a sense that the modern world was too complicated, the stakes too high, for the future to be left to "chance" or "blind hope."[17] This concern was only intensified by the pressure of "the Bomb" and America's increasing world power in the 1940s and 1950s. As one advocate of marriage education wrote in 1946, "Man must learn to control his destiny and prevent recurring depressions and wars or suffer the decline of this civilization." And, he continued, we must not limit our attention to the sweeping forces of war and economy, for the "intimate aspects of . . . personal living" must also be controlled. In personal life, as well, he thought, the needs had become "so pressing and the issues so complex" that individuals must have the assistance of experts.[18]

These specialists in "the art and science of family living" (as the founder of the movement referred to their calling[19]) were honestly concerned about the problems of youth in the modern world. They often looked back sentimentally to a stable and idyllic society where courtship and marriage were grounded in the family and local community. But for all their attempts to alleviate the impact of modernization, they were products of the same forces that had unsettled the family, and furthermore, they had actively linked their fortunes to these forces.

By casting their lot with the planning movement, the marriage experts also put on that movement's strengths and weaknesses. Its strengths — the desire to control those forces that lay waste to human lives and resources, and the faith that America could be improved —

appear in the marriage-education movement's attempts to recreate a
stable family in the modern world. Its weaknesses — the arrogance and
insensitivity that sometimes plagued expert definitions of good and
bad, and the wresting of control from individuals and communities —
are inseparable from the often-noble goals of the marriage education
movement.

Official histories place the origin of marriage education courses at
the University of North Carolina in 1927, when a group of senior men
requested a "practical" marriage course and Ernest Groves, a sociologist of the family with a strong interest in psychology, was hired to
teach it.[20] Ernest Groves spent the rest of his life promoting marriage
education (which he and others understood to include courtship), and
was hailed as the father of the movement even by later practitioners
who found his approach not scientific enough. Of course, this was not
the first instance of functional marriage education in the United States.
Many progressive-era programs had similar goals and methods: the
eugenics movement, which sought to transform mate selection from
an "experiment" to a "science" by instructing youth in the principles of
"eugenical matings"; the home economics movement in colleges,
which trained women in scientific housewifery; settlement-house
courses on child care and nutrition; the controversial public school
sex-and-hygiene courses.[21] In 1904, the Iowa House of Representatives
considered a bill that would have provided free instruction in the "art
of successful matrimony" to all students in the state, and in 1912 *Good
Housekeeping* "open[ed]" in the magazine a "school of practical guidance" on marriage, using experts from various fields as instructors.[22]
The heritage of all these previous attempts to cope with changing
forms of American courtship and marriage helped shape the new marriage education movement, and in fact it remained flexible, adapting
to and incorporating the changes in American society over the period
of its ascendency.

In 1927, however, the University of North Carolina was especially
fertile ground for marriage education. Groves came to a sociology department dominated by Howard Odum, who was most interested in
the relation between planning and culture. Odum's research was on
southern regionalism and its place in the national system, a practical
concern that gave him entré to policy makers and foundation grants,
but his theoretical concern applied directly to marriage education:
how can social scientists help a culture change to fit the modern
world? Odum's answer, like the eventual answer of the marriage education movement, was fourfold: research, experts, planning, and edu-

cation. This theoretical concern and its practical answers, which were shared by those with power and resources to implement programs in the 1930s and 1940s, help explain the rise of marriage education in the United States.[23]

And the rise of marriage education, measured by its numbers alone, was impressive. Ernest Groves, in a 1938 *American Magazine* article, predicted that within a generation almost every American college would have a complete course in marriage.[24] It looked as if he was right. In 1937, ten years after the first practical course began at UNC, over 200 of America's 672 colleges and universities offered similar courses. A 1949 survey found over 500 U.S. colleges and universities gave courses on marriage relations. The *New York Times* reported in 1958 that over 700 institutions had fully accredited courses on marriage, and by 1961 a *Mademoiselle* writer found that 1,200 American colleges — "of academic rank ranging from southern junior to Ivy League" — offered "self-help" marriage courses.[25]

Hundreds of thousands of college students, at institutions that did indeed range from southern junior to Ivy League, had some brush with marriage courses. "Preparation for Marriage" was mandatory for seniors at the University of Miami in the 1940s. Michigan State College's course, offered through the Basic College's Department of Effective Living, enrolled 3,350 students in 1948, and the University of Minnesota enrolled 2,000 students in its course that same year. Vassar and the University of Michigan began their courses as extracurricular lecture series in the 1930s, and even used the same "experts" as lecturers. The University of California at Berkeley offered the course for students and nonstudents, and registered 12,000 between 1939 and 1946. At Stephens College in Missouri (a two-year college bordering on finishing school) 60 percent of eligible students took the marriage course, and credit usually transferred to four-year institutions. The administration of Purdue University limited enrollment, and instructors were obliged to spend four weeks each year screening applicants on the basis of written applications, interviews, and "knowledge" tests. (At Purdue, 81 percent of female students and 74 percent of male students thought the marriage course should be required.) In 1940, Lake Erie College's marriage course enrolled the entire senior class — twenty students. Both Northwestern University and the University of Illinois offered marriage courses through the campus YWCA-YMCA, and the University of Chicago held summer institutes. Smith College offered marriage courses, and so did Brooklyn College and the Asheville (N.C.) Normal and Teachers' College. Loyola had one, and so did Syracuse, Colgate, Haverford, Connecticut College for Women,

Cornell, Ohio State, Stockton Junior College, and the University of Utah. By the 1950s, most states had instituted some form of marriage training in their high school curricula.[26] The marriage-education movement was not narrowly based.

Nevertheless, formal marriage and courtship training reached only a small percentage of American youth. Even in the post–World War II GI Bill college explosion, only about 15 percent of young people between the ages of eighteen and twenty-four went to college, and *Marriage and Family Living* itself admitted in 1953 that only about 2 percent of American college students were taking a marriage course in any given year.[27] But the beliefs underlying marriage courses — that scientific knowledge could improve courtship and marriage — reached a much wider audience. The popular media gave a platform to the movement, profiling marriage courses and their leaders, reporting on research findings, and employing the marriage experts as advice columnists.

When *American Magazine* ran an article on college marriage courses and the scientific approach to love in 1937, it prompted thousands of letters from readers and a follow-up article by Professor Groves.[28] The same year, *Good Housekeeping* offered a "College Course on Marriage Relations" in its pages, with the first "lecture" given by Groves. A *Ladies' Home Journal* version, with the more catchy title "How to Be Marriageable," ran in the 1950s.[29] Also in the 1950s, a *Newsweek* article entitled "Bringing Up Mother" quoted Dr. Mirra Komarovsky, chair of Barnard's Sociology Department, that "all colleges, including those for men, must offer a course on marriage and the family."[30] Several other magazines and newspapers, including *Mademoiselle, Collier's,* and the *New York Times,* carried favorable articles on marriage education during the 1940s and 1950s.[31] The publicity seems to have been effective, for the 110th *Woman's Home Companion* poll (1955) found that most American women believed that, for the "best chance" in marriage, a woman should have taken a "serious marriage course and . . . read at least one good book on marital love."[32]

Even those who did not learn about the virtues of formal marriage courses might still have felt the impact of the movement. Increasingly, advisers turned to scientific studies for answers — and for authority. Even teen advisers looked to the literature of the field. One columnist for *Seventeen* magazine told readers she based her advice on social science studies of dating preferences on high school and college campuses.[33] Maureen Daly, perhaps the best-known adviser of youth in the 1940s and 1950s, frequently used data from the Purdue Opinion

Polls of Youth.[34] Also, the marriage educators themselves translated research results for popular audiences. For example, Clifford Adams, Ph.D., who wrote the "Companion Marriage Clinic" in *WHC* and "Making Marriage Work" in the *LHJ* (and who taught the marriage course at Pennsylvania State College), made it clear to readers that his advice was not based simply on common sense but on research and professional judgment.[35] Finally, many magazines offered their readers scientific tests — often tortured out of shape and context from some social science research scale — of sex appeal, marriageability, compatibility, and other crucial attributes.

Thus, college marriage courses, though directly reaching only a small number of people, were highly visible in American society. Because they caught the popular imagination, because they were the nucleus around which the experts coalesced, and because they provide for us the clearest view of how these experts tried to influence American courtship, their importance exceeded their immediate reach. These courses, both as they were offered to students and as they were presented to the general public outside the colleges and universities, illustrate the ideal of "scientific courtship" that was presented to American youth.

There is no "typical" marriage course to examine; the institutions offering them were too disparate, and often professors and other experts brought to the courses priorities and understandings from their disciplines of origin. Still, marriage education was a unified movement with a clearly articulated program. The courses fostered by the movement differed in many specifics, but they all reflected the general presumptions — and shared in the strange coexistences and tensions — of the larger movement.

Three major characteristics defined the marriage courses. They were "functional" — that is, they rejected "academic" education for a practical program leaders sometimes compared to vocational education. They stressed the "personal." Courses were designed to foster "rapport" between student and instructor so that instructors could use personal authority to counsel individual students. In a different but related emphasis, the courses located importance in the individual: material was deemed useful only insofar as a student recognized a personal relation to (or interest in) what was presented. Finally, quantitative social science research on "normal" American courtship and marriage served as the basis for prescription and proscription in these courses.

Functionality was the main characteristic the marriage educators themselves used to define their courses and to distinguish them from the "other" marriage courses. Those who wrote for professional journals and for popular consumption constantly stressed that their purpose was to "prepare" youth for marriage, that the courses were as "practical" and "functional" as they could make them, and that they should not be confused with academic (nonfunctional, impractical) courses that looked at marriage as a historical and social institution.

The Subcommittee on College Courses of the movement's professional organization, the Committee on Education for Marriage and the Family, made this point clearly in its 1941 guidelines for college marriage courses. "The objective of a course in preparation for marriage should be to present those scientific findings and to cultivate those attitudes which contribute most toward the achievement of successful marriage," the subcommittee recommended, stressing that "the course should be functional." Furthermore, they warned, "there is a difference between preparation for marriage, education for family living in the broader sense and understanding marriage as an institution." Functional marriage courses are not intended to replace nor to compete with "traditional" sociology courses on the family, for "the two courses have quite different objectives."[36] Throughout their writings, the marriage educators made it very clear which objective they considered more valuable.

The marriage educators were not a voice in the wilderness when it came to "functional" education. Instead, they were the most visible examples of a larger movement for functional education for America's youth. Functional education sometimes was deemed part of the general education movement, which stood in opposition to the rising tide of academic professionalism and "overspecialization" in American colleges and universities, and under which fell a spectrum of often-contradictory methods and understandings.[37] General education found its first home at Columbia after World War II, but its most famous expression was Hutchins' College at Chicago through the 1930s and 1940s.[38]

Not all of general education was devoted to great books, however, nor to great students. In the 1930s, the University of Minnesota organized an Institute for Social Intelligence (later renamed the General College) for students who lacked the ability for a conventional liberal arts program.[39] Here they could study practical matters — not vocational studies, exactly, but courses that would make them more "at home in their complex modern world."[40] Other colleges and universities followed suit, either setting up "general" or "basic" colleges of their own, or integrating such programs into their curricula. These programs offered courses "based on the functions which contemporary men and women perform," and offered concrete training for students' future roles in society.[41]

The goals of functional education seemed even more appropriate in the years after World War II, when the GI Bill opened college to a much larger and more diverse group. College should no longer be "merely the instrument for producing an intellectual elite," concluded the President's Commission on Higher Education in 1947, in a report aptly subtitled "Higher Education for American Democracy," but should "become the means by which every citizen, youth and adult, is enabled and encouraged to carry his education, formal and informal, as far as his native capacities permit."[42] Functional education seemed to offer a truly *democratic* possibility.[43]

All the rhetoric and programmatic statements about functional education, as is often the case in educational theory, give little sense of how the program looked in practice. In the case of marriage education, "functional" basically meant student oriented and student controlled. In part the student centering made sense, for marriage education grew largely through student agitation and demand.[44] College students, along with other segments of American society, had placed their faith in the possibilities of scientific expertise and actively sought the new authority that marriage experts offered. The original course at UNC was due to a student petition; the widely praised course at Berkeley came out of a student referendum in the face of administration opposition; at other universities, marriage courses came through the efforts of joint faculty-student committees. With students in founding roles, they could reasonably request some voice in shaping the courses.

Howard E. Wilkening, leader of Purdue University's marriage course (which was based in its own Marriage Department), wrote to his colleagues in *Marriage and Family Living*: "Inasmuch as *students* supplied the activating force, it was considered no more than democratically right for them to have a major voice in future policies of the course." Purdue therefore created the post of student coordinator. Student coordinators were chosen by a joint committee of students and faculty on the basis of "poise, general ability in handling people, and tactfulness." Scholarship "was not a basis for selection because it was felt that for such duties personality and social presence were more important." Those "duties" included helping to determine the content of the course, selecting which students, on the basis of "educational and emotional maturity," could fill the course's forty slots, editing class notes, and acting "in conjunction" with the professor to "determine final grades." Under this system, Wilkening wrote, the faculty member "always is made conscious of the students' needs and demands."[45]

Students normally exercised a great deal of control in the marriage courses. The "experts" often abdicated control of their courses to students, saying, in effect, that only those concerned — the students themselves — could know what material was functional. A 1946 survey of the content and teaching methods employed in both high school and college marriage courses found that many teachers "attempted to make their courses more functional" by asking students or prospective students just what they wanted to learn.[46] One of the most influential books of the marriage education movement was Laura Drummond's *Youth and Instruction in Marriage and Family Living* (1942), a badly written, Chi-Square Test–laden former dissertation that attempted to discover what young men and women wanted to learn in marriage courses.[47] Many marriage educators agreed with Michigan State professor Judson Landis, who wrote in *M&FL* that "we feel in general that the student is in a position to judge what is meeting his needs in marriage education."[48]

And this belief was put into practice. In the Michigan State course, student opinion was allowed to overrule staff judgments. For example, staff rated a lecture on "Contemporary Religious Views of Marriage" second in importance among class lectures, while married and single students respectively rated it ninth and tenth (out of ten lectures). The next year it was replaced by a more "practical" lecture on mixed religious marriages. Likewise, an anthropological lecture on marriage among South Sea Islanders was "soon dropped" (even though staff thought it was "of importance because of its sociological implication") because "students did not feel that it offered much that would help them make a successful marriage."[49]

Landis admitted that it was sometimes difficult to know whether to follow student opinion or staff opinion about a subject's importance — a remarkable statement from an "expert" in the field. At Michigan State, however, the course was intended to be practical, and, as Landis explained, "If the students do not feel that their needs are being met, they will show little interest in the course."[50]

In this way, functional marriage education fell prey to one of the dangers of any democratic form: its leaders, dependent on the support of their constituents, were bound to the constituents' demands and interests. And students often were interested only in the short-term, the exciting, the easy answer. Students demanded direct answers to complicated questions such as: "What types of attitudes and behavior between men and women before marriage are appropriate today?" and

"Should a married woman work?" They complained when lecturers didn't "get down to 'brass tacks.'" They rejected lectures on budgets and family finances as boring, and redefined "functional" as "immediately useful." (One University of Michigan student objected to the course of lectures because the material presented would not be useful to him for at least five years.[51]) Finally, many students had a more down-to-earth view of what was practical than the founders of the movement envisioned. One girl complained that she wanted "more discussion on the ways to get a husband . . . in other words, how to attract men so they will want to marry you," and *Mademoiselle* urged that personal appearance courses should be offered for credit in U.S. colleges.[52]

What is interesting here is that student demands did not encounter much opposition. Certainly a few educators continued to include some sociological and historical analysis, and kept a tight rein on their classes. But the instructors of the most visible courses — visible both in professional journals and in the popular press — were full collaborators. Paul Popenoe, a flamboyant proponent of marriage education and one of the most-demanded marriage lecturers in the 1940s, distributed pamphlets such as "Are You Husband Hunting?"; "Why Don't You Make Him Propose?"; and "How Do You Know It's Love?" The teacher of Occidental's marriage course insisted to a *Mademoiselle* writer in 1944: "I'm not a bit academic."[53] The head instructor at the University of Illinois reported to colleagues that he released students from a term paper if they did six hours of baby-sitting during the term, and at Stephens College a wedding plan was an acceptable term paper.[54] Courses gradually shifted their emphasis to the more immediately useful subjects — courtship and the first years of married life — and one professor not unreasonably proposed instituting courses concerned only with dating.[55]

The antiacademic bias was set forth clearly by the conference's Committee on College Education for Marriage, which concluded in 1942 that some college teachers "depend too much upon intellectual verbalization, at which they themselves might be very adept, but which does not carry over to students who have to face actual life problems."[56] Marriage educators, seeking a method that would free them from abstract formulations that students felt had little to do with actual life, turned more and more to an approach that emphasized the personal — personal relevance of material, personal application of information, and even a personal relationship between instructor and student.

The personal orientation of marriage education was in many ways a by-product of its stress on functionality. By giving students so much say in structuring marriage courses, educators gave full play to teenage shortsightedness. Students often accepted as important only what they felt as personally relevant, and that emphatically did not include the institutional, the historical, and the context of a larger society. When confronted with the abstract, most students transformed it into the personal. And educators endorsed that process — even when it revealed a self-centeredness that now seems blatantly dysfunctional or at least antisocial. One teacher explained proudly to the December 1941 National Conference on Family Relations how she focused on students' personal concerns in her course:

> After the announcement of a state of war, it was observed that some of the girls came into the classroom, put their heads down on their desks, and were silent. Fear had entered their lives to stay for a while — fear from which Mother and Father could not shield them. . . . This teacher, who was guiding the girls in courtship practices and into marriage, gave this answer to their fear: "If you react so decidedly now when dangers are yet at a distance, what will you do in the face of emergencies in marriage — when John may say that he does not like your cooking and is going home to Mother." Heads lifted and faces became set with determination.[57]

The comparison of World War II to a burned roast — with the roast winning out in importance — shows how completely students and teachers were willing to put the personal above the societal. Students seemed incapable of hearing about any subject without converting it to a personal issue. In fact, by 1958, 72 percent of American college students felt the main purpose of a college education was to help them acquire well-rounded personalities.[58] Most marriage educators sidestepped the negative implications of the personal emphasis: after all, the stated "ultimate goal" of marriage education was "changed conduct," and conduct would change only if students applied what they learned to their own lives.

To support and encourage students' personalized understandings of course material, many colleges integrated personal counseling into their courses. A "How to Do It" symposium on marriage education in 1946 noted approvingly that "almost inevitably questions raised in class discussion create a desire in the students to discuss personal implications with the teacher or some other counselor."[59] Different instructors played on that desire in different ways.

E. E. LeMasters, one of the most sophisticated and thoughtful of the marriage educators, informed students in his 1957 text that it was their "responsibility" to tell the instructor if they needed counseling.

He illustrated his point with the tale of a young man who "sweat[ed]" through the lecture "reviewing Terman's data related to sexual climax in married women" because he was having that precise "difficulty" with his own wife. LeMasters admitted that he had not known that the student was having difficulties, and in fact had not intended the lecture to apply to any individual. However, he praised the student's maturity in coming in and "unburden[ing] himself of his marital woes," and assured readers that he had made some suggestions that helped the student and his wife with their "sexual adjustment." [60]

Henry Bowman, head marriage instructor at Stephens College and one of the most prolific writers in the field, set up his courses to encourage "rapport" between students and instructor. By fostering a sense of personal relationship, he hoped to encourage his students to bring their personal problems to him. In the 1941 *Marriage and Family Living* he reported his successes: in the preceding three years he had recorded 313 "confidential conferences" with 182 students. Students had consulted him on everything from dysmenorrhea to unattractiveness to which of two boys to marry — and about a wide range of sexual fears, anxieties, and guilts. Bowman referred those with "serious personality maladjustments" or medical problems to other experts, and also used the services of grooming clinics and dancing classes. He admitted that many of these problems would probably have been cured by time or by the young persons involved, but warned that "in numerous cases, just such problems as these constitute the fork in the emotional adjustment or maladjustment roads for many an individual," and that "there is no way of foretelling which problems will be solved and which will be the first step toward personal or marital failure." [61]

At Purdue, instructors evidently took Bowman's warning to heart, for counseling was not left to the students' initiative. Purdue students were required to write a 5,000-word "personal history" exploring their attitudes toward sex and marriage and the factors that might have determined them. Two individual counseling sessions were required of each student, in which they met with instructors on a "personal basis" to discuss problems. From this aspect of the course, at least, the powerful student coordinators were barred, for students, the professor reported, refused to have them "brought in on personal confidences entrusted to the faculty coordinator." [62]

The terms these various teachers use to describe the counseling process — words such as *rapport* and *unburdened*, the phrase "personal confidences entrusted to" — suggest the ambiguity of the counseling relationship. Was it to be modeled on the professional relation

between therapist and client? Was it, in fact, to be a personal relationship, with youth seeking advice from trusted older persons? Was it a
legitimate requirement that students confess their most intimate (often
sexual) problems and concerns to their professors? And finally, why,
though by-and-large not trained therapists, did marriage educators
embrace the role of counselor so willingly?

The answers to these questions are inextricably tied up with the
fundamental justification for marriage courses. Their founders were
trying to invent a new model of education for the modern world — one
that applied the authority of expertise and science to the private and
the personal. They did not reject the personal, they simply shifted its
location and its meaning.

So, in a way, marriage educators were trying to fill many roles.
They were, as they understood it, standing in for the students' own
parents, whose authority had been discredited by modernization.
Many marriage educators sought an often ill-defined personal relationship with their students, hoping that young people would come to
them with problems, just as they once might have sought advice from
a parent or elder in the community. In this way, professors sought an
authority beyond that of expert, scientist, or professor-who-assigns-
grades. The professors reached for some level of *personal* authority in
students' lives. They hoped that scientific information, coming from a
trusted elder, would be doubly influential in shaping attitudes and
forming behavior patterns.

Thus, marriage educators were to provide the role models lacking
in students' own lives. The professional organization, as well as individual members writing for colleagues and for the general public, repeatedly stressed that competence in subject matter was not enough to
qualify men and women to teach courtship and marriage. The professor's personal life was to be as open to scrutiny as his or her publication record. In 1940, *Living* went on record that it was of the "utmost
importance" that marriage instructors have an "integrated personality"
and "emotional maturity and security . . . preferably within marriage." [63] At the University of Iowa, marriage courses were staffed with
"many experts who are well-adjusted personalities." [64] And in 1949,
Boston University professor Harold Lamson warned his colleagues:
"We must be sure that we do not attract into this field unadjusted persons and those who have made a flop of their own married life and
who are seeking personal salvation in saving others. In this field we
cannot afford to have many crackbrained and 'wackie' persons." [65]

Just as vehemently as they claimed personal qualifications, however, these educators asserted their professionalism. The personal relationship between professor and student was to be held confidential, of course (and the model offered was the doctor and not the priest).[66] But their claim to professionalism centered elsewhere: these men and women were experts; they dealt in science. The information garnered from students was important data for their scientific research. Whether submerged into a statistic or reproduced as an anecdote in a marriage text, these individual stories could increase the fund of knowledge and improve American courtship and marriage. In combining the forces of personal authority and scientific expertise, the leaders of the movement hoped to come up with a model of education for marriage suited to the modern world.

The critical ingredient in marriage education was its claim to scientific truth. Claims to functionality, to helping students prepare for real-life situations, clearly were based on a strongly held belief that scientific research was yielding answers that would improve American courtship and marriage. But the other key characteristic of marriage education — its personal orientation — was also bound up with faith in science.

One of the earliest manifestos of the movement warned against applying abstract formulations to individual students' problems. Counseling was, ideally, to be nonjudgmental, nonprescriptive, based on "insight-giving rather than advice-giving."[67] But the experts and educators believed they could discover answers — the right answers — through research. Why, then, not direct students to the right course? In the context of this faith, the counseling that professors offered to their students was more often prescriptive than nonjudgmental — and it often had more to do with abstract formulations than with individual circumstances. With the volume of students passing through marriage courses, it was very difficult to learn enough about a student's individual circumstances to offer truly personal (in the sense of individualized) counseling. Instead, in personal counseling, in the classroom, and in marriage texts, professors fell back more and more on the growing body of social science research. For example, Ernest Burgess's notes for a lecture to his University of Chicago class in the late 1940s read:

Hamilton. Research in Marriage
  Measurement of Satisfaction
Terman. Psychological Factors
  personality vs. sex

"how to get couples"
Burgess and Wallin
     Life History Material[68]

All too often, however, statistical studies of probability were transformed into how-to guides by professors eager to offer truth and students willing to personalize everything. One of the most widely used texts, Judson Landis's *Building a Successful Marriage,* is an instruction book in social science language. Students could consult tables summarizing data from five studies of the "best age" for marriage; they learned that couples who were married in church would be more likely to have a happy marriage than those who married elsewhere, that premarital intercourse would likely ruin chances for marital adjustment altogether.[69] What all this — the presentation of probabilities and statistical description as prescription for behavior — meant was that educators offered the normative as the right and proper and desirable.

The studies on which such prescription and proscription were based usually derived from survey research conducted at northeastern and midwestern colleges and universities. Inevitably, these studies of normative behavior reflected a white, middle-class bias. But when a Southern Illinois University professor wrote in *Marriage and Family Living* in 1953 that his colleagues should consider some of the problems of prescribing middle-class norms as proper behavior for all, especially considering that the college population had recently broadened to encompass many students from the lower and lower middle classes, his argument was quickly refuted. A "comment" directly following his article asserted, "This is no place to debate the 'middle-class bias,' but it should be stated in fairness to teachers and texts that even the lower middle and lower class students in college today aspire to middle-class patterns — or they would not be in college."[70]

With very few exceptions (one being Vassar's Folsom, who wrote in the 1930s that change was so rapid and regional and religious variation so great he could not simply state current mores and urge the reader to follow them "loyally") these experts accepted the authority of the norm and the results of their studies as Truth.[71] There was very little discussion of how the norms, the truths, even the truthfulness of the answers subjects gave to the social science surveys were culturally determined, nor of whether or not the existing norms were "good" ones. The goal of functional education was to prepare students for the *actual* roles they would play in society, to help them adjust to existing conditions.[72]

Thus, as research demonstrated that marriages of mixed religion —

much less mixed race or nationality — were likely doomed, Landis included a thirty-two-page chapter on mixed marriage in his text. He closed the chapter by saying that his consideration of the subject "forces the conclusion" that mixed marriages involve "serious hazards to success." [73] Likewise, as researchers had uncovered the "Psychological Factors in Marital Happiness" (for example, women who "do not object to subordinate roles" make "happier" wives), Landis furnished readers with the list of traits that "in general" characterized the happy and the unhappy spouse. [74]

The normative studies with which his and other texts were filled were definitely intended as models for student behavior. One professor, hoping to "modify behavior in a larger proportion of cases," recounted approvingly the student comment: "My wife read the books and now cooperates more effectively." [75]

One of the most widely known and used products of social science research was the Burgess-Wallin Marriage Prediction Schedule, which could yield the subject's "probability of marital adjustment" based on Burgess's previous determination of the correlation between various factors and future marital adjustment. Burgess, in his proposal for the study, wrote that he hoped that increasing accuracy of prediction would make counselors and educators better able to influence young people against marriage when test results indicated the "presence of factors almost certain to imperil marital adjustment." Thus, he wrote, if a couple could not decide whether or not to get engaged, the "expectancy table" might help them decide — and if it helped them decide to end the relationship, they might experience "less emotion, strain and regret than would otherwise be the case" because they knew their decision was based on "science." [76]

But even surpassing their faith in science, for many marriage educators, was a sense of mission. They were conscious that they had assumed roles previously held by other arbiters of convention and morality in society. While they believed that the *ability* of individuals and institutions — parents, church, and community — to educate the young had been undermined, their authority discredited, that did not mean they believed the old answers were outmoded. Much of the work of these social scientists and educators in the era of marriage education was concerned with providing new scientific underpinnings for the religious and moral sanctions they had grown up with and firmly believed in. As an early column in *Living* explained:

> Even the expert knowledge about wise ways of living together is not so new in one sense. It is new in that hitherto it has not been presented in this country by professional advisers in keeping with the different needs and conditions

of our urbanized, industrial modern life. But the able scientists in the field who are formulating this body of knowledge now did not pull it out of the air or make it up themselves. In one form or another it has been in the world and has been serving human beings for time immemorial.[77]

This timeless knowledge, not surprisingly, most often had to do with sexual morality. Faced with loosening codes of sexual morality — which seemed to most observers blatantly dysfunctional — the marriage experts attempted to bring their modern enlightenment to the defense of traditional morality. According to the experts, premarital sex would hamper future marital adjustment. The scientific phrasing was (as Burgess submitted to his Courtship and Marriage students on a true/false test): "The consequences of immorality are harmful to personality and to the members of society."[78]

Thus, American students were taught that "too much petting creates revulsion"; that "unchastity will bring biological and psychological reactions which may entirely prevent the normal functions of marriage"; that "sexual activity tends to divert couples from the 'primary function of dating and courtship'"; that "unless they work for [a happy marriage] by exercising complete self-control" before marriage, "they may wreck their entire lives." They also learned that in a good relationship there will be "normal sex attraction but no desire for sex relations until after marriage," and that should a woman acquiesce to intercourse, her partner will be less attracted to her afterward.[79]

Many marriage educators were even willing to challenge social science research in the service of conventional — functional — sexual morality. Judson Landis, in the 1958 edition of his text, acknowledged that it was "necessary" to discuss Kinsey's research on sexual behavior in the human female. Landis, however, was determined to show that Kinsey's findings — especially that premarital sexual experience increased the likelihood that women will enjoy coitus early in marriage — should not be taken as a guide to behavior. Kinsey's sample was not representative of the American college population, Landis explained, and anyway, most women eventually achieved successful sexual response. Elsewhere in the text Landis presented studies done fifteen or twenty years earlier — thus on a sample not representative of contemporary college students — as perfectly adequate models for conduct.[80] When *Mademoiselle* surveyed U.S. marriage courses in 1961, the author of the article found that the reading assigned in most courses was "likely to sidestep Kinsey in favor of authors who chose their statistics to prove a point that is compatible with middle-class morality." [81] The new arbiters of American morality were not going to betray their trust — even for Science.

The 1961 *Mademoiselle* article, titled "College Marriage Courses: Fun or Fraud?" offers a clue to marriage education's fall from prominence. This article, unlike those from the previous decades, attacked the movement and everything for which it stood. Marriage education, with its scientific defense of "timeless truths," its location of authority in expertise and institutional surroundings, was increasingly on the defensive in the 1960s. Youth's changing mores and sexual morals, the cultural rejection of the normative — indeed, of any form of authority — undercut the very premises of marriage education. To fully explain the movement's demise, then, is as complicated as explaining the origins of "the Sixties." Still, a partial explanation lies in the movement itself: marriage education succumbed to its own paradoxes.

The marriage education movement in the United States was a complicated one, never completely clear in its priorities, pulled this way and that by the internal demands of a developing discipline and the external demands of the society these experts and educators sought to serve. They were never quite sure if they were scientists or counselors, conservators or pathbreakers, experts or role models. They had many difficulties to contend with: the study of marriage and family life was struggling for academic legitimacy, but even though science was their keystone, the movement never completely gained academic respectability because of its functional orientation. The persona of moral authority affected by many practitioners did not neatly mesh with that of objective social scientist. There is an awkwardness in the rejection of the societal (not to mention the historical) context, in the abdication of control to students, in the way scientific research was transformed into Dear Abby-style advice. All these problems show the difficulty of creating an authority and an education about personal matters that was suited to the emerging modern society.

As the tensions and contradictions within the movement were played out, they shed light on one aspect of American courtship — the struggle for the power to define propriety, the struggle to hold final authority, to become arbiters of morality and convention. This struggle is separate from the bipolar accommodations made by the genders to the new forms of courtship that arose in the twentieth century, but the experts' successes and failures are a mediating force in these private and public struggles and accommodations.

Still, there is one final note — one that might serve as a postscript to this entire study. Certainly it mattered what the experts said. Certainly the arbiters of convention had a profound impact on the way youth understood courtship. Certainly it made a difference that modern youth received advice with the imprimatur of science and not of religion or of custom. But the power of forces other than convention, science, and expertise, other than the struggle for control in courtship, cannot be overlooked. In what must have been one of the most poignant moments in the history of marriage education, Burgess scrawled on the back of his marriage prediction study proposal:

Once they are in love? [82]

Epilogue

It has been more than a quarter of a century since the dating system lost its coherence and its dominance. The public language of courtship is different, if uncertain, today. "Conventional" courtship bears little resemblance to the complicated rituals of the mid-twentieth century. Many of the problems faced by previous generations persist; the dramas and acts of love continue, but once again the context has shifted.

What has replaced courtship's metaphor of economy? What structures our public language and behavior today? Anyone who has spent time glancing through popular magazines in the grocery store checkout line could volunteer the obvious answer: sex. Sex appears to be the normal, if not unproblematic, medium of contemporary courtship. Perhaps we can trace the shift in courtship to the sexual revolution.

Today, looking back, the normalization of "revolutionary" sexual practice obscures the concreteness of the sexual revolution as an event — an event that seemed to many observers overwhelmingly sudden. Of course, the revolution did not come out of nowhere, and it was not nearly so sudden as it seemed. Over the years, as we learn from studies such as the Kinsey reports, the sexual experiences of individuals and groups had been less and less in line with public conventions. The buttresses had been crumbling slowly and finally could no longer support this structure of meaning. The true revolution was, perhaps, not in sex, but in the metaphor that gave it meaning.

In the "culture of abundance" that was postwar America, economic metaphors for society were less instrumental — more, they made little sense. In the midst of abundance, why must value be defined through scarcity? If sexuality is abundant, why must it be conserved?

By presenting the sexual revolution as a revolution in meaning, I don't mean to imply that the changes in experience were unimportant. The acts of courtship certainly changed. "Technical virginity" declined in importance. More people had premarital sex; intercourse replaced petting as a convention of youth. It is easy to forget how rigidly controlled sex was in the postwar era, and how closely a woman's value was linked to her sexual morality. The sexual revolution was not just about the right to have sex with a stranger met at a singles' bar and to depart the next morning uncommitted and guilt-free. It was also about the right of unmarried people to express love sexually, and centered around a rejection of the understanding that equated a woman's value with her "virtue."

In contemporary America, living together has become a conventional step in the path to marriage and an acceptable arrangement on its own terms. Sexual intercourse is a conventionally assumed part of long-term relationships (even among teenagers, for better or worse), and a clear possibility on first dates. These conventional behaviors are not universally observed, and are loudly protested by many Americans. But even today, in the age of AIDS and the not-unrelated impulse toward monogamy or chastity, the sexual legacy of the revolution is not really threatened. When *Newsweek* tried to come to grips with contemporary courtship, it quoted New York trend-spotter Faith Popcorn's opinion that "we are seeing a return to traditional values and practices — people want to know the background of the next person they sleep with."[1] That knowing a person's background would seem to define "traditional" values shows how far down the road we have come.

If the sexual revolution had stopped at sex, I would say that concepts of abundance came to define the public acts of courtship. (Calls for chastity today are calls for restraint in the midst of plenty.) Instead, I hold on to the sexual revolution — with the emphasis on revolution. I propose — suggestively, and not definitively — that just as metaphors of economy replaced metaphors of home and family (paralleling courtship's shift from private to public spheres) in the early twentieth century, metaphors of revolution (granted, *sexual* revolution) emerged in the 1960s to replace economy. In the late 1960s, in the streets as well as in the bedrooms of America, revolution came to the fore. Change was in the air, and power, unmasked, was at stake.

The contestation for power was no less significant between the sexes than between generations, classes, and races. The sexual revolution was not only about sex. It was about the struggle for power and for freedom, equality, and autonomy — a struggle in which sex played a key role. The struggles between the sexes, the struggles over the meaning of sex and of gender, took place in so many spheres — economic, familial, personal, political — the boundaries blur. The results, I believe, were increased freedom for both women and men. The blessings of freedom are not unmixed. There is much potential for exploitation in this system, and it is quite reasonable to ask if the revolution has offered anyone *true* freedom. But a form of freedom we have got, together with its attendant perils, responsibilities, pleasures, and problems.

The new freedoms, which were not at all restricted to sexual behavior, had a profound impact on courtship. Freedom made courtship less certain. It undermined the rules. Metaphors of economy offered a wonderfully coherent system: models based on cause and effect, clear and logical rules. Metaphors of revolution are the opposite. They offer change and struggle as a way of seeing. Conventions are no longer so coherent, their meaning no longer so clear.

Can you say, today, what it means if a middle-class girl in Middle America picks up the phone and calls a boy? Can you say for sure what it means if a thirty-five-year-old man or woman offers a member of the opposite sex his or her business card at a social gathering? If you know that two people slept together last night, do you know how they define their relationship? The uncertainties are staggering, complicated enough for those who observe, possibly debilitating for those who participate.

The vast uncertainties of contemporary courtship have produced a flood of nostalgia. We look longingly, in our popular culture, back to the "traditional" courtship of the postwar era — when rules were rules. According to *Mademoiselle* in 1986, "Dating was probably never fun. But it wasn't navigating shark-infested waters, either. . . . If you wanted sex, you got married; society required it — it was not optional. Men pursued women ardently and openly; women pursued men ardently and covertly. The game was clear to all players."[2] Even if the rules were stifling, it seems, at least we knew what they were — and the consequences of breaking them.

This nostalgia is misplaced. Our past does not contain a golden age of courtship, and the "security" of the postwar era was bought at great price. Besides, we are not those people. We are too far from their understandings of the world. For all the problems with modern relationships, we have made gains in freedom and equality; for all our fears in facing an uncertain world, we have incorporated the revolution into our ways of seeing. And it is a revolution we are still fighting.

Notes

Introduction

1. Christopher Lasch, "What's Wrong with the Right?" *Tikkun* 1 (1), n.d., pp. 24–25.

2. "The New Mating Games," *Newsweek*, 2 June 1986, p. 58; "Dating Is Hell," *Mademoiselle*, November 1986, p. 177.

3. The point of "What Ought to Be and What Was" is well taken, and historians are rightly very careful in using prescriptive literature as historical evidence these days. Still, I believe prescription and convention are related to individual experience, even if the connection is not direct and uncomplicated.

4. Theodore Peterson, *Magazines in the Twentieth Century* (Urbana: University of Illinois Press, 1964), pp. 4–5, 47–49.

5. Ibid., pp. 62, 57, 45.

6. In my research, I looked at prescriptive and descriptive articles and columns in twenty-nine mass- and high-circulation magazines. I read more than eighty advice and etiquette books, and followed scholarly works as they made their way into popular culture. I examined texts used in high school and college marriage courses as well as the professional journals of the educators and scholars who taught the courses. Finally, I looked at the culture of colleges, both as it appeared locally — in college newspapers, magazines, and handbooks, and as it was presented to a national audience through national magazines. I did not use fiction as a source because I believe that the fictional portrayals of courtship are very different from the nonfiction sources I examined, involving a much more explicit element of fantasy. Fiction and fantasy unarguably played a role in determining convention and provided another layer of context for individual experience; I suspect that fiction would supply the romantic dimension often lacking in the material I used. But the difficulty of weighing the different meanings and roles of fiction and nonfiction as evidence could well have undercut the validity of this work.

7. Colleges offered accessible local cultures to compare to each other and to national conventions to see if the conventions I describe as national hold across the board. Also, college culture exerted influence and carried a symbolic

145

weight much greater than the actual number and roles of college students would justify. Even in the early years of the twentieth century, the conventions and customs of college students were presented to the nation in minute detail by popular magazines and found a fascinated audience. College customs probably influenced the culture-at-large as much as vice versa.

8. Joseph F. Kett, *Rites of Passage: Adolescence in America: 1790 to the Present* (New York: Basic Books, 1977), p. 216. Much of my discussion of youth is drawn from Kett, especially chapters 1, 5, 6, 8, and 9, and from Paula Fass, *The Damned and the Beautiful* (New York: Oxford University Press, 1977). I have, to some extent, conflated the terms *youth* and *adolescence*.

9. "Bobby-Sock Forum," *Newsweek*, 30 October 1944, p. 89.

10. Thomas B. Morgan, "Teenage Heroes: Mirrors of Muddled Youth," *Esquire*, March 1960, p. 71.

11. The term *middle class* has drawn a lot of fire lately, especially in relation to the "rising middle class" of America's nineteenth century. The term presents fewer problems in discussing mid-twentieth-century America, a society that contained an expanding economic middle class and that self-consciously labeled itself a middle-class nation. In this work I draw on the argument made by Stuart M. Blumin in "The Hypothesis of Middle-Class Formation in Nineteenth-Century America: A Critique and Some Proposals," *American Historical Review (AHR)* 90 (April 1985): 299–338.

12. H. H. Remmers, R. E. Horton, and Sverre Lysgaard, "Teenage Personality in Our Culture," *Purdue Opinion Panel* (Lafayette, Ind.: Purdue University, May 1952), pp. 10a–11a. Burton Bledstein, in *The Culture of Professionalism* (New York: W. W. Norton & Co., 1976), p. 3, quotes a 1940 *Fortune* magazine survey that revealed that 79.2 percent of all Americans thought of themselves as middle-class. For a fuller discussion of this redefinition of class or desire for classlessness, see Roland Marchand, "Visions of Classlessness, Quests for Dominion: American Popular Culture, 1945–60," in Robert H. Bremner and Gary W. Reichard, eds., *Reshaping America* (Columbus: Ohio State University Press, 1982).

Calling Cards and Money

1. Alexander Black, "Is the Young Person Coming Back?" *Harper's*, August 1924, p. 340. The author of the *Ladies' Home Journal (LHJ)* "Good Manners and Good Form" column advised a young woman who had been invited to the theater to greet her escort with her hat on, though without her wrap and gloves. Mrs. Burton Kingsland, *LHJ*, August 1909, p. 39.

2. "Some Expert Opinions on Dating," *McCall's*, August 1961, p. 125. Quote is from Professor Ruth Shonle Cavan.

3. Ibid. See also Robert M. Eret, "Marriage Need Not Be a Gamble," *LHJ*, September 1956, p. 80; David R. Mace, "A Radical Proposal," *McCall's*, August 1961, p. 96.

4. Quote is from Allyn Moss, "Whatever Happened to Courtship?" *Mademoiselle*, April 1963, p. 151. See also Ernest W. Burgess and Paul Wallin, *Engagement and Marriage* (Chicago: J. B. Lippincott Co., 1953), p. 64; Evelyn Millis Duvall, Ph.D., *Facts of Life and Love for Teenagers* (New York: Association Press, 1956), p. 276 (this work went through four printings in five

months); and Paul H. Landis, *Your Dating Days* (New York: Whittlesey House/McGraw-Hill Book Co., 1954), p. 10.

5. For the extended discussion on the concepts I draw on here, see Blumin, "Middle-Class Formation," pp. 299–338.

6. By the turn of the century, America had a category of popular magazines. They did not yet reach a mass audience, but were low in price, appealed to a middle ground of public taste, and were read by many Americans. The *Ladies' Home Journal* advice column, "Side Talks with Girls," received 158,000 letters from readers in a sixteen-year period bracketing the turn of the century. Peterson, *Magazines*, pp. 13, 14, 59.

7. See especially *Ladies' Home Journal* columns by Mrs. Burton Kingsland ("Good Manners and Good Form") ; by Mrs. Stickney Parks ("Girls' 'Affairs'"); by "The Lady from Philadelphia"; and Alice Preston's columns for working girls. For etiquette books, see: Florence Howe Hall, *The Correct Thing* (Boston: Dana Estes & Co., 1902), pp. 34–57; Professor Walter R. Houghton, A. M. et al., *American Etiquette* (Chicago: Rand, McNally & Co., 1882), pp. 127–40; C. L. Snyder, *Decorum* (New York: Union Publishing House, 1881), pp. 70–90.

8. Mrs. Burton Kingsland, "Good Manners," *LHJ*, February 1907, p. 54; "Lady from Philadelphia," *LHJ*, July 1905, p. 35; Eleanor H. Phillips, "What Girls Ask," *LHJ*, March 1912, p. 42. On refreshments: Helen L. Roberts, *Putnam's Handbook of Etiquette* (New York: G. P. Putnam's Sons, 1913), p. 71; Kingsland, *LHJ*, March 1907, p. 48. On chaperonage: Florence Howe Hall, "Etiquette for Men," *Harper's Bazaar*, November 1907, p. 1096; "The Lady from Philadelphia," *LHJ*, February 1904, p. 25; Roberts, *Putnam's Handbook*, p. 64. On conversation and leavetaking: "The Lady from Philadelphia," *LHJ*, February 1904, p. 255.

9. For examples see letter from "Country Girl" to Kingsland, *LHJ*, June 1907, p. 44; letter from "Ignoramus" to "The Lady from Philadelphia," *LHJ*, February 1904, p. 25.

10. See letter from "I.D." to Kingsland, *LHJ*, January 1907, p. 46; Hall, "Etiquette," pp. 1095–97.

11. "How May a Girl Know?" *LHJ*, January 1914, p. 9. See also letter to Mrs. Stickney Parks, "Girls' 'Affairs'," *LHJ*, May 1914, p. 58.

12. Sir William Craigie and James R. Hulbert, eds., *A Dictionary of American English*, vol. 2 (Chicago: University of Chicago Press, 1940), p. 726. On Ade, see Carl S. Smith, *Chicago and the American Literary Imagination* (Chicago: University of Chicago Press, 1984), p. 181.

13. As Alexander Black had noted after telling his story of the call that turned into a date. Black, "Is the Young Person Coming Back?" p. 340. See also Kathy Peiss, *Cheap Amusements: Working Women and Leisure in Turn-of-the-Century New York* (Philadelphia: Temple University Press, 1986), p. 75.

14. Alice Preston, "After Business Hours — What?" *LHJ*, February 1907, p. 31.

15. Hull House Oral History Project Tapes, Jane Addams-Hull House, University of Illinois, Chicago Campus.

16. Peiss, *Cheap Amusements*, pp. 75, 51–52.

17. Ibid., p. 51.

18. Kathy Peiss, "'Charity Girls' and City Pleasures," in *Powers of Desire,*

ed. Ann Snitow, Christine Stansell, and Sharon Thompson (New York: Monthly Review Press, 1983), pp. 81, 83; Lewis Erenberg, *Steppin' Out* (Westport, Conn.: Greenwood Press, 1981), especially 60–87, 139–42. On nineteenth-century chaperones, see Ellen Rothman, *Hands and Hearts* (New York: Basic Books, 1984), pp. 207–9. Radcliffe's rules of conduct in the early twentieth century were popularly called "chaperone rules" and did indeed require chaperones for student dates.

19. Erenberg, *Steppin' Out*, pp. 60–87, 139–42.

20. A Girl, "Believe Me," *LHJ*, July 1914, p. 7.

21. Kingsland, *LHJ*, May 1907, p. 48.

22. Although nineteenth-century young people had more unchaperoned time than our stereotypes acknowledge, the shared experience of urban nightlife, with its sexual overtones and sense of escape, was significantly different.

23. Helen Lefkowitz Horowitz, "Women and the City," talk at Chicago Historical Society, 17 May 1984.

24. "The Lady from Philadelphia," *LHJ*, February 1904, p. 25; July 1905, p. 35; Kingsland, *LHJ*, August 1907, p. 39; November 1907, p. 60.

25. *Red Book*, Radcliffe College, 1923, p. 47; 1930, pp. 57–58; 1937–38, p. 66. In 1923, chaperone rules did not apply to girls with their fiancés, but the engagement had to have been publicly announced.

26. Robert S. Lynd and Helen Merrall Lynd, *Middletown* (New York: Harcourt, Brace & World, 1929), pp. 114, 134–35, 137–38, 141. See also Burgess and Wallin, *Engagement and Marriage*, p. 13. While recognizing the importance of other factors, they emphasize the impact of the automobile and look to rural and small-town culture for the change. Duvall simply says that the car changed courtship. Duvall, *Facts of Life and Love*, p. 276.

27. Kingsland, *LHJ*, May 1909, p. 58.

28. Kingsland, *LHJ*, January 1907, p. 46.

29. "The Lady from Philadelphia," *LHJ*, January 1904, p. 31. A 1938 etiquette book, *Safe Conduct*, still observed that "theoretically" it was a woman's "privilege" to ask a man to call. Margaret Fishback, *Safe Conduct* (New York: Harcourt, Brace & Co., 1938), pp. 74–75.

30. Cecil-Jane Richmond, *Handbook for Dating* (Philadelphia: Westminster Press, 1958), p. 11.

31. Marjorie Vetter and Laura Vitray, *The Questions Girls Ask* (New York: E. P. Dutton & Co., 1959), p. 79.

32. Betty Cornell, *Betty Cornell's All about Boys* (Englewood Cliffs, N.J.: Prentice-Hall, 1958), p. 18; Richmond, *Handbook*, p. 24.

33. Steven Hart and Lucy Brown, *How to Get Your Man and Hold Him* (New York: New Power Publications, 1944), p. 89.

34. Kingsland, *LHJ*, October 1907, p. 60.

35. Ruth Rosen and Sue Davidson, eds., *The Maimie Papers* (Old Westbury, Conn.: Feminist Press, 1977), pp. 191–98. See also Peiss, *Cheap Amusements*, p. 54.

36. Ruth Rosen, *The Lost Sisterhood: Prostitution in America, 1900–1918* (Baltimore: Johns Hopkins University Press, 1982), p. 151. Kathy Piess, in "'Charity Girls' and City Pleasures" (pp. 81–82), discusses the sexual exchange practiced by late nineteenth- and early twentieth-century "charity girls" —

distinguished from prostitutes because they did not accept money directly but exchanged sexual favors for presents and entertainment.

37. William Johnston, "Why Men Won't Marry," *Collier's*, 14 March 1925, p. 23.

38. Black, "Is the Young Person Coming Back?" p. 342.

39. "The Too-High Cost of Courting," *American Magazine*, September 1924, pp. 27, 145–50.

40. Ibid.

The Economy of Dating

1. Margaret Mead, *Male and Female* (New York: William Morrow, 1949; reprint ed., New York: Morrow Quill Paperbacks, 1967), p. 285. Mead first gave the substance of this book as the Jacob Gimbel Lectures in Sex Psychology in 1946. The *Ladies' Home Journal* also ran much of Mead's discussion in 1949, including her description of dating as a "competitive game." (Margaret Mead, "Male and Female," *LHJ*, September 1949, p. 145.)

2. Willard Waller, "The Rating and Dating Complex," *American Sociological Review* 2 (1937): 727–34. Woman's popularity was described as associational — she received status as the object of man's choice. Undoubtedly, the right clothes, the right connections, and all the intangibles that come from the right background purchased male attention in the first place, but popular and scholarly accounts consistently slighted this angle.

3. Fass, *Damned and Beautiful*, p. 201.

4. Ibid., p. 226.

5. Michael Gordon, "Was Waller Ever Right?" *Journal of Marriage and the Family (JMF)* 43 (February 1981): 67–75. Gordon questions the validity of Waller's model based on the atypicality of his sample. I do not insist that rating-dating actually governed individual acts and choices of either Penn State students or the population at large (although it may have), but it did provide a vocabulary for and a way of understanding the dating system for participants and observers alike. The language of rating-dating appears widespread in both college and noncollege sources, though with a significant time lag between colleges and the general population.

6. Mary Ellen Green, "Advice to Freshmen," *Mademoiselle*, August 1939, p. 88.

7. Fass, *Damned and Beautiful*, p. 200. Fass found the Northwestern arrangement reported in the *UCLA Daily* (13 November 1925). I found an apocryphal version of the story in "If Your Daughter Goes to College," *Better Homes and Gardens (BH&G)*, May 1940.

8. Norton Hughes Jonathon, *Guidebook for the Young Man about Town* (Philadelphia: John C. Winston Co., 1949), pp. 129–31.

9. Betty Strickroot, "Damda Phi Data Sorority Rates BMOC's by Their Dating Value," *Michigan Daily*, 25 March 1936.

10. Editorial, "Where Do You Make Your Date?" Massachusetts *Collegian*, 10 October 1935, p. 2.

11. Elizabeth Eldridge, *Co-ediquette* (New York: E. P. Dutton & Co., 1936), p. 224. The author based her book on personal research and experience

at several U.S. colleges and universities. This volume went through four printings in June-August 1936.

12. Anna Streese Richardson, "Dates in Christmas Socks," *Woman's Home Companion (WHC)*, January 1940, p. 7.

13. Usage does change. The name Gay Head comes from the cliffs of Martha's Vineyard, where, as *Senior Scholastic (SS)* revealed in its teachers' supplement, Gay had been christened by a male editor with a bottle of raspberry soda (20 February 1937). In 1937, *Senior Scholastic* was used by 6,200 teachers in high school classrooms, and the teachers reported that "Boy Dates Girl" was extremely popular with students (Teachers' Supplement, 29 May 1937, p. A-3).

14. Gay Head, "Boy Dates Girl: The First Reel," *SS*, 19 September 1936, p. 18.

15. "Blind as a Bat," *LHJ*, December 1944, p. 8.

16. Gay Head, "Boy Dates Girl Jam Session," *SS*, 22–27 February 1943, p. 29; "Should High School Students Go Steady?" *SS*, 20 October 1941, p. 38; "Jam Session," *SS*, 28 February–4 March 1944, p. 32. *Senior Scholastic* began its jam session polls in 1941; the first was on dutch dating.

17. Eldridge, *Co-ediquette*, pp. 203, 211. Being engaged, of course, removed both man and woman from the dating system, and thus from competition. Engagement, however, was not presented as an immediate social goal.

18. Dorothy Dayton, "Anxious Ladies," *Mademoiselle*, February 1938, p. 34.

19. *Daily Northwestern*, 27 September 1940, p. 12.

20. Paul Popenoe, "How Can Colleges Prepare Their Students for Marriage?" *Journal of Home Economics*, March 1930, p. 173.

21. Millicent Fenwick, *Vogue's Book of Etiquette* (New York: Simon & Schuster, 1948), pp. 79–80.

22. Alice Leone Moats, *No Nice Girl Swears* (New York: Alfred A. Knopf, 1933), pp. 84–85.

23. Virginia Hanson, "Party-Girl — Princeton Style," *Mademoiselle*, May 1938, p. 46; Margaret Culkin Banning, "What a Young Girl Should Know," *Harper's*, December 1933, p. 50.

24. Jan Landon, "The Dateline: Every Dance with the Same Boy?" *Good Housekeeping (GH)*, March 1955, p. 100. In the South, the cut-in system persisted longer, but as *Esquire* noted in 1958, "Cutting in is the outer limit of poor form almost everywhere else in America" (Nicholas David, "Courtship on the Campus," *Esquire*, February 1958, p. 49).

25. Cameron Shipp, "The Strange Custom of Going Steady," *WHC*, March 1956, pp. 44–45.

26. The term *unwilling virgins* comes from J. B. Rice, M.D., "The Unwilling Virgins," *Esquire*, May 1949, p. 127.

27. Ernest Rutherford Groves and William Fielding Ogburn, *American Marriage and Family Relationships* (New York: Henry Holt & Co., 1928), pp. 130, 193.

28. Gretta Palmer, "Marriage Is a Career," *Mademoiselle*, May 1938, p. 43.

29. "U.S. at War: Women," *Time*, 26 February 1945, p. 18. Of course, women living near military installations could have the opposite experience — too many men in too short a time. For a description of victory girls, see Studs Terkel, *The Good War* (New York: Pantheon Books, 1984), pp.

242–46. Despite pockets of abundance, the war left most women with less male companionship.

30. Editorial, "Can Sacrifice Be Related to Comfortable College Life?" *Daily Northwestern*, 27 February 1945, p. 2.

31. "The Sound and the Fury" (letters to the editor), *Esquire*, November 1946, p. 10. This letter from a British WREN complained about American servicewomen.

32. *U.S. Selective Service and Victory* (Washington, D.C.: Government Printing Office, 1948), p. 91.

33. Women's colleges, which had previously offered such a society, had long ago lost their identity as communities of women. In *Harper's* a woman author compared her class (1915) with the class of 1930. Unlike her classmates, who were close to each other and saw men as outside their community, the girls in the class of 1930 talked about men all the time, went away six weekends a quarter, and thought that events only counted if men came (Agnes Rogers Hyde, "Men in Women's Colleges," *Harper's*, December 1930, pp. 11–12). See also Helen Lefkowitz Horowitz, *Alma Mater* (New York: Alfred A. Knopf, 1984), p. 287.

34. Naomi Riol, "Somebody's After Your Man," *GH*, November 1943, p. 25.

35. Florence Howitt, "A Place for the *Extra* Woman," *GH*, April 1945, p. 29.

36. "Lo, the Poor Coed," *Newsweek*, 29 April 1946, p. 86. *Mademoiselle's* college-issue "Handbook for Freshmen" noted that roommates would be very important "'count of we'll be seeing lots of each other these dateless nights — c'est la manpower shortage" (Joan Epperson and Marilyn Mayer, "Handbook for Freshmen," *Mademoiselle*, August 1944, p. 189).

37. Shirley Spring, "Ratio Favors Girls for Dance Dates," Massachusetts *Collegian*, 6 December 1945, p. 1. The University of Massachusetts at Amherst was founded in 1863 as Massachusetts Agricultural College. In 1931 it became Massachusetts State College, and in 1948 the University of Massachusetts. The freshman class of 1915 had included only 9 women among its 201 entering students.

38. "Handbook, 1946–47," University of Massachusetts, pp. 53, 55–60.

39. Spring, "Ratio," p. 1.

40. "Junior Prom Date Bureau to Open Today," *Daily Northwestern*, 19 January 1945, p. 1; "Want Car, Coed for Prom? Phone Scott Date Bureau," *Daily*, 24 January 1945, p. 1; Bill Brown, "Coeds Face Dateless Prom," *Daily*, 31 January 1945, p. 1. Note that all are first-page articles.

41. Editorial, "Sacrifice," *Daily Northwestern*, p. 2.

42. "Featuring NU" (cartoon page), reprint from *Esquire*, *Daily Northwestern*, 1 March 1945, p. 3.

43. Herb Hart, "Men, Cokes Rationed for War," *Daily Northwestern*, 19 May 1949, p. 1 (series on NU's first 100 years); "Deering Becomes Date Bureau for Co-eds and Navy," *Daily*, 1 March 1945, p. 3. The University of Washington, also near a military installation, had a date bureau to introduce servicemen to coeds. Rayanne D. Cupps and Norman S. Hayner, "Dating at the University of Washington," *Journal of Marriage and Family Living (M&FL)* 9 (Spring 1947): 30–31. Tom Koch, "Poll Reflects Girls' Morale as Navy Boys Go on Leave," *Daily Northwestern*, 3 November 1944, p. 5.

44. Bart R. Swopes, letter to the editor, "Use Pancake, He Says. . . ." *Daily Northwestern*, 8 February 1945, p. 2.

45. The Harvard Faculty of Arts and Sciences assumed responsibility for Radcliffe educational policies in 1943. All Harvard classes were opened to Radcliffe students. *De facto* joint instruction began then, but did not become official policy until 1947 (*The Radcliffe Guide, 1978–79*, p. 10).

46. "Crimson Myth Refuted: Initiative Upheld at War-Time Radcliffe," *Radcliffe News*, 21 December 1944, pp. 1, 3.

47. Ibid.

48. "Marriage Total High Show Recent Radcliffe Vital Statistics," *Radcliffe News*, 8 December 1944, p. 4.

49. Early in the war, some Northwestern sorority women had a similar reaction to the man shortage. See DeeDee Laughead, "NU Coeds Busily Engaged," *Daily Northwestern*, 1 May 1942, p. 3.

50. Lucy Greenbaum, "In Marriage It's a Man's Market," *New York Times Magazine*, 17 June 1945, p. 14.

51. Judith Chase Churchill, "Your Chances of Getting Married," *GH*, October 1946, pp. 38–39. The numbers don't tally, but it was an attention-getting blurb.

52. Jean and Eugene Benge, *Win Your Man and Keep Him* (Chicago: Windsor Press, 1948), p. 3.

53. Rice, "The Unwilling Virgins," p. 127.

54. "Counting 150,000,000 Noses," *SS*, 1 February 1950, p. 7.

55. Churchill, "Your Chances," pp. 38, 313; Merrill Panitt, "Those English Girls," *LHJ*, September 1945, p. 5.

56. Eleanor Perenyi, "Women of America, Now Is the Time to Arise: 'Maybe(?)'," *Esquire*, July 1962, p. 37.

57. For examples of desertion stories (and explanations for the phenomenon), see Betty South, "The Secret of Love: Have American Girls Forgotten?" *Esquire*, February 1951, pp. 23, 112–13. Gallup poll reported in Joseph Goulden, *The Best Years: 1945–1950* (New York: Atheneum, 1976), pp. 31–32; organized pressure in Judson T. Landis and Mary G. Landis, *Building a Successful Marriage* (New York: Prentice-Hall, 1953), p. 52; army regulations in "German Girls," *Life*, 23 July 1945, p. 38. The *Life* story also noted that the English word *rape* had entered the German vocabulary and that German women suffered a "serious man-shortage." More concrete proof of fraternization were the 90,000 German-American children born in the American zone of occupation in the first year after the war. See Reinhold Wagnleitner, "Propagating the American Dream: Cultural Policies as Means of Integration," unpublished paper, 1983.

58. *The 'N' Book, 1945–46*, p. 48. Fifteen hundred veterans registered at NU in September, 1945. The *Daily* explained, "Those strange two-legged creatures you have been seeing around campus are men! . . . Peace, it's wonderful!" (quoted in Herb Hart, "Peace Brings Expansion, Vets," *Daily Northwestern*, 20 May 1949). By 1947, 1 million of the 2.4 million students enrolled in American colleges were veterans.

59. Goulden, *Best Years*, p. 70.

60. Ibid., p. 73.

61. Ibid., p. 72.

62. "WSGA to Hear Noted Beauty Consultant," Massachusetts *Collegian*, 1 November 1945, p. 1.

63. "McCann to Lead Forum on Co-ed–Veteran Relations," *Daily Northwestern*, 21 February 1945, p. 1.

64. Anna Marie Barlow and Bobbie Baker, "I Want a Girl," *Mademoiselle*, August 1944, p. 209. This theme also appeared in fiction. In a *McCall's* short story, a veteran said, "After you'd been away from civilization for a while, separated from everything except the grim details of winning a war, you stopped thinking of a girl as just a date" (Ruth Adams Knight, "Pattern for a Kiss," *McCall's*, March 1945, pp. 24–25).

65. Sergeant Gene Philip Fortuna, "The Magnificent American Male," *Esquire*, July 1945, p. 147. See also Leland Stowe, "What's Wrong with American Women," *Esquire*, September 1948, p. 93.

66. Robert C. Ruark, "Cupid Has Two Heads," *Esquire*, January 1951, p. 123.

67. Victor Dalliare, "The American Woman? Not for This G.I.," *New York Times Magazine*, 10 March 1946, p. 15. *Collier's* in response to a spate of letters and articles complaining about "demanding, spoiled" U.S. women, in a 1944 editorial said that girls shouldn't worry. There's nothing wrong with being demanding and expecting to have money spent on you, the editors advised, because that's what is responsible for the steady rise in the average U.S. standard of living. So, the editors concluded, keep on demanding, "after, of course, catching your man by acting like a nondemanding homebody if that's what his war experiences have led the lug to think he wants in you" ("Our Demanding Women," *Collier's*, 1 July 1944, p. 70).

68. For a public announcement of the new record, see "U.S. Marriage Rate Zooms to All-Time High," *Science Digest* 22 (October 1947): 17; for discussion of the phenomenon, Susan Hartmann, *The Home Front and Beyond: American Women in the 1940s* (Boston: Twane Publishers, 1982), pp. 164–80. Hartmann gives figures per 1,000 unmarried women (148 / 1,000 in 1946); the ones I quote are per 1,000-population — as they appeared in national media at the time and were quoted in marriage texts.

69. "The Falling Off of the Marriage Market," *Literary Digest* 116 (22 July 1933): 7.

70. The term is Margaret Mead's, from *Male and Female*, p. xvi.

71. There are many popular sources that noted the decreasing average age at marriage. See, for example, Lowell S. Trowbridge, "No 'Right Age' for a Girl to Marry," *New York Times Magazine*, 19 October 1952, pp. 19–20; "U.S. Campus Kids of 1953: Unkiddable and Unbeatable," *Newsweek*, 2 November 1953, p. 53; and the marriage text, Landis and Landis, *Building*, p. 38.

72. "Another Myth Blows Up," *Collier's*, 5 August 1939, p. 54.

73. See Phyllis I. Rosenteur, *The Single Woman* (Indianapolis: Bobbs-Merrill Co., 1961), p. 58; James H. S. Bossard, "The Engagement Ring — A Changing Symbol," *New York Times Magazine*, 14 September 1958, p. 74; "The Family: Woman's World," *Time*, 14 June 1963, p. 66.

74. "The Married Student," *Newsweek*, 4 March 1957, p. 49. Purdue spent $10 million to build 908 apartments to house married students, but still couldn't provide for 2,000 (of 13,000 total enrollment) of them. Also see "More Marriages at Younger Ages," *M&FL* 19 (May 1957): 141, and "Couples Out in Cold," *Michigan Daily*, 2 March 1948.

75. "Life Goes to a Pansy Breakfast," *Life*, 23 July 1945, pp. 90–93.

76. "Profile on Youth: Subsidized Marriage," *LHJ*, December 1949, p. 58.

77. Hildegarde Dolson, "How Young America Lives," *LHJ*, January 1953, p. 131.

78. Abbot Mills, "Campus Romance," *LHJ*, July 1957, p. 112. This was a profile of a couple at the University of Wisconsin.

79. For example, see discussion of the *Life* article, "To Love, Honor, Obey . . . and Study," Michigan *Daily*, 21 May 1955.

80. Gay Stadler, "Men Named Motive of Women at College," *Daily Northwestern*, 19 April 1949, p. 5. In 1953, the *Daily* reported that, of 640 freshmen coeds, 80 were pinned or engaged (Gee Gee Geyer, "Honors, Pins Won by Freshman Girls," *Daily Northwestern*, 22 May 1953, p. 3). Note choice of word *won.*

81. "Chez E Phi," 21 January 1961. In A E Phi Scrapbook, 1949–50, Northwestern University Archives.

82. Polly Weaver, "Pursuit of Learning . . . and the Undaily Male," *Mademoiselle*, January 1958, p. 80. See also, "The Best College for Me," *Mademoiselle*, January 1954, pp. 116–17.

83. 1917 class song, *Handbook of Radcliffe College, 1915*, p. 42. Every other Wednesday at 1:00 P.M. college song practice was held in the theater and all students were expected to attend. At the song competition (held in the spring on the steps of Agassiz House) each class sang two songs, one of which was original in both words and music.

84. "The Only Man," *Students' Handbook*, Radcliffe College, 1909, pp. 29–30. It also appeared in an article, "College Songs We Ought to Know," in the *Radcliffe News*, 26 November 1915, p. 5.

85. *Red Book*, 1931, p. 88.

86. "Radcliffe Mothers," *Red Book, 1954–55*, p. 109. The *Radcliffe News* (9 March 1951) ran an article titled, "'Cliffites to Become Grandmothers at 40 Pres. Jordan Predicts." The changes at Radcliffe closely coincided with the beginning of the joint instruction system and a self-conscious attempt to shake off the image of the "blue stocking." Another 1947–48 song ended:

So Radcliffe really is the best
No jeans in class, we're neatly dressed
And the blue-stockinged gal of yesterday
Is gone, and we are here to stay.

In 1950, Miss Joan Projansky (Radcliffe '49) was appointed as director of the college publicity office. Miss Projansky, who was also studying interior decorating, said she wanted to "put across the idea that the blue-stockinged days are far behind us" (*Radcliffe News*, 23 September 1950, p. 3).

87. *Red Book, 1954–55*, p. 153. Another entry (which didn't win) included the stanza:

Tech men take us dancing in Boston
Dartmouth takes us to ski in Vermont.
Yalies will wine us and Princeton men dine us
So who wants to get into Lamont?

It was by Holly Butler and Barbara Williams and sung to the tune of "I'm in

Love with a Wonderful Guy" (*Red Book, 1953–54*, p. 108). There were exceptions to the convention – but the vote went to marriage.

88. *Red Book, 1951–52*, pp. 96–97; *Red Book, 1957–58*, p. 90.

89. *Red Book, 1955–56*, p. 96.

90. *Red Book, 1956–57*, p. 82.

91. Howard Whitman, "Sex and Early Marriage," *BH&G*, August 1947, p. 147; "Profile on Youth: Subsidized Marriage," *LHJ*, December 1949, pp. 195–96.

92. Whitman, "Sex and Marriage," pp. 147, 40; David R. Mace, "Is Chastity Outmoded?" *WHC*, September 1949, p. 101. Dr. Mace was professor of Human Relations at Drew University and wrote frequently for *Woman's Home Companion* and *McCall's*.

93. Tony Barlow, "Possible Ways to Provide More Eligible Husbands in the Marriage Market," from *Collier's*, reprinted in Landis and Landis, *Building*, p. 61.

94. Jhan and June Robbins, "One Hundred Twenty-nine Ways to Get a Husband," *McCall's*, January 1958, pp. 28, 89. The authors explained that "brainstorming" was a technique used by "business, industry and our armed forces to sell goods, solve production problems and plan strategy."

95. For statistical analyses, see Hilda Holland, comp., *Why Are You Single?* (New York: Farrar Straus & Co., 1949), especially pp. 67–68; Rosenteur, *Single Woman*, pp. 13, 88–89; Jean Van Evera, *How to Be Happy While Single* (New York: J. B. Lippincott Co., 1949), p. 11.

96. See Frances Bruce Strain, *Love at the Threshold: A Book on Social Dating, Romance, and Marriage* (New York: Appleton-Century-Crofts, 1952), p. 20; Hart and Brown, *Get Your Man*, p. 35.

97. Dorothy Barclay, "Encouraging Teen-Age 'Dates,'" *New York Times Magazine*, 26 July 1953, p. 35.

98. Ruth Imler, "The Sub-Deb: The Late Dater," *LHJ*, September 1955, p. 54; Dorothy Barclay, "When Boy (Age Twelve) Meets Girl," *New York Times Magazine*, 23 January 1955, p. 39; "The Pre-Teens," *Time*, 20 April 1962, p. 68; "Going Steady at Twelve," *Newsweek*, 18 December 1961, p. 90. See also David R. Mace, "Let's Take a Sane Look at the Hysterical Quest for a Husband," *McCall's*, September 1962, p. 54.

99. Mead, *Male and Female*, p. xvi.

100. One teenage bride, quoted in *LHJ*, said, "When you're fifteen you feel so confused and alone. You think if you get married you won't be alone, you'll *have* somebody" ("Why So Many Early Marriages?" *LHJ*, March 1960, p. 155). On military service, see LeMasters, *Modern Marriage* (New York: Macmillan, 1957), pp. 209–10. See also Sidonie M. Gruenberg, "Why They Are Marrying Younger," *New York Times Magazine*, 30 January 1955, p. 38.

101. See, for example, G. O. Schultz, "Are Our High Schoolers Snobs?" *BH&G*, February 1941, p. 86; and Henrietta Ripperger, "Maid in America: Going Steady – Going Where?" *GH*, April 1941, p. 70. In the 1930s and early 1940s, *Senior Scholastic* argued that going steady would divert teens from achieving their ambitions. A 1939 argument against going steady went: "In our modern, high-speed civilization, it is safe to say that physical maturity usually arrives long before emotional maturity . . . and before most young men are vocationally established and capable of supporting a wife, let alone a family. The educational process for professional or business success today often re-

quires the full concentration of thought and energies for a long time before love and marriage can be seriously considered" ("Readers' Forum," *SS*, 11 February 1939, p. 3).

102. Psychologists warned that going steady (unless leading directly to marriage) could have a "permanent emotional effect that makes later marriage anticlimactic, since it is 'make believe'" ("Going Steady . . . a National Problem," *LHJ*, July 1949, p. 131).

103. Robert D. Herman, "The Going Steady Complex: A Re-examination," *M&FL* (February 1955): 37. The mid-1950s saw a proliferation of studies reevaluating Waller's concept. See the *Journal of Marriage and Family Living* throughout the decade.

104. Maureen Daly, ed., *Profile of Youth* (New York: J. B. Lippincott Co., 1949), p. 30.

105. Herman, "Going Steady Complex," p. 38.

106. "Going Steady," *LHJ*, p. 44.

107. Clark W. Blackburn, "True Love versus Sexual Curiosity," *Cosmopolitan,* October 1960, p. 60.

108. All figures from Purdue Opinion Polls of high school youth. H. H. Remmers and Ben Shimberg, *Purdue Opinion Panel (POP)* (Lafayette, Ind.: Purdue University, November 1948), p. 26; R. D. Franklin, M. H. Maier, H. H. Remmers, "Youth Looks at Education," *POP,* March 1959, p. 11; R. D. Franklin, *POP,* May 1959, pp. 21a–22a. A 1966 study of elementary school students found that, of the eleven-year-old girls studied, 30 percent had dated or gone steady (cited in Everett D. Dyer, *Courtship, Marriage, and Family: American Style* [Homewood, Ill.: Dorsey Press, 1983], pp. 50–51).

109. "Boy Dates Girl," *SS*, 18 April 1951, p. 16.

110. LeMasters, *Modern Marriage,* pp. 97–98.

111. For descriptions of the protocol of going steady, see "Going Steady," *LHJ*, p. 44; Betty Coe Spicer, "If You Don't Go Steady You're Different," *LHJ*, December 1959, pp. 68–69; Shipp, "Strange Custom," p. 44; "Profile on Youth: Iowa Teen-agers Step Out," *LHJ*, July 1949, p. 42; Jan Landon, "The Date Line" *GH*, October 1956, p. 21; Thomas B. Morgan, producer, "How American Teen-Agers Live," *Look*, 23 July 1957, pp. 21–32.

112. See sources cited in note 111, especially *Ladies' Home Journal* articles.

113. Daly, *Profile,* p. 30. Also quoted in LeMasters, *Modern Marriage,* p. 123.

114. Jan Landon, "The Date Line," *GH*, June 1957, p. 20; Landon, "The Date Line," *GH*, October 1954, p. 18; Beverly Brandow, *Date Data* (Dallas: Banks Upshaw & Co., 1954), p. 100.

115. Richard M. Gummere, Jr., "(1) Money (2) Books (3) Going Steady," *New York Times Magazine,* 3 June 1962, p. 30.

116. "Father Carey's Chickens," *Time*, 8 March 1963, p. 52. The principal of St. Mary's High School in Lynn, Massachusetts, barred any student who went steady from holding positions of leadership or honor in the school or in school organizations. Also "Love and Marriage," *SS*, 6 December 1956, p. 2T.

117. Landis and Landis, *Building,* pp. 64–65.

118. Morgan, "American Teenagers," pp. 28–29.

119. Helen Louise Crounse, *Joyce Jackson's Guide to Dating* (Englewood Cliffs, N.J.: Prentice-Hall, 1957), p. 101. Crounse's name appeared nowhere on the book — it was supposedly written by teenage J. J.

120. For example, see Gay Head, "Boy Dates Girl: Fresh Date," *SS*, 18 February 1939, p. 31.

121. For an extended discussion, see "Sex Control" in this volume.

122. A sociologist, E. E. LeMasters, attempted to gauge the change from random dating to going steady by exploring the "dating experiences (or at least the *memories* of such)" of parents who were members of study groups he led over five years during the 1950s. LeMasters, *Modern Marriage*, p. 120.

123. John J. Morgenstern, Ph.D. (Chief Clinical Psychologist, Warren County Mental Hygiene Association, Glens Falls, N.Y.), letter to the editor, *New York Times Magazine*, 15 September 1957, p. 12.

124. Daly, *Profile*, p. 29; Rosenteur, *Single Woman*, pp. 57–58.

125. Herman, "Going Steady Complex," p. 40; John R. Crist, "High School Dating as a Behavior System," *M&FL* 15 (February 1953): 26.

126. "Going Steady," *LHJ*, p. 44.

127. Herman, "Going Steady Complex," p. 40.

128. Popularity — especially in the debate over going steady — was frequently referred to in business terms. See, for example, Gay Head, "Boy Dates Girl," *SS*, 2 March 1949, p. 28.

129. Cornell, *All About Boys*, pp. 89–91. Morgan, "American Teenagers," pp. 28–29. Even the later sexual revolution appeared dull to some observers. *Newsweek*, in an article titled "The Morals Revolution," said: "In their serious and earnest quest for love and sex, many college couples lead social lives about as full of zest as a Ph.D. thesis in epistemology. Even amid the excitement and color of New York, monogamy often takes on the gray tone of monotony." "So terribly middle-class" and "middle-aged" was *Newsweek*'s verdict ("The Morals Revolution," *Newsweek*, 6 April 1964, p. 56).

130. Art Unger, ed., *Datebook's Complete Guide to Dating* (Englewood Cliffs, N.J.: Prentice-Hall, 1960), p. 32.

131. Cecil Jane Richmond, *Handbook for Dating* (Philadelphia: Westminster Press, 1958), p. 55.

132. See, for example, "What Parents Say about Teen-agers," *Look*, 2 September 1958, p. 65; and Morgan, "Heroes," p. 65.

133. Strain, *Love*, p. 25.

134. Rosenteur, *Single Woman*, p. 58.

135. Crounse, *Joyce Jackson's Guide*, pp. 94–95.

136. Unger, *Datebook's Guide*, p. 34.

The Worth of a Date

1. Richard Wightman Fox and T. J. Jackson Lears, eds., *The Culture of Consumption* (New York: Pantheon Books, 1983), p. xii. The culture of consumption, as Lears and Fox describe it, emerged in roughly the same period as the dating system. Its origins lie in the late nineteenth century, with the maturation of a national marketplace; the development of a new stratum of professionals, managers (experts), and organizations; and the emergence of a "gospel of therapeutic release" that replaced an older morality with ideals of self-fulfillment and immediate gratification. For a full discussion, see Fox and Lears, pp. ix–xvii.

2. Elizabeth Woodward, "The Sub-Deb: I'm Fed Up," *LHJ*, January 1944, p. 8. A *WHC* article similarly equated the date and being paid for: "Keeping in

circulation is the surest way to fill your date nights. If no lad ever sees you at a school dance or perched on a drugstore stool or floating out of the movies, he'll think you don't enjoy that fare. *He'll spend his money on a girl who does* [emphasis added]" (Judith Unger Scott, "No Date Is No Disgrace," *WHC*, November 1946, p. 159).

3. Gay Head, "Boy Dates Girl Jam Session," *SS*, 11 April 1951, p. 24.

4. Ibid.

5. Letters to *Senior Scholastic* throughout the period suggested this strategy, as did Gay Head and other advisers, including the social director of the Illini Union at the University of Illinois. See Irene Pierson, *Campus Cues* (Danville, Ill.: The Interstate, 1956), pp. 39–40, 86.

6. Margaret Mead, "Male and Female," *LHJ*, September 1949, p. 145.

7. Gladys Denny Shultz, "Are Our High Schoolers Snobs?" *BH&G*, February 1941, p. 86; Enid Haupt, *The* Seventeen *Book of Etiquette and Entertaining* (New York: David McKay Co., 1963), p. 45.

8. Scott, "No Date," p. 158.

9. Everett Ryder, "In Defense of the Bird Dog," *Mademoiselle*, August 1957, pp. 367–68.

10. Gay Head, "Boy Dates Girl," *SS*, 19 November 1938, p. 36.

11. "Time on Their Hands," *Recreation*, September 1941, p. 361. The average American family spent $152.

12. Dan C. Fowler, producer, "Her First Date," *Look*, 13 December 1953, pp. 124–29.

13. "Blind Date," *McCall's*, April 1956, pp. 24, 26.

14. Allyn Moss, "Whatever Happened to Courtship?" *Mademoiselle*, April 1963, p. 151.

15. "Boy Dates Girl Jam Session: How Does the High Cost of Dating Affect You?" *SS*, 4 November 1953, p. 26.

16. Shipp, *Strange Custom*, p. 107.

17. "Profile on Youth: The High Cost of Dating," *LHJ*, September 1949, p. 46.

18. Ibid.

19. "Boy Dates Girl Jam Session: Are High School Proms Getting Too Expensive?" *SS*, 10 May 1950, p. 24.

20. R. W. Heath, M. H. Maier, and H. H. Remmers, "Youth's Attitudes toward Various Aspects of Their Lives," *Purdue Opinion Panel*, April 1957), p. 32. Results were based on a questionnaire administered to 10,000 students in December of 1956, from which a balanced sample of 2,000 was selected for analysis. Thirty-seven percent of the girls spent over $30 on the prom, and only 4 percent spent $5 or less.

21. Ibid. An additional 34 percent spent between $5 and $30. Statistics are remarkably consistent across income levels and geographical location, suggesting how powerful a national ideal extravagant proms had become. In a rough translation to 1984 dollars, median family income equals $16,107, and the $15 prom date translates into about $56.

22. Thomas Gutowski, "The High School as Adolescent-Raising Institution: An Inner History of Chicago Public Secondary Education, 1856–1940," (Ph.D. diss., University of Chicago, 1978), p. 256.

23. Richard L. Frey, "The High Cost of Dating," *GH*, August 1953, p. 225.

24. "Ten Ways to Spend a Quiet Evening," *Mademoiselle*, August 1954, p. 309.

25. Frey, "High Cost," p. 224. A 1952 study of a large state university and a small junior college found "routine" dates cost $2 to $3 and "special" dates ran $20 to $30 (Ruth Connor and Edith Flinn Hall, "Dating Behavior of College Freshmen and Sophomores," *Journal of Home Economics* 44 [April 1952]: 279).

26. "Figures Show $80,000 Yearly Spent for Dances by Students," *Michigan Daily*, 19 December 1924.

27. "Coeds Refuse to Walk," *Daily Northwestern*, 25 January 1904, p. 4.

28. Elizabeth Eldridge, *Co-ediquette* (New York: E. P. Dutton & Co., 1936), p. 29.

29. "Prom Season Begins Tomorrow," *Massachusetts Collegian*, 14 April 1926, p. 1; "Junior Prom Is Big Social Event of the Season," 21 April 1926, pp. 1, 2.

30. Stan Frankel, "Mr. Average Student," *Daily Northwestern*, 17 October 1939, p. 4.

31. "I-F Ball Reduces Ticket Cost," *Daily Northwestern*, 18 October 1930, p. 1.

32. M. S., "Public Be Damned," *Daily Northwestern*, 3 November 1939, p. 4.

33. Lois Jean McElroy, "She Wants Corsages," *Daily Northwestern*, 31 October 1939, p. 4.

34. Bob Salveson and Dick Rhein, "Students Oppose Attempted Corsage Ban at Formals," *Daily Northwestern*, 15 February 1940, p. 2.

35. "Corsages Banned at Interhouse Spring Formal," *Daily Northwestern*, 9 May 1941, p. 1; "I-H Ball Will Feature Gardenias," *Daily Northwestern*, 3 May 1940, p. 1.

36. "No Corsages, Chairmen Ask," *Daily Northwestern*, 4 February 1949, p. 1.

37. For example, see Frey, "High Cost," p. 225. The *Radcliffe News* of November 19, 1937, reported that the origin of corsages on campus was the Harvard-Yale game of 1912. The man usually brought two red chrysanthemums that cost $1 each.

38. William B. Powell, "If You Say It with Flowers," *Esquire*, January 1936, p. 84.

39. Moss, "Courtship," p. 151.

40. See, for example, Frank Richardson, M.D., "When a Girl Marries," *WHC*, May 1941, p. 15; discussion in marriage text by Henry A. Bowman, *Marriage for Moderns* (New York: Whittlesey House, 1942), p. 155.

41. Mum advertisement in *Esquire*, June 1941, p. 119. In contrast, as Mum ad for women in *WHC* (November 1939, p. 38) read: "Ed — with another girl and he used to be mine! . . . It isn't always the *pretty* girls who win! For even a pretty girl can spoil her chances, if she's careless about underarm odor. . . ." [their ellipses].

42. Gay Head, "Boy Dates Girl," *SS*, 23 February 1948, p. 27; 22 September 1948, p. 36.

43. Frey, "High Cost," p. 225.

44. For example, see Brandow, *Date Data*, p. 177.

45. "A Tale of Not-So-Flaming Youth," *Literary Digest* 105 (10 May 1930): 70.

46. "Profile on Youth: How Perfect Can You Get?" *LHJ*, October 1949, pp. 52–53; Franklin, "Teen Culture," *POP*, May 1959; Elaine Landau, "The Teen Guide to Dating" (New York: Julian Messner, 1980), p. 51.

47. Gay Head, "Boy Dates Girl," *SS*, 25 October 1950, p. 21.

48. "Views and Reviews: LaConga, Drake Form Fanciest New Clubs," *Daily Northwestern*, 27 September 1940, p. 5.

49. Gay Head, "Boy Dates Girl Jam Session," *SS*, 15–20 December 1941, p. 35.

50. Jonathon, *Guidebook for the Young Man*, p. 13.

51. Robert Benton and Gloria Steinem, "The Student Prince; or How To Seize POWER though an UNDERGRADUATE," *Esquire*, September 1962, p. 83.

52. Ryder, "Bird Dog," p. 368.

53. Marie Torre, "A Woman Looks at the Girly-Girly Magazines," *Cosmopolitan*, May 1963, p. 43. The author concluded: "The disturbing thing about the entire situation is that there are millions of so-called 'men' who are digesting these stultifying ideas." *Esquire*, from its beginnings, had much potential for influencing men. A 1936 poll at the University of Michigan ranked *Esquire* as men's favorite magazine (Michigan *Daily*, 11 January 1936). During World War II, *Esquire* enlarged its potential audience by sending hundreds of sets of pinups to Special Service officers to use in decorating recreation rooms and day rooms.

54. Peterson, *Magazines*, p. 274. For a sketch of *Esquire* history, see pp. 273–81.

55. "Crossing the Dateline," *Esquire*, February 1948, pp. 54–55.

56. "Man, Mode, and Manners," *Esquire*, February 1945, p. 108; R. T. Nimmons, "Orchids for the Lady," *Esquire*, January 1951, p. 50.

57. Peterson, *Magazines*, p. 317.

58. Quoted in Torre, "Girly-Girly Magazines," p. 46. *Playboy*'s first printing of 70,000 (1953) nearly sold out, and by 1956 it was the largest-selling urban men's magazine in the United States with a circulation of 1,100,000. For a profile of *Playboy*'s readership, see "Meet the *Playboy* Reader," *Playboy*, April 1958, pp. 63, 76, 77. Barbara Erenreich, in *The Hearts of Men* (pp. 42–45), describes how *Playboy* advocated the "new consumer ethic" or "fun morality," and argues that "nothing could have been more in conformity with the drift of American culture than to advocate a life of pleasurable consumption."

59. Torre, "Girly-Girly Magazines," p. 46.

60. Margaret Mead, *Male and Female*, pp. 286–87; she uses the same image in the *LHJ* article.

61. "The Younger Generation," *Time*, 5 November 1951, p. 48.

62. Herb Graffis, "The *Esquire* Girl, 1951 Model," *Esquire*, January 1951, p. 54.

63. Ibid.

64. See Lois W. Banner, *American Beauty* (New York: Alfred A. Knopf, 1983), p. 283. On conformity, see George Ade, "Today's Amazing Crop of Eighteen-Year-Old Roués and Nineteen-Year-Old Vamps," *American Magazine*, March 1922, p. 5.

65. Cora Carlyle, *How to Get a Husband* (n.p.: Hedgehog Press, 1950), p. 82.

66. "Billions of Dollars for Prettiness," *Life*, 24 December 1956, p. 121. This article appeared in a special issue on the American woman.

67. Louise Paine Benjamin, "What Is Your Dream Girl Like?" *LHJ*, March 1942, p. 114; Curt Riess, "Beauty Is a Bore," *Esquire*, March 1940, p. 27; Banner, *American Beauty*, pp. 271–73.

68. Abigail Wood, "How to Hold a Boy without Hanging On," *Seventeen*, August 1963, p. 216.

69. Gay Head, "Boy Dates Girl," *SS*, 27 November 1944, p. 34.

70. Elizabeth Woodward, "The Sub-Deb: Extra! Extra!" *LHJ*, May 1942, p. 6.

71. Juliet Farnham, *How to Meet Men and Marry* (New York: Simon Publications, 1943), p. 15.

72. Gay Head, "Boy Dates Girl: The Dickens," *SS*, 4 February 1939, p. 29.

73. Perfume ad quoted in Robert F. Winch, *The Modern Family* (New York: Henry Holt & Co., 1952), p. 383; Carlyle, *Get a Husband*, p. 3.

74. Norman W. Hamilton, *How to Woo, Win, and Keep Your Man* (New York: William-Frederick Press, 1955), p. 13.

75. Margaret Mead writes: "A girl has no excuse for relaxing in despair because initially she lacks a good figure or the right-shaped eyebrows. Proper diet or a carefully cut girdle will correct the one, proper cosmetics the other" (Mead, "Male and Female," *LHJ*, September 1949, p. 145).

76. T. F. James, "The Truth about Falling in Love," *Cosmopolitan*, June 1958, p. 26. The sweater-girl look began during World War II (sweater-girl contests began in 1943), but the breast craze culminated later (Hartmann, *Home Front*, p. 198).

77. James, "Falling in Love," p. 30.

78. "The Bosom in Hollywood," *Playboy*, August 1959, p. 72.

79. "Dear Playboy," *Playboy*, May 1958, p. 5.

80. Victor Warren Quale, "Beauty and the Bust," *Esquire*, June 1954, p. 85.

81. Amram Schienfeld, "Our Ideal Physiques," *Cosmopolitan*, April 1960, p. 31; "Do Americans Commercialize Sex?" *LHJ*, October 1956, p. 69.

82. Quale, "Beauty and The Bust," p. 109.

83. Of course, there were many other ways women competed by consuming, and makeup is probably chief among them. The most extreme statement of this principle I've come across is a *Cosmo* article titled, "Why I Wear My False Eyelashes to Bed" (1968). The author writes: "More makeup disappears [in bed] than anywhere else. And the bed is where you need it most! Every girl having an affair should have a magnifying mirror and her *essentials* makeup kit hidden under the bed. While her lover sleeps, she can make repairs" (reprinted in Helen Gurley Brown, ed., *The Cosmo Girl's Guide to the New Etiquette* [New York: Cosmopolitan Books, 1971], pp. 26–31). While this article is surely somewhat tongue-in-cheek, it seems less funny when read side by side with other, definitely serious advice. *Seventeen*, in a 1963 article titled "School Day Beauty on the Go" (February 1963, p. 113), advised girls to freshen or totally re-do their makeup four times *during* the school day — and they don't just mean fresh lipstick.

84. Vina Delmar, "Midnight of a Bridesmaid," *LHJ*, March 1955, p. 62–63.

This observation had very little to do with the story itself, but was pulled out as the teaser-quote at the front of the story anyway.

85. See, for example, the advertisement featuring Mrs. F. Martin Smith of Chicago in *WHC* (May 1941, p. 8). The ad tells about her wedding and honeymoon and shows her wedding reception at the Algonquin Hotel.

86. This ad appeared in *LHJ* (March 1942, p. 37). Engagement rings, which *Look* described as "courtship's greatest prize," symbolized the material goods that came with marriage. Ernest Havemann, "Modern Courtship, the Great Illusion," *Look*, 15 September 1961, p. 128. Today, the diamond jewelry industry runs ads with the headline: "Two Months' Salary. For a diamond as valuable as the love you've found" (*Bride's*, October-November 1984, p. 152).

87. These figures from Rosenteur, *Single Woman*, p. 81. For discussions of weddings and consumption, see Kitty Hanson, *For Richer, for Poorer* (New York: Abelard-Schuman, 1967) and Marcia Seligson, *The Eternal Bliss Machine: America's Way of Wedding* (New York: William Morrow & Co., 1973). A *Vogue* magazine survey in the late 1950s found that the typical middle-class father would spend one-fifth of his yearly income on his daughter's wedding — not counting her trousseau (Hanson, *Richer, Poorer*, p. 17).

88. "Double Wedding . . . Double Glamour," *Look*, 17 September 1957, pp. 124–27.

89. Rosenteur, *Single Woman*, p. 79. A Gorham Sterling ad in *Mademoiselle* (June 1940, p. 17) made the same connection: "Is there moonmagic in your life this spring . . . moon-magic and a shopping list as long as your arm?"

Sex Control

1. See Rothman, *Hands and Hearts*; Peter Gay, *Education of the Senses* (New York: Oxford University Press, 1984); Carl Degler, "What Ought to Be and What Was: Women's Sexuality in the Nineteenth Century," *AHR* (December 1974): 1467–90; Daniel Scott Smith, "The Dating of the American Sexual Revolution," in Michael Gordon, ed., *The American Family in Social-Historical Perspective* (New York: St. Martin's Press, 1978), pp. 426–38; Peter Filene, *Him/Her/Self: Sex Roles in Modern America* (Baltimore: Johns Hopkins University Press, 1986), pp. 131–32.

2. See Kett, *Rites of Passage*, and Fass, *The Damned and the Beautiful*, for discussions of these trends.

3. Joseph Kett, on page 6 of *Rites of Passage*, discusses the "massive reclassification" of young people as "adolescents," including the reassignment of traits normally assigned to girls to cover boys also under this new mantle of adolescence. Common experience and more association between boys and girls and between young men and women furthered their own belief in the common interests and traits of young people as opposed to their elders. Paula Fass's work on the production of "youth" is especially useful here. She quotes a 1922 *Atlantic Monthly* editorial, which noted that the "old and the young" were "as far apart in points of view, code, and standard, as if they belonged to different races" (p. 19), and notes that much concern about youth was based on a "frantic fear of sexual promiscuity" (p. 25).

4. Polly Weaver, "College and Career One Hundred Years Ago," *Mademoiselle*, January 1956, p. 63.

5. Lois Kimball Matthews, *The Dean of Women* (Boston: Houghton-Mifflin Co., 1915), pp. 3–9, 151–52.

6. "Alas, That Co-eds Should Spoon," *The Northwestern*, 25 March 1904, p. 1.

7. "Puppy Love," *LHJ*, September 1907, p. 44; Mrs. Burton Kingsland, "Good Manners and Good Form," *LHJ*, April 1907, p. 54.

8. See Fass, *Damned and Beautiful*, p. 25.

9. In the late nineteenth and early twentieth centuries, unmarried young people were more carefully chaperoned than in any other period of American history (Rothman, *Hands*, p. 208).

10. "Snuggle-Pupping," *Ann Arbor Times-News*, 24 March 1922.

11. Mitford M. Matthews, *A Dictionary of Americanisms on Historical Principles* (Chicago: University of Chicago Press, 1951), p. 1228. The equivalent of petting was done in the nineteenth century and before, especially between engaged couples, but was not celebrated in popular song, and was not considered *conventional*, normative behavior.

12. Ernest R. Groves (as told to Jerome Beatty), "Too Much Kissing?" *American Magazine*, December 1939, p. 23; Gladys D. Shultz, "Down with Chaperones," *BH&G*, July 1939, p. 46; text mentioned is LeMasters, *Modern Marriage*, p. 200.

13. For a discussion of this practice, see Henry Seidel Canby, "Sex and Marriage in the Nineties," *Harper's*, September 1934, pp. 427–36.

14. Floyd Dell, "Why They Pet," *Parents*, October 1931, p. 18.

15. LeMasters, *Modern Marriage*, p. 191. He compared petting to wearing lipstick — both were "expected" of women. See also Strain, *Love at the Threshold*, p. 176.

16. Claudia Hatch, "First Big Romance . . . First Kiss," *Seventeen*, September 1957, p. 131.

17. Gay Head, "Boy Dates Girl Jam Session," *SS*, December 1943, p. 45.

18. LeMasters, *Modern Marriage*, p. 192.

19. One book attacked the "authorities [who] either bemoan or condone the fact that our moral code is changing, that few girls are virgins when they reach the altar, that more and more women are acceding to the demands made on them by men. It is a grave mistake to publish this information," the author argued, for "when women read that their competitors are giving something away, they feel obliged to do likewise, and when men read of the courtesies extended to their brothers, they naturally expect the same for themselves" (Nina Farewell, *The Unfair Sex* [New York: Simon & Schuster, 1953], p. 14).

20. Henry F. Pringle, "What Do the Women of America Think about Morals?" *LHJ*, May 1938, pp. 14–15; Gay Head, "Boy Dates Girl Student Opinion Poll #2," *SS*, 11 February 1939, p. 30; Remmers, "Parent Problem," *Purdue Opinion Panel*, 1949, p. 5; Remmers, "Courtship," *Purdue Opinion Panel*, 1950, pp. 32–33. Pressures from proscriptive conventions certainly show up in these polls. Although 81 percent of the 1949 POP sample said necking or petting was at least sometimes all right, a 1952 POP found that 57 percent of high school youth (47 percent of males and 67 percent of females) said that if they "heard that some friends of mine had not followed the morals or

rules relating to the behavior of unmarried people" they "would not consider them good friends anymore."

21. Jack Shepherd, "The *Look* Youth Survey," *Look*, 20 September 1966, p. 48.

22. Robert O. Blood, Jr., *Anticipating Your Marriage* (Glencoe, N.Y.: Free Press, 1955), p. 126. Blood's text was used widely and went through three printings between 1955 and 1957. LeMasters, *Modern Marriage*, p. 183.

23. "Fashions for Romantics Only," *Mademoiselle*, February 1954, p. 78.

24. "Fifty-nine Hundred Forty Women," *Time*, 24 August 1953, p. 51; Barbara Benson, "What *Women* Want to Know about the *Kinsey Book*," *LHJ*, September 1953, pp. 52–53; Letters to the Editor, *Look*, 20 October 1953, p. 12.

25. Eugenie A. Leonard and Margaret Bond Brockway, "Must a Girl Pet to Be Popular?" *Parents*, June 1932, p. 20.

26. Gutowski, "High School," pp. 118–20.

27. See issues of *Senior Scholastic* through the World War II years.

28. Roy Dickerson, "Prepare Them for Marriage," *Parents*, December 1937, p. 73.

29. Gutowski, "High School," p. 239.

30. Maureen Daly, "The Sub-deb: Pick a Problem," *LHJ*, January 1950, p. 28.

31. Matthews, *Dean of Women*, p. 248.

32. *University Regulations Concerning Student Conduct* (Ann Arbor: University of Michigan, 1962), esp. p. 13. Curfews changed at slightly different rates in different parts of the country, and between private, religious, and public schools, but students often cited regulations at other universities in making the case to relax their own.

33. Quote from the *Handbook* of the University of Massachusetts, Amherst. The 1956–57 edition dropped the proscription against "immodest dancing and offensive intimacy" that had previously appeared in the formula, but unintentionally confessed trepidation about student conduct. The statement read: "Behavior unbecoming to ladies and gentlemen, as defined by the prevailing standards of reputable places of entertainment and the homes of students, will be expected at all social events" (p. 24). The women's rule book at the University of Michigan in the 1950s was called "Judy Be Good"; at Northwestern in the 1940s it was called "Read and Be Right" and was given to men as well.

34. Kernel, "Serenading Season Has Finally Opened," Michigan *Daily* 26 May 1927; "University Regulations Concerning Student Conduct," 1962, p. 12.

35. "Student Handbook," Northwestern University, 1951–52, p. 59.

36. "U-M Radio Listeners Must Have Chaperones," *Detroit Free Press*, 18 October 1947; Joan Katz and Naomi Stan, "Cloister or College?" Michigan *Daily*, 15 October 1947.

37. "Stockwell Residents Polled to Solve Lounge Problems," Michigan *Daily*, 26 February 1952.

38. *Red Book*, 1951–52, p. 99.

39. Stephen O. Saxe, "The Coming of Age in Radcliffe: Joint Education Turns the Tide," Harvard *Crimson* (preregistration issue), September 1956, p. 14.

40. "Where People Go When They . . . Take a Date," *Pulse*, September

1937, p. 20. The piece begins: "Students like to play, and their No. 1 amusement is Sex." For those who care, the spots included: "the west entrance to Classics (heated and always open); the chapel steps by the outdoor pulpit; Classics 16 (for philosophy students with keys); and Social Sciences (Hide away in a corner until they lock up around 10:30. You can get out, but not in)."

41. Sallie Bingham, "Winter Term," *Mademoiselle*, July 1958, p. 94. I am not using fiction for evidence in most cases, but this story was written by a Radcliffe senior and spells out what other sources imply.

42. Grace Hechinger and Fred M. Hechinger, "College Morals Mirror Our Society," *New York Times Magazine*, 14 April 1963, p. 22.

43. "In Defense of Courting," *Recreation*, January 1940, p. 588; "Love in Atlanta," *Newsweek*, 16 November 1953, pp. 32–33. For a sample of pictures of couples kissing in cars, see *LHJ*, June 1944, p. 42; Abigail Wood, "How Much Kissing Is Too Much Kissing?" *Seventeen*, July 1963, p. 86; Margaret Widdemer, "Cad's Paradise," *GH*, October 1950, p. 55.

44. A sociology professor at the University of Wisconsin suggested that universities should establish "lovers' paradises," complete with comfortable benches and good lighting, where "responsible and mature students could do a bit of romancing in private — with reasonable supervision." Students at the University of Michigan, where the plan was briefly discussed, saw that "supervision" was undoubtedly the operative term (Vernon Emerson, "Supervised Woo Plan Gets Cold Shoulder Here," Michigan *Daily*, 20 October 1951).

45. This was a complicated amalgam of understandings without one clear source. These understandings are not new, and I am not arguing that they were unique to twentieth-century America. Instead, I am demonstrating how these systems of meaning *functioned* in twentieth-century America to control sexual expression among youth.

46. Strain, *Love*, p. 169.

47. "The Lady from Philadelphia," *LHJ*, July 1905, p. 35.

48. Mrs. Stickney Parks, "Girls' 'Affairs,'" *LHJ*, May 1914, p. 58.

49. Anne Bryan McCall, "The Tower Room: Love and the Girl Who Blundered," *WHC*, June 1919, p. 37.

50. Joseph Kirk Folsom, ed., *Plan for Marriage* (New York: Harper & Bros., 1938), p. 109.

51. Kiowa Costonie, *How to Win and Hold a Husband* (New York: Kiowa Publishing Co., 1945), p. 45.

52. Gay Head, "Boy Dates Girl," *SS*, 4 February 1946, p. 28.

53. Unger, *Datebook's Guide*, p. 93. See also Crounse, *Joyce Jackson's Guide* (1952), pp. 88–89.

54. "If a Man Takes Liberties — Is It *Always* the Girl's Fault?" *WHC*, March 1916, p. 10.

55. Irene Pierson, *Campus Cues* (Danville, Ill.: The Interstate, 1956), p. 101.

56. Landis and Landis, *Building*, pp. 20–21.

57. "Hearing in Student's Case Continued," *Ann Arbor News*, 25 January 1947.

58. "Is the Younger Generation in Peril?" *Literary Digest* 69 (14 May 1921): 10. In 1921 the YWCA press department sent photos of posed models, illustrating "morals in dress and conduct" to newspapers and magazines. This quote appeared as a headline for one of these pictures in the New York *Evening*

World. The caption read: "The girl on the right is really reading. She is demure and reserved, strictly minding her own business. Please note *The Literary Review,* enough to frighten any man away."

59. J. P. Edwards, "Do Women Provoke Sex Attack?" *Cosmopolitan,* March 1960, p. 38.

60. Ibid. *Cosmopolitan* printed no letters to the editor in response to this article.

61. Alan Hynd, "How to Protect Your Family," *Cosmopolitan,* January 1962, p. 47. A 1949 advice book told the story of a girl who was afraid to go out at night because she had been "jumped" one night while taking a shortcut through the park. The author said: "A girl with no more sense than that deserves to be jumped at." Van Evera, *Happy While Single,* p. 82.

62. Quote from Elizabeth Woodward, "The Sub-deb: Alone Together," *LHJ,* July 1942, p. 8.

63. Albert Ellis, *Sex and the Single Man* (New York: Lyle Stuart, 1963), p. 12.

64. Ibid., endpages.

65. Ibid., p. 15.

66. Ibid., p. 75.

67. Ibid., p. 83. Though not advocating "literal" rape, Ellis believed rape was a normal response in a culture that prohibited men's free sexual expression (Albert Ellis, *The Folklore of Sex* [New York: Grove Press, 1951], p. 170). Ellis considered rape to be an example of a sex act that is not "dangerous or health destroying" in and of itself, but that "society insists on viewing . . . as such and making them so." Rape, he explained, "actually inflicts no harm on adult victims if they are raised to view it lightly; but if they are raised to look upon it as a heinous attack, they may actually be seriously harmed by it." He insisted that rape, though "undesirable," was not perverted: "There is nothing, for example, necessarily neurotic or perverted about an individual's robbing a bank or picking a fistfight with his fellow citizens — at least, in some circumstances. Yet, we would not ordinarily encourage such acts. Similarly, my own prejudices lead me to believe that such acts as rape and sexual assault should definitely be discouraged, although I should rarely consider a rapist as a pervert" (Albert Ellis, *The American Sexual Tragedy* [New York: Lyle Stuart, 1954], p. 81).

68. Abigail Van Buren, "Things My Mother Never Told Me — Blue Jean Biology," *McCall's,* September 1959, p. 132. See also Brandow, *Date Data,* p. 188.

69. Evelyn Millis Duvall, Ph.D., *Why Wait Till Marriage?* (New York: Association Press, 1965), pp. 208–9.

70. Paul Popenoe, *Preparing for Marriage* (Los Angeles: Institute of Family Relations, 1939), p. 6.

71. Ferdinand Lundberg and Marynia F. Farnham, Ph.D., *Modern Woman: The Lost Sex* (New York: Harper & Bros., 1947), p. 286.

72. Landis and Landis, *Building* (1953), pp. 67–68.

73. Unger, *Datebook's Guide,* pp. 14–15.

74. Since biblical times, a woman's value was equated with her virtue, so this was a strong force even in the face of the seeming contradiction of women's increasing freedom and autonomy. This understanding was com-

plicated further when the same cultural sources that stressed a woman's virtue also demanded that she be sexual.

75. Landis and Landis, *Building*, p. 22; Brandow, *Date Data*, p. 165; Gay Head, *SS*, 6 April 1949, p. 32; Anne Hirst, *Get Your Man — and Hold Him* (New York: Kinsey & Co., 1937), p. 25; Carlyle, *Get a Husband*, p. 92; Gay Head, *SS*, 1945, p. 28; Emily Post, *Etiquette* (New York: Funk & Wagnalls, 1937), p. 355; Duvall, *Why Wait?* p. 20; Elizabeth Woodward, "Sub-deb: Bargain Buys," *LHJ*, May 1942, p. 8.

76. April Taylor, *Love Is a Four Letter Word* (New York: Beechhurst Press, 1948), p. 17.

77. Costonie, *Hold a Husband*, pp. 71, 46.

78. Farewell, *Unfair Sex*, p. 88.

79. Leonard and Brockway, "Must a Girl Pet," pp. 20, 61.

80. Bettye Butler, *If It's a Husband You Want* (n.p.: Jupiter Books, 1956), p. 13.

81. Juliet Farnham, *How to Meet Men and Marry* (New York: Simon Publications, 1943), p. 13.

82. Duvall, *Why Wait?* p. 69.

The Etiquette of Masculinity and Femininity

1. Peg Bracken, *I Try to Behave Myself: Peg Bracken's Etiquette Book* (New York: Curtis Publishing Co., 1959; reprint ed., New York: Harcourt, Brace & World, 1964), pp. 111–12. See similar comment on flirting, "How Good a Flirt Are You?" *Seventeen*, February 1963, p. 24.

2. Quote is from a 1967 *American Medical Association* journal, cited in Vance Packard, *The Sexual Wilderness* (New York: David McKay Co., 1968), p. 14. Similar language was used frequently in many sources from the 1940s through the 1960s. See also an earlier edition of Filene, *Him/Her/Self*, pp. 144.

3. Judson T. Landis and Mary G. Landis, "The U.S. Male . . . Is He First-Class?" *Collier's*, 19 July 1952, p. 22.

4. James B. Harrison uses the term *causal nexus* to discuss the relation between biology and sex roles in "Men's Roles and Men's Lives," *Signs* 4 (Winter 1978): 326.

5. Elizabeth Hardwick, "The Feminine Principle," *Mademoiselle*, February 1958, p. 133. The quote ran as a blurb for her article.

6. Clyde W. Franklin, II, *The Changing Definition of Masculinity* (New York: Plenum Press, 1984), pp. 2–3. See also Janet Saltzman Chafetz, *Masculine/Feminine or Human? An Overview of the Sociology of Gender Roles* (Itasca, Ill.: F. E. Peacock Publishers, 1978), p. 12. I use the definitions offered by Franklin and Chafetz, although there is some disagreement between sociologists about which term designates culture and which nature. See Harrison, "Men's Roles," pp. 324–25.

7. Peter Stearns, *Be a Man! Males in Modern Society* (New York: Holmes & Meier Publishers, 1979), p. 37.

8. Term comes from E. Anthony Rotundo, "Manhood in America: Middle-Class Masculinity in the Northern United States, 1770–1910" (Ph.D. diss., Brandeis University, 1981), p. 445. See also H. Carleton Marlow and Harrison

M. Davis, *The American Search for Woman* (Santa Barbara, Ca.: Clio Books, 1976), p. 27; and Ruth H. Bloch, "Untangling the Roots of Modern Sex Roles: A Survey of Four Centuries of Change," *Signs* 4 (Winter 1978): 239–46.

9. Marlow and Davis, *Search for Woman*, p. 17.

10. Ibid., p. 70.

11. Ibid., pp. 35–41. See also John S. Haller, Jr., and Robin M. Haller, *The Physician and Sexuality in Victorian America* (Urbana, Ill.: University of Illinois Press, 1974), pp. 70–71.

12. Joe L. Dubbert, *A Man's Place: Masculinity in Transition* (Englewood Cliffs, N.J.: Prentice-Hall, 1979), pp. 11, 29–33, 96. See also Jeffrey Hantover, "Sex Role, Sexuality, and Social Status: The Early Years of the Boy Scouts of America" (Ph.D. diss., University of Chicago, 1976).

13. Dubbert, *Man's Place*, p. 19; Rotundo, "Manhood in America," pp. 181, 189.

14. Dubbert, *Man's Place*, p. 125. In Northwestern Univerity's English F course in 1903, male students repeatedly wrote essays attacking women students for their "non-domesticity" and "masculinity." "Co-eds Score the Men," *The Northwestern*, 16 November 1903, p. 1.

15. Haller and Haller, *Physician and Sexuality*, pp. 78–79.

16. Sigmund Freud, "The Psychogenesis of a Case of Homosexuality in a Woman," *The Standard Edition of the Complete Works of Sigmund Freud*, trans. James Strachey (London: Hogarth Press, 1957), 18:171.

17. Most of this argument appears in Freud's *New Introductory Lectures on Psycho-Analysis*. There are many very important contemporary feminist analyses of Freudian theory that I have ignored here, obviously not doing justice to the topic. However, I am only concerned here with the simple versions of Freudianism that passed into popular culture and influenced popular understandings of masculinity and femininity. These understandings are comparable to the popular Freudianism (and inaccurate Freud) that provided a rationale for a freer code of sexual behavior in the 1920s in America.

18. Marlow and Davis, *Search for Woman*, p. 81.

19. Lawrence Frank, "Preparation for Marriage in the High School Program," *Living* 1 (January 1939): 9.

20. Mary Pinchot, "Credits for Love," *Mademoiselle*, August 1944, p. 253.

21. Bowman, *Marriage for Moderns*, pp. 1–26.

22. LeMasters, *Modern Marriage*, p. 493. See also Landis and Landis, *Building*, chap. 2.

23. Mead, *Male and Female*, p. 318.

24. Arthur Schlesinger, Jr., "The Crisis of American Masculinity," *Esquire*, November 1958, p. 62.

25. "Playboy Panel: The Womanization of America," *Playboy*, June 1962, p. 142.

26. Lawrence K. Frank, "How Much Do We Know about Men?" *Look*, 17 May 1955, p. 56.

27. Amram Scheinfeld, "How 'Equal' Are Women?" *Collier's*, 18 September 1943, p. 74.

28. Louis Lyndon, "Uncertain Hero: The Paradox of the American Male," *WHC*, November 1956, pp. 41, 107.

29. Amaury DeRiencourt, "Will Success Spoil American Women?" *New York Times Magazine*, 10 November 1957, p. 32.

30. On the creation of the concept of masculine businessmen, see Stearns, *Be a Man!* pp. 83–86; see also Joe Dubbert, *A Man's Place*, pp. 242–59.

31. Carl N. Degler, *At Odds* (New York: Oxford University Press, 1980), p. 418–19.

32. Ibid.

33. LeMasters, *Modern Marriage*, pp. 484–513.

34. "Playboy Panel," pp. 43–44. See also Edith G. Nesser, "Is Marriage the Trap?" *Mademoiselle*, December 1955, p. 131. Nesser was a "specialist in the field of marriage and family relations."

35. David Boroff, "Sex: The Quiet Revolution," *Esquire*, July 1961, p. 99. By another account, homosexuality could stem from "feminine" acts — a boy who was allowed to grow up expressing love for "pretty things" would be "practically forced [into homosexuality] by his looks, his dress and his manner" (Leslie B. Hohman, M.D., "As the Twig Is Bent," *LHJ*, January 1941, p. 60). Dr. Hohman was an associate in psychiatry at the Johns Hopkins Medical School.

36. J. B. Rice, M.D., "She Gets Away With Murder," *Esquire*, April 1949, pp. 140–41.

37. George Frazier, "The Entrenchment of the American Witch," *Esquire*, February 1962, p. 100.

38. Phyllis Bottelle, "The Non-Woman: A Manhattan Enigma," *Cosmopolitan*, March 1962, p. 63. Quote is from Phyllis Rosenteur, author of the best-seller, *The Single Woman*.

39. Moss, "Courtship," p. 151.

40. Katharine Fullerton Gerould, "Treat 'Em Rough," *Harper's*, October 1922, p. 611. Similar labels for American men abound after World War II.

41. For example, Lynn White, Jr.'s book, *Educating Our Daughters* (New York: Harpers, 1950). White, the president of Mills College, advocated a "firm nuclear course in the family," including such subjects as "the theory and preparation of a Basque paella, of a well-marinated shish kebob, lamb kidneys sauteed in sherry." For an overview of the movement, see Marion Nowack, "'How to Be a Woman': Theories of Female Education in the 1950s," *Journal of Popular Culture* 9 (Summer 1975): 77–83; or the chapter titled "Scientific Truth . . . and Love" of this work.

42. David Boroff, "The Graduate Limbo," *Mademoiselle*, October 1960, p. 111.

43. Clifford R. Adams, "How Feminine Are You to Men?" *WHC*, May 1946, p. 34.

44. Jack Harrison Pollack, "How Masculine Are You?" *Nation's Business*, June 1950, pp. 53–55.

45. Oscar Homolka, letter to the editor, *Cosmopolitan*, August 1959, p. 6.

46. "What's Your Biggest Problem?" *SS*, 10–15 January 1944, p. 32.

47. "Housewifely Husbands," *WHC*, June 1919, p. 54.

48. Richard Gehman, "Man's Private World," *Cosmopolitan*, May 1961, p. 39. Gehman also explores the fantasy private worlds, looking at the popularity of *Playboy* magazine and the now defunct Playboy Club (established in Chicago in 1960 and grossing over $1 million in its first year).

49. Vance Packard, "The Manipulators," *Playboy*, December 1957, p. 62.

50. Dubbert, *Man's Place*, p. 9.

51. Myron Brenton, *The American Male* (New York: Coward-McCann, 1966), p. 30.

52. Hugh Hefner, "The Playboy Philosophy," *Playboy*, December 1964, p. 218. This section was also part of a roundtable discussion, "Trialogue," on New York radio station WINS.

53. Barbara Ehrenreich, *The Hearts of Men* (Garden City, N.Y.: Anchor Press/Doubleday, 1983), pp. 42–51.

54. Hugh Hefner, "The Playboy Philosophy," p. 217.

55. Arthur Schlesinger, Jr., "The Crisis of American Masculinity," pp. 64–65.

56. Betty Freidan, "I Say: Women Are *People* Too," *GH*, September 1960, p. 162.

57. "*Senior Scholastic* Student Opinion Poll," *SS*, 11 February 1939, p. 30.

58. Marie Watters, "The Evolution of Flint's Co-ed Night," *Recreation*, October 1939, pp. 396–97.

59. "The Kind of a Boy That Girls Like," *SS*, 25 March 1940, p. 32. Girls led off with "courteous," etiquette came in fourth, and "respectful" sixth. Boys were most concerned with girls' appearance, but etiquette was the eighth most popular response. The student stress on etiquette appears in *Senior Scholastic* throughout the 1930s and 1940s.

60. *Daily Northwestern*, 7 February 1945, p. 1; notice for freshman meeting to revise the etiquette section of the "'N' Book."

61. The term *repulsive* comes from Norman W. Hamilton, *How to Woo, Win, and Keep Your Man — How Not to Drive Him into Other Women's Arms* (New York: William-Frederick Press, 1955), p. 9. The author was director of Hamilton's Counseling Service, White Plains, New York.

62. Of course, the binding clothes are even more extreme symbols and tools of women's submission. The difference is that twentieth-century women, by and large, shed the immediate symbol (and the actuality of restrained movement) but desired the symbolic act to continue.

63. Brandow, *Date Data*, p. 56. See also Helene Wright, "Teens of Our Times: Let *Him* Pay," *GH*, June 1945, p. 11; Dorothy Dayton, "Proposing Is a Proposition," *Mademoiselle*, January 1983, p. 66. Dayton says of dutch dating: "Men never did share our love of bargains."

64. Eldridge, *Co-ediquette*, p. 216.

65. Jonathon, *Guidebook for the Young Man*, p. 49; Lawrence Frank and Mary Frank, *How to Be a Woman* (New York: Bobbs-Merrill Co., 1954), p. 30.

66. Philip Morris advertisement, *Massachusetts Collegian*, 18 March 1955, p. 3.

67. "This Can't Be Love . . ." *SS*, 11 February 1939, p. 30.

68. Purdue poll cited in Evelyn Ruth Millis Duvall, Ph.D., *The Art of Dating* (New York: Association Press, 1958), pp. 138–39.

69. "Boy Dates Girl Jam Session," *SS*, 9 January 1948, p. 32; 11 April 1951, p. 24. Although in 1937 *Senior Scholastic* had listed "Dutch Dates without Embarrassment" as one of its goals in advising youth (teachers' pages, 15 May 1937), in the didactic stories of the "Boy Dates Girl" column male characters frequently made comments such as "Maybe I'm old-fashioned, but I want to wear the pants" (3–8 April 1944, p. 28); "I'd rather be King Bee!" (14–19 February 1944, p. 24); and one story pictured "Juliet" excusing herself to the

"dressing room" while "Romeo" pays the check (9 January 1937, pp. 22–23).

70. *Esquire Etiquette* (New York: J. B. Lippincott Co., 1953), p. 261.

71. Brandow, *Date Data*, p. 45.

72. Fishback, *Safe Conduct*, p. 47.

73. William Moulton Marston, Ph.D., "The Reaction of a Man to a Woman," *GH*, February 1941, p. 27.

74. Lois Mattox Miller, "Dining Out," *Mademoiselle*, February 1938, pp. 28–29.

75. Bettye K. Butler, *If It's a Husband You Want* (n.p.: Jupiter Books, 1956), p. 117.

76. Pierson, *Campus Cues*, p. 40.

77. Hart and Brown, *Get Your Man*, p. 89.

78. "Maryland Coeds Demonstrate Do's and Don'ts of Campus Etiquette," *Life*, 17 February 1941, p. 41. Quoted from the University of Maryland Etiquette Book, *That Is the Question*.

79. "How Loveable Are You?" *LHJ*, June 1959, p. 51.

80. Kay Corinth and Mary Sargent, *Male Manners: The Young Man's Guide* (New York: David McKay Co., 1969), p. 91.

81. Landis and Landis, *Building*, p. 24.

82. Hart and Brown, *Get Your Man*, p. 26.

83. Farnham, *How to Meet Men*, p. 81.

84. Paul Popenoe, "What Do You Know about Marriage?" *LHJ*, February 1944, p. 133.

85. "Profile on Youth: Jim Brown, Class of '50," *LHJ*, December 1949, p. 55.

86. Judson T. Landis and Mary G. Landis, "What You Should Know about Women Even If You're a Woman," *Collier's*, 24 November 1951, p. 19. See also George Lawton, Ph.D., "Are Women as Intelligent as Men?" *SS*, 5 February 1945, p. 30.

87. Susan Ware, *Holding Their Own: American Women in the 1930s* (Boston: Twane Publishers, 1982), pp. 6–8.

88. Elizabeth Hawes, *Why Women Cry, or Wenches with Wrenches* (New York: Reynat Hitchcock, 1943), cited in Pamela Neal Warford, "The Social Origins of Female Iconography: Selected Images of Women in American Popular Culture: 1890–1945" (Ph.D. diss., St. Louis University, 1979), pp. 107–8.

89. See chapter 2 for a fuller discussion. For statistics, see Churchill, *GH*, pp. 38, 313; Panitt, "English Girls," p. 5.

90. Brandow, *Date Data*, p. 66.

91. Ibid., p. 185. See also, for condemnation of aggressiveness, "How Good a Flirt Are You?" p. 24; Dayton, "Anxious Ladies," p. 34.

92. In 1935 an *Esquire* article argued that women often compete with men "passively" by being so weak and helpless that men have to take care of them (W. Beran Wolfe, M.D., "Men, Women, and Marriage," *Esquire*, June 1935, p. 137).

93. Nell Giles, *Susan Tells Stephen* (Boston: Hale, Cushman & Flint, 1942), p. 65.

94. Corinth and Sargent, *Male Manners*, pp. 91–92.

95. See, for example, Helen Lawrenson, "Old Fashioned Men," *Esquire*, February 1951, pp. 114–15; Elizabeth Honor, "The Fight for Love," *Cosmopolitan*, July 1960, p. 46.

Scientific Truth . . . and Love

1. Russell M. Cooper, "Marriage Courses in General Education," *M&FL* 8 (Spring 1946): 32.

2. Ernest W. Burgess and Emily H. Mudd, "Changes in Attitudes to the Family and in Sex Mores," paper presented to the ACLS conference, 25–26 April 1952, p. 22. Burgess Papers, Box 1.

3. Ernest W. Burgess, "Research," *M&FL* 8 (Summer 1946): 64.

4. James R. McGovern, "The American Woman's Pre–World War I Freedom in Manners and Morals," *JAH* 55 (September 1968): 315–33.

5. See chapter 2 for a full discussion.

6. Burgess and Mudd, "Changes in Attitudes," p. 22.

7. LeMasters, *Modern Marriage*, p. 9. This is probably the most cogent statement of an attitude held from the beginning of the movement. For an earlier statement, see the first issue of *Living*: "Editorial Comment: Work of the Conference," *Living* 1 (January 1939): 25.

8. Ernest R. Groves, "Report of Committee on Education for Marriage and Family Living," *Living* 2 (Spring 1940): 47–48.

9. Ernest W. Burgess, lecture for Sociology 351, n.d., p. 29. Burgess Papers, Box 28.

10. Howard Odum, "Editor's Introductory Note," in Ernest Rutherford Groves and William Fielding Ogburn, *American Marriage and Family Relationships* (New York: Henry Holt & Co., 1928), p. vi.

11. LeMasters, *Modern Marriage*, pp. 9, 13.

12. Ibid.

13. Burgess and Mudd, "Changes in Attitudes," p. 20.

14. For discussion of the role of planning in twentieth-century America, see Barry D. Karl, *The Uneasy State* (Chicago: University of Chicago Press, 1983).

15. Jerome Beatty, "Taking the Blinders off Love," *American Magazine*, December 1937, p. 22.

16. Henry Bowman, "Education for Marriage and Family Life," *M&FL* 8 (Summer 1946): 63.

17. Cooper, "Marriage Courses," p. 32.

18. Ibid.

19. Groves, "Report," p. 47.

20. Donald S. Klaiss, "Ernest Rutherford Groves, 1877–1946," *M&FL* 8 (Autumn 1946): 93. Also see Beatty, "Blinders," p. 22; E. R. Groves, "So You Want to Get Married?" *American Magazine*, April 1938, pp. 15–16, 151; and Joseph Kirk Folsom, ed., *Plan for Marriage* (New York: Harper & Bros., 1938), p. xi. Groves wrote the first college textbook on marriage in 1926, the year before he was called to UNC, and founded the movement's professional organization, the Conference on the Conservation of Marriage and the Family, in 1934.

21. See, for example, Charles B. Davenport, *Heredity in Relation to Eugenics* (New York: Henry Holt & Co., 1911; reprint ed., New York: Arno Press, 1972), pp. 4–7. For home economics, see Helen Horowitz, *Alma Mater* (New York: Alfred A. Knopf, 1984), pp. 295–302. For sex education, see Gutowski, "High School," pp. 124–25. The Chicago public schools system instituted sex hygiene lectures in 1913. The twenty-two-lecture series was given

in English, Polish, Russian, and Bohemian. First 2,210 parents attended, then the series was given to 21,534 students in sex-segregated groups. The series was dropped in 1914 after a protest by the Catholic Church.

22. "College May Aid Cupid," *The Northwestern*, 2 March 1904, p. 3; Rev. Samuel McComb, D.D., "Who Should Marry?" *GH*, March 1912, p. 344.

23. For Odum's views, see issues of *Social Forces* throughout the 1930s.

24. Groves, "Get Married?" *American Magazine*, April 1938, p. 155.

25. Beatty, "Blinders," p. 22; Abraham Stone, M.D., "Marriage Education and Marriage Counseling in the United States," *M&FL* 11 (Spring 1949): 38; James H. S. Bossard, "The Engagement Ring—A Changing Symbol," *New York Times Magazine*, 14 September 1958, p. 32; Mary Anne Guitar, "College Marriage Courses—Fun or Fraud?" *Mademoiselle*, February 1961, p. 126.

26. This information comes from the *Journal of Marriage and Family Living*, especially the personal information column and the following articles: "Teaching Marriage Courses," *M&FL* 8 (Spring 1946): 32–41; Howard E. Wilkening, "The Purdue University Marriage Course," *M&FL* 7 (Spring 1945): 35–38; "Marriage Education Courses and Interdepartmental Relationships at Four Universities," *M&FL* 11 (Winter 1949): 9–13; and Beatty, "Blinders," p. 22. On high school courses: Donald S. Longworth, "Certification of Teachers of Family Living," *M&FL* 14 (May 1952): 103–4.

27. Henry Bowman, "A Critical Evalution of College Marriage Courses," *M&FL* 15 (November 1953): 304–8.

28. Beatty, "Blinders," p. 22.

29. "College Courses on Marriage Relations," *GH*, September 1937, pp. 28–29; "How to be Marriageable," *LHJ*, March 1954, pp. 46–47; April 1954, pp. 48–49.

30. "Bringing Up Mother," *Newsweek*, 15 June 1953, p. 58.

31. Dean Jennings, "Sex in the Classroom," *Collier's*, 15 September 1945, p. 22 (a profile on Berkeley); Jane Whitbread and Vivien Cadden, "Dating and Marriage," *Mademoiselle*, August 1954, p. 332; Bossard, "Engagement Rings," p. 32.

32. "Marrying Girls Need Experience with Men, Work," *WHC*, June 1955, p. 11. The *WHC* poll began in 1941. It polled a group of 2,000 selected from its readership and frequently revised to give an accurate picture of what its readership (4,343,000 by 1953) thought about current issues. See *WHC*, January 1946, p. 7.

33. See, for example, Clifford Adams, Ph.D., "The Companion Marriage Clinic," *WHC*, July 1946, p. 34. He prints a "test" he gives to couples who come to him for advice, which, he claimed, enabled him to "judge with real accuracy the compatibility of a courting couple."

34. Abigail Wood, "Must Dating Always be a Game?" *Seventeen*, September 1963, p. 154.

35. Maureen Daly, ed., *Profile of Youth* (New York: J. B. Lippincott & Co., 1949). Daly began writing the *LHJ* "Sub-deb" column in 1945. She previously had written the *Chicago Tribune* column, "On the Solid Side," for teens.

36. Henry Bowman, "Report of Committee on College Courses in Preparation for Marriage," *M&FL* 3 (Spring 1941): 37.

37. Christopher Jencks and David Reisman, *The Academic Revolution* (Garden City, N.Y.: Doubleday & Co., 1968), p. 494. Conflation of functional

education with the Chicago model of general education is odd, for Hutchins blamed presentism and scientism (two undeniable characteristics of functional education) for the defeat of his own program. Still, both attempted, in very different ways, to prepare young people for their eventual roles in a democratic society.

38. John S. Brubacher and Willis Rudy, *Higher Education in Transition: An American History, 1636–1956* (New York: Harper & Bros., 1958), p. 255.

39. Robert Lincoln Kelly, *The American College and the Social Order* (New York: Macmillan Co., 1940), p. 187. Kelly was the director of the Association of American Colleges from 1917 to 1937.

40. Brubacher and Rudy, *Higher Education,* p. 269.

41. Ibid., pp. 269–70.

42. Oscar Handlin and Mary F. Handlin, *The American College and American Culture* (New York: McGraw-Hill Book Co., 1970), p. 73. Russell Cooper (in "Marriage Courses in General Education," *M&FL* 8 [Spring 1946]: 32) stresses that general education is not designed for "an intellectual elite."

43. See Wilkening, "Purdue Marriage Course," p. 35; he repeatedly uses the term *democratic* to characterize his course.

44. Groves, "Get Married?" pp. 15–16.

45. Wilkening, "Purdue Marriage Course," pp. 35–38.

46. Paul Popenoe, "Trends in Teaching Family Relations," *M&FL* 8 (Spring 1946): 35–36.

47. Laura Winslow Drummond, *Youth and Instruction in Marriage and Family Living* (New York: Bureau of Publications, Teachers' College, Columbia University, 1942).

48. Judson T. Landis, "An Evaluation of Marriage Education," *M&FL* 10 (Fall 1948): 81.

49. Ibid., pp. 81–82.

50. Ibid., p. 82.

51. "Marriage Relations Course Comments," Marriage Relations Course file, Michigan Historical Collection, Bentley Library, University of Michigan; J. Stewart Burgess, "The College and the Preparation for Marriage and Family Relations," *Living* 1 (Spring/Summer 1939): 39.

52. Beatty, "Blinders," p. 182; Bernice Peck, "It Ought to Be Taught," *Mademoiselle,* August 1955, p. 276. *Mademoiselle* frequently praised Stephens College (where personal appearance was taught for credit) for its "practical" orientation in the 1940s and 1950s.

53. Mary Pinchot, "Credits for Love," *Mademoiselle,* August 1944, pp. 253, 162.

54. "News and Notes," *M&FL* 9 (Winter 1947): 19; Henry Bowman, "The Marriage Course at Stephens College," *M&FL* 3 (Winter 1941): 9.

55. Samuel Harman Lowrie, "Dating, a Neglected Field of Study," *M&FL* 10 (Fall 1948): 90–91.

56. Henry Bowman and Florence Schroeder, "College Courses in Preparation for Marriage," *M&FL* 4 (Spring 1942): 31.

57. Louise Ramsey, "Education for Marriage and Family Life in the High School as a Means of Strengthening National Defense," *M&FL* 3 (Summer 1942): 52. This paper was read at the National Conference of Family Relations. Ramsey was making a case to college marriage educators for more marriage

training in high school because most high school students did not attend college.

58. "I Am a Student," *Look,* 14 October 1958, p. 35.

59. Cooper, "Marriage Courses," p. 34.

60. LeMasters, *Modern Marriage,* pp. 10–11.

61. Henry Bowman, "The Marriage Course at Stephens College," pp. 8–11.

62. Wilkening, "Purdue Marriage Course," pp. 35–37.

63. Groves, "Get Married?" p. 15.

64. Groves, "Report," p. 46.

65. Moses Jung, "The Course in Modern Marriage at the State University of Iowa," *Living* 1 (Spring/Summer 1939): 50.

66. Herbert D. Lamson, "Next Steps in College Education for Marriage," *M&FL* 11 (Spring 1949): 46.

67. Groves, "Report," p. 48.

68. Ibid.

69. "Lecture on Prediction in Marriage." Burgess Papers, Box 28. No date — included with materials from the late 1940s.

70. Judson T. Landis and Mary G. Landis, *Building a Successful Marriage* (New York: Prentice Hall, 1948), pp. 110, 167, 212–19. This text went through seven editions between 1948 and 1977.

71. Herman R. Lantz, "Problem Areas in Marriage Education," *M&FL* 15 (May 1953): 116–18; Earl Lomon Koos, "Comment," pp. 118–19. In the same issue, in an article titled, "Some Fringe Problems of Teaching Marriage in Negro Colleges," J. S. Himes, Jr., noted that his own research suggested that the social science findings were not "universally applicable" (pp. 114–16).

72. Joseph Kirk Folsom, ed., *Plan for Marriage* (New York: Harper & Bros., 1938), p. 107.

73. Landis and Landis, *Building,* 1948, p. 162. The conclusion was slightly toned down in the 1958 edition (p. 266).

74. Data from Lewis M. Terman, *Psychological Factors in Marital Happiness* (New York: McGraw-Hill Book Co., 1938), pp. 142–66, quoted in Landis and Landis, *Building,* 1948, pp. 90–91. This scale also was reproduced, in part, in the *Woman's Home Companion* as a "quiz" on "popular fallacies" now debunked by sociologists, statisticians, educators, and psychologists. Judith Chase Churchill, "What Do You Know about Marriage?" *WHC,* September 1950, p. 42.

75. Herbert D. Lamson, "Quiz on a Marriage Course," *Journal of Home Economics* 40 (December 1948): 584.

76. Ernest W. Burgess, Proposal for Marriage Study, handwritten draft, n.d., pp. 11b–12. Burgess Papers, Box 31.

77. "The Future Adventure," *Living* 2 (January 1939): 17.

78. Examination for Sociology 8 course, "The Family: Courtship and Marriage," Burgess Papers. Question refers to Evelyn Millis Duvall and Reuben Hill, *When You Marry* (New York: Association Press, 1948), which Burgess used as a text in this course.

79. Groves, "Get Married?" pp. 152, 154; Guitar, "College Marriage Courses," p. 144; Groves, "Get Married?" p. 153, Ralph G. Eckert, "Highlights of a Marriage Course," *M&FL* 8 (Spring 1946): 39, 40.

80. Landis and Landis, *Building,* 1958, pp. 133, 274, for examples.

81. Guitar, "College Marriage Courses," p. 144.
82. Burgess, Proposal for Marriage Study, p. 16.

Epilogue

1. "The New Mating Games," *Newsweek*, 2 June 1986, p. 58.
2. "Dating Is Hell," *Mademoiselle*, November 1986, p. 177.

Index

BETH L. BAILEY teaches history at the University of Kansas. Formerly she taught at the University of Hawaii at Manoa.

From Front Porch to Back Seat

Designed by Ann Walston.

Text composed by Capitol Communication Systems, Inc., in Paladium.
Display type composed by The TypeWorks in Gill Sans Italic.

Printed by The Maple Press Company on 55-lb. S. D. Warren's Antique Cream and bound in Joanna Arrestox and G.S.B. cloth.